Writer's Guide to 2010

Writer's Institute Publications ™

Editor: Susan M. Tierney

Contributing Writers:

Jacqueline Adams
Judy Bradbury
Jan Czech
Jacqueline Diamond
Sue Bradford Edwards
Carmen Goldthwaite
Christina Hamlett
Mark Haverstock

Veda Boyd Jones
Kelly McClymer
Sharelle Byars Moranville
Cindy Rogers
Mary Rosenblum
Katherine Swarts
Leslie J. Wyatt

Cover images supplied by Jupiterimages.

Contributing Editor: Marni McNiff

Copy Editor: Meredith DeSousa

Cover design: Joanna Horvath

Publisher: Prescott V. Kelly

International Standard Book Number 978-1-889715-51-3

1-800-443-6078. www.writersbookstore.com
e-mail: services@writersbookstore.com

Printed and bound in Canada.

Table of Contents

The Good, the Bad, and the Hopeful

The Year in Magazines & Books

By Susan Tierney

No mirror, mirror on any wall can prophesy how and when publishing will emerge from the economic stresses of the last two years. Looking directly at the year's publishing news, however, is like looking in a mirror that reflects many realities, some ugly. Lo and behold, it also reveals some beauty, in the form of positive change, growth, and hope.

A clear-eyed look at the past year cannot hide the truths of an industry continuing to struggle through business woes and a still new and unfolding media universe. For writers, keeping apprised of the industry's overall state is important. Up-to-date information helps writers to take advantage of opportunities that present themselves; to be realistic about what will be difficult to write and sell; and to be prepared for the future—which undoubtedly will be significantly different from the past. Understanding the dynamic changes in the industry makes writers more capable of adjusting, and looking fruitfully into their own career and artistic mirrors.

Good news first, or the bad? Let's start with the good.

Magazines: Keep Them Coming

Publishing is suffering as much as any sector, sometimes more. But it is also an industry blessed with creative entrepreneurs, and by a unique period of transformation. Transformation is double-edged, however, as controversial remarks by *New York Times* Publisher Arthur O. Sulzberger Jr. spotlighted. Sulzberger told *New York Magazine* that the print media are functioning under a *"Titanic* Fallacy." Jada Yuan asked him for advice for young people interested in journalism, and reported his response:

> "The best analogy I can think of is—have you ever heard of the *Titanic* Fallacy? . . . Even if the *Titanic* came in safely to New York Harbor, it was still doomed," he said. "Twelve years earlier, two brothers invented the airplane."

Sulzberger likened the publishing industry's transformation to an attempt "to convert shipping companies to airplane companies." While the business—transportation in one instance, communication in the other—remains the same, the costs, operations, personnel, and more are changing. He concluded, "So print will still be here, I believe, decades from now. But will it be the driving force? No." (Jada Yuan, http://nymag.com/daily/intel/2009/10/times_publisher_arthur_sulzber.html)

The progress of publishing is very visible, even if the ultimate destination is only a distant silhouette. It has become essential to start a website to accompany a print launch, but the overlap of print and Web editorial today varies widely with each publication. More magazines are foregoing print altogether and starting up primarily, if not completely, online.

But even in a difficult environment and with formats changing, the number of magazine start-ups over the past year is impressive. Some have come and gone (*New Mexico Family Magazine &*

Guide); some have come and gone and come again, like a cat with nine lives (*Vibe*). Those start-ups listed in the sidebar on pages 12 to 18 were born, still have heartbeats (some strong, some irregular), and, some are already growing. Some are glossy and well-funded. Some are small and carving a niche, pinning hopes on interesting slants and new audiences. Many of the magazines are looking for submissions. Here is a general breakdown of the sidebar list by category:

➤ **Glossies:** The big launches of the year—slick, with lots of money behind them, from major companies—are *BBC Knowledge Magazine; Cesar's Way* (IMG and the Dog Whisperer, Cesar Millan); *Children's Health* (Rodale Press); *Food Network Magazine* (Hearst Publications); *ForbesWoman; Mixing Bowl* (Meredith Corporation); *TheWrap* (online).

➤ **On wheels:** Notable is the number of debut publications that cover cycling, motorcycles, and cars: *Bicycle Times; Go for a Ride; Moto Retro Illustrated; Racing World; Racin' Today; She Pedals: The Journal of Women in Cycling; Women's Cycling.*

➤ **Young people:** New publications for and about children and teens include *Children's Health; East Texas Teen; GirlMogul* (with *GirlMogul Mom*); *Susie; Xplor; University Link,* for college students.

➤ **Parenting and family:** *Acara Mia; Fit Parent; Long Island Parent; Observer Playground; Single Parent 101; StrollerTraffic; Well Now;* and *Your Teen* are all new.

➤ **Regionals:** The hundreds of regional publications across North America have been joined in the past year by *1859 Oregon's Magazine; Alpine, A Green Living Magazine* (Nevada); *ArtSync* (North Carolina); *Avenues* (the Ozarks); *b-Metro* (Birmingham); *Blush* (Canada); *Brava* (Wisconsin); *Capital Style* (Ohio women); *Coast Drive* (Pacific Coast

Highway); *Hunt Alaska; Ke Ola* (Hawaii); *LasVegas.net Magazine; Maine; Maine Ahead; Make It Better* (North Shore, Chicago); *Minnesota Poker; OakBook* (Oakland, CA); *Portland Spaces* (Oregon); *Queens Karma* (New York); *Scottsdale Health* (Arizona); *Seven Cities* (Virginia); *Southern Indiana Business Source; Southern Vermont Arts & Living; Valley Faith* (Red River Valley); *WV Living; Zone 4, Living in the High Country West.*

> **Arts, architecture, culture:** *Arabella; ArtSync; Blurt* (music); *Clavier Companion; Southern Vermont Arts & Living; Modern.*

> **Bridal:** *Get Married; Serendipity* (Asian American brides); *Southern Weddings.*

> **Fashion:** *Acara Mia* (children); *Arise* (African); *Gladys.*

> **Food, shelter, lifestyle:** *Drink Me; Edible Queens; The Food Magazine; Food Network Magazine; Guitar Aficionado; Hearts of the Country; Mixing Bowl; Modern; Modern Home + Living; Urban Living.*

> **Politics and business:** *The Baffler; DoubleX; Forbes-Woman; Smart Girl Nation.*

> **Religion:** *Bible Study; Rejoice, a Multicultural Christian Magazine; Susie; The Tablet; Travel with Spirit; Valley Faith.*

> **Sports and recreation:** *The Fourth Period* (hockey); *Golf Today, Northwest Edition; Indie Game; Minnesota Poker; Mountain Sports + Living.*

> **Travel:** *Afar; Big World; Travel with Spirit.*

> **Miscellaneous:** *Anthropology Now; Charity Times; Native Legacy; Sky* (Delta in-flight magazine); *Simply Handmade; Vehicle* (storytelling); *Teaching Canada's History; TechKnow.*

Magazines with the Will to Live

Companies are trying many routes to survive and grow, even if slowly. Publishers cut back on staff across the board or via the departure of a few highly paid, high-profile executives. *New York Magazine,* American Media (which publishes *Star* and *Shape*), and Hachette Filipacchi Media (*Woman's Day, Car & Driver, Elle*) apologetically left the trade organization Magazine Publishers of America (MPA), to save expenses. Sometimes magazine salvation has meant reducing the number of issues, changing print schedules, or reworking the online-print synergy. It has also meant bankruptcy and restructuring when the figures do not add up.

Numbers from the Audit Bureau of Circulations (ABC) leave no doubt that magazine sales and advertising declined in the first half of 2009, but May and June saw a newsstand bump that the industry hoped presaged an upswing. In addition to lower revenues, however, magazines faced higher production costs and smaller marketing budgets. The newsstand distribution system is also now weaker because of sales declines for major titles (*Newsweek, Family Circle, Life & Style, In Touch, OK!, Star, W*), and the loss of others.

Other magazines with large circulations held their own overall, according to rate base (the guaranteed circulation figure on which a magazine sells advertising). *Newsweek*'s sales may have been down on the newsstand but it maintained its rate base at midyear, as did *Reader's Digest, AARP,* and *Maxim.*

By late in the year, magazines that had increased newsstand sales were *The Week, Time* (slightly), and *Inc.* Fashion magazines seem to have taken the largest hit as a category, with sales about 12 percent lower than in the preceding year. *W, In Style,* and *Vogue* were all down. Condé Nast closed *Men's Vogue,* apart from two special issues to be packaged with *Vogue.* In October, it also closed *Gourmet, Cookie, Elegant Bride,* and *Modern Bride,* and converted *Bride* to a monthly to cover the category.

An American publishing icon, *Reader's Digest* maintained its rate base in the first half of the year, but the publisher was hurting.

Reader's Digest Association had stretched well beyond that compact magazine's traditional collection of articles, pleasant jokes, and Americana. Over the decades since its founding in 1922, Reader's Digest expanded to publish many other magazines and books, acquire educational publishers, partner with other publishers, run sweepstakes, and more.

On August 24, Reader's Digest Association, once publisher of the best-selling magazine in the country, filed for bankruptcy. It had already laid off hundreds of employees and put divisions up for sale. Its curriculum publishing company, Gareth Stevens, was sold to Roger Rosen, the owner of the school and library publisher, Rosen Publishing. (Gareth Stevens and Rosen Publishing will not be affiliated.) Reader's Digest retained the classroom magazine company, Weekly Reader Publishing Group. It sold the World Almanac line, which published *The World Almanac, Book of Facts,* and *The World Almanac for Kids,* to Infobase Publishing.

Early 2009 plans had included the launch of a quarterly home improvement magazine called *Fresh Home*, but by the end of the year, the website and publication were still "under construction." Along the way, the company had decided to shift back toward more conservative coverage of lifestyle and issues. Among its larger efforts in this direction was a partnership with pastor Rick Warren to begin a quarterly print and online presence called *Purpose Driven Connection.* But November brought an announcement that after four print issues, publication would "move to an expanded, fully Web-based, digital format in January 2010 . . . ."

Changing Tack, Sailing Ahead

Struggling companies like Reader's Digest must, as Sulzberger might say, change tack to meet and serve their readerships. What follows is in essence a navigational chart to the past year's industry news.

Big publications create an environment that impacts smaller ones. Independent publishing flourishes in places, and drowns in others. In this period of survival, it is not a question of everyone for himself. How will publishers, editors, and writers make it to the distant shore? At least in part, by exploring all the potential routes and variations available.

➤ The July/August issue of the 300-year-old *Saturday Evening Post* introduced a redesign that aimed at making it both more contemporary and truer to its legacy than recent incarnations. Publisher Joan SerVaas said, "We plan to build on tradition by bringing our important historical magazine content more into the mainstream, so we can better understand and reflect how we've evolved culturally as a country." The new Editor in Chief is Stephen George, who had been at *Better Homes & Gardens*.

➤ The Children's Better Health Institute (CBHI), part of the Saturday Evening Post Society, saw considerable change last year. The nonprofit, now named U.S. Kids, consolidated the number of its children's magazines from five to three, serving ages three to twelve with *Turtle, Humpty Dumpty*, and *Jack and Jill.* The re-branding included a format redesign that Editor Terry Harshman believes is fresh, more contemporary, and more interactive. After years of being relatively closed to submissions, the magazines are now wide open to freelancers.

➤ *OK! Magazine* has struggled on the newsstands, and its response about a year ago was reportedly to move away from gossipy entertainment news and toward more of a lifestyle magazine. *OK!* has been through a series of top editors but as of the end of 2009, the lifestyle shift had not yet taken strong hold.

➤ Some of the big media companies know which way the wind is blowing. Hearst Corporation's *Food Network Magazine* had the strongest magazine launch since the *O Magazine* juggernaut.

New Magazines

➤ **1859 Oregon's Magazine:** www.1859magazine.com. Regional lifestyle quarterly with a focus on sustainability, recreation, entrepreneurship, history of Oregon. Freelance writers contribute most articles.

➤ **Acara Mia:** www.acaramiamagazine.com. Online magazine about fashion for infants through age 10, targeting affluent parents and grandparents.

➤ **Afar:** www.afar.com. International, "experiential," cultural travel.

➤ **Alpine, A Green Living Magazine:** http://alpinegreenliving.com. Regional quarterly on green living, from health to technology to recreation. Northern Nevada, Sierra foothills, Lake Tahoe.

➤ **Anthropology Now:** www.anthronow.com. Making anthropology clear, accessible, and part of contemporary issues and debates. Debuted in early 2009.

➤ **Arabella:** www.arabelladesign.com. Quarterly on Canadian art, architecture, design, and fine living.

➤ **Arise:** www.arisemagazine.net. African designers and culture, international. Glossy.

➤ **ArtSync:** www.artsyncmag.com. Quarterly on the arts in North Carolina.

➤ **Avenues:** www.areawidenews.com. Regional monthly from Area Wide News in the Ozarks, Arkansas. People, places, homes, businesses. Launched in September 2009.

➤ **The Baffler:** www.thebaffler.com. A highly liberal political magazine published from 1988 to 2003 that is being revived. As of the closing date of *Writer's Guide*, the website was only taking subscription addresses. The first issue was scheduled to appear in October 2009, but was delayed.

➤ **BBC Knowledge Magazine:** www.bbcknowledgemagazine.com. A science, nature, and history magazine launched in the U.K., which expanded to the U.S. in 2009.

➤ **Bible Study:** www.biblestudymagazine.com. Articles for the average reader on biblical studies, archaeology, and history, including profiles and interviews with pastors and scholars.

➤ **Bicycle Times:** www.bicycletimesmag.com. Covers "your everyday cycling adventure." Companion publication to *Dirt Rag*.

New Magazines

> *Big World:* www.bigworldmagazine.com. Travel, culture, ideas, food, people, essays. Open to submissions.

> *Blurt:* www.blurt-online.com. Music quarterly.

> *Blush:* http://blushmom.com. Canadian magazine for mothers, with an emphasis on being green.

> *b-Metro:* www.b-metro.com. City monthly for Birmingham, Alabama.

> *Brava:* www.bravamagazine.com. Madison, Wisconsin, women's magazine. New owners relaunched in August 2009, after publishing from 2002 through April 2009. Open to submissions about regional women and places.

> *Capital Style:* www.capital-style.com. Columbus, Ohio, quarterly women's magazine.

> *Cesar's Way:* http://channel.nationalgeographic.com/series/dog-whisperer/all/Overview58#tab-cesars-way-magazine. The lifestyle magazine based on the Dog Whisperer, Cesar Millan, debuted in September 2009. Published by IMG.

> *Charity Times:* www.charitytimesmagazine.ca. National Canadian magazine about charity issues, raising awareness about philanthropy.

> *Children's Health:* www.rodale.com. A special interest from Rodale Press, publisher of *Men's Health* and *Women's Health*. It appeared on newsstands in September 2009 and has the possibility of becoming an ongoing publication.

> *Clavier Companion:* www.claviercompanion.com. Bimonthly for piano teachers, performers, enthusiasts. Debuted in January 2009.

> *Coast Drive:* www.coastdrivemagazine.com. Luxury magazine for the Pacific Coast Highway region. First issue was November 2009.

> *DoubleX:* www.doublex.com. Web magazine for women spun off from *Slate*. Politics, cultures, sex. In November, however, the editors "retreated" and turned *DoubleX* back into a blog.

> *Drink Me:* http://drinkmemag.com. Lifestyle, epicurean magazine focused on "the art of and cultures of the world of alcohol." San Francisco bimonthly. Open to submissions.

> *East Texas Teen:* www.easttexasteen.com. Bimonthly for teen girls; fashion, health, conservative viewpoint. Published two issues. As of the end of 2009, the website indicated a restructuring with a new name, and national publication was underway.

New Magazines

➢ *Edible Queens:* www.ediblecommunities.com. Companion publication to *Edible Manhattan* and *Edible Brooklyn.* Covers the food culture of Queens, New York. Uses freelance writers.

➢ *Fit Parent:* www.fitparentmagazine.com. Healthy active families.

➢ *The Food Magazine:* www.thefoodmag.com. Launched January 2009. Profiles of celebrity chefs, recipes, travel.

➢ *Food Network Magazine:* www.foodnetwork.com/food-network-magazine/package/index.html. Had the largest launch numbers since *O Magazine.* Published by Hearst Corporation.

➢ *ForbesWoman:* www.forbes.com/forbeswoman. A website and print magazine published three times in 2009; packaged with *Forbes* and mailed to female subscribers.

➢ *The Fourth Period:* www.thefourthperiod.com/magazine. Lifestyle magazine for hockey fans. Quarterly relaunched in June 2009. Has been online for ten years. Looking for team correspondents.

➢ *FT Wealth:* www.ft.com/ftwealth. Britain's *Financial Times,* which re-launched last year, started publishing the quarterly *FT Wealth* in the U.S. in October 2009.

➢ *GetMarried:* www.getmarried.com. Online and television media company launched a national magazine in October 2009, with trends and products for weddings.

➢ *GirlMogul:* www.girlmogul.com. Bimonthly for girls 7 to 13 who are leaders active in their communities. Looking for writers for *GirlMogul* and *GirlMogul Mom.*

➢ *Gladys:* www.gladysmagazine.com. Quarterly on beauty, motivation, dreams, fashion, travel, luxury, for women. Went national with its third issue.

➢ *Go for a Ride:* www.gofarmag.com. Monthly motorcycle magazine out of Tampa, Florida. Launched late 2008, early 2009.

➢ *Golf Today, Northwest Edition:* www.golftodaynw.com. Golf in the Pacific Northwest. Monthly sister publication to *Golf Today, West Coast Edition*, which has been published for 22 years.

➢ *Guitar Aficionado:* www.guitaraficionado.com. Upscale lifestyle magazine, primarily for men, with a focus on guitars.

➢ *Hearts of the Country:* www.heartsmag.ca. Rural Canadian women.

➢ *Hunt Alaska:* www.huntalaskamagazine.com. Semiannual for Alaskan hunters. Companion publication to *Fish Alaska*.

➤ *Indie Game:* www.indiegamemag.com. Bimonthly, online and print. For video game developers and players. Very welcoming to submissions.

➤ *Ke Ola:* www.keolamagazine.com. Bimonthly about life on the Big Island of Hawaii.

➤ *LasVegas.net Magazine:* www.lasvegas.net. Online magazine that recently debuted a print version. Covers people, places, events in Las Vegas.

➤ *Long Island Parent:* www.liparentonline.com. Regional family magazine in New York.

➤ *Maine:* www.themainemag.com. Regional that replaced *Port City Life* in September 2009. Profiles of people, restaurants, homes, events. Accepts submissions online.

➤ *Maine Ahead:* www.maineahead.com. Business magazine with a November 2009 launch. Print and digital.

➤ *Make It Better:* www.makeitbetter.net. Regional lifestyle magazine for family and community on the North Shore of Chicago and its suburbs.

➤ *Minnesota Poker:* www.mnpokermag.com/magazine.php. Launch issue in July 2009.

➤ *Mixing Bowl:* www.mixingbowl.com/home. Meredith Corporation publication on food and friends based on its social website. One issue in July 2009, may go quarterly.

➤ *Modern:* www.idealmodern.com. Contemporary design. Glossy quarterly for high-end collectors of art, antiques, decorative arts. Brant Publications.

➤ *Modern Home + Living:* www.modernhomeandliving.com. Glossy, celebrity-based shelter magazine.

➤ *Moto Retro Illustrated:* www.motoretroillustrated.com. Magazine on classic motorcycles.

➤ *Mountain Sports + Living:* www.highcmedia.com. Relaunch of a quarterly lifestyle magazine covering mountain culture, sports, resorts, products, events.

➤ *Native Legacy:* www.nativelegacymag.com. Quarterly about the cultures, arts, and history of the Great Plains Indians.

➤ *OakBook:* www.theoakbook.com. Bimonthly about Oakland, California.

➤ *Observer Playground:* www.observer.com/playground. Packaged in the *New York Observer*. For affluent New York mothers and expectant mothers. Premiered fall 2009.

New Magazines

➤ *Portland Spaces:* www.portlandspaces.net. Architecture in Portland, Oregon, from home designs to neighborhoods, the city, and region. A bimonthly from the publisher of *Portland Monthly* and *Seattle Metropolitan*. Open to submissions.

➤ *Queens Karma:* www.queenskarma.com. Quarterly on holistic health, yoga, food. Distributed in Queens, New York, but articles are not limited to the borough. Launched in Fall 2009. Companion publication to *Gay Parent*. Open to submissions.

➤ *RacingWorld:* www.racingworldnj.com. Six issues yearly about auto racing in the Northeast.

➤ *Racin' Today:* www.racintoday.com. Online publication about motorsports, aiming to pick up on coverage where newspapers leave off. From experienced racing journalists.

➤ *Rejoice, a Multicultural Christian Magazine:* www.rejoicemag.com. Multidenominational; interviews and profiles. Open to submissions.

➤ *Scottsdale Health:* www.allyouneedforhappiness.com. Regional health and fitness magazine, Scottsdale, Arizona.

➤ *Serendipity, Inspirations for the Asian Bride:* http://theserendipity-magazine.com. Bridal magazine, weddings of Southern Californian Asian American brides. Welcomes submissions.

➤ *SevenCities:* www.24sevencities.com. Regional for Hampton Roads, Virginia. Launched in spring 2009. Open to submissions.

➤ *She Pedals: The Journal of Women in Cycling:* www.shepedalsmagazine.com. Quarterly; first issue mailed December 2009.

➤ *Simply Handmade:* http://scrapbooktrendsmag.com/handmade.html. New bimonthly. Seeking submissions of "creations."

➤ *Single Parent 101:* http://singleparent101mag.com. Published two print issues in 2009. The Maryland regional offers articles with advice from experts and parents.

➤ *Sky:* http://deltaskymag.delta.com. In-flight magazine from Delta Airlines. See contact page for editorial submissons.

➤ *Smart Girl Nation:* http://smartgirlnation.com. Online magazine about conservative politics for a community of women.

➤ *Southern Indiana Business Source:* www.sibusinesssource.com. Regional business magazine, for Chamber of Commerce members. Open to story ideas.

New Magazines

➢ **Southern Vermont Arts & Living:** www.vermontartsliving.com. In a region with a high number of artists, a quarterly for locals and visitors that covers the arts.

➢ **Southern Weddings:** www.swsmag.com. First issue, January 2009. Biannual. Emphasis on Southern traditions and weddings, but distributed nationally.

➢ **StrollerTraffic:** www.strollertraffic.com. Online resource and e-newsletter for city mothers.

➢ **Susie:** www.susiemagazine.com. Teen Christian girls.

➢ **The Tablet:** www.tabletmag.com. A daily online publication about Jewish news, ideas, and culture. Accepts pitches online.

➢ **Tame Pet Magazine:** www.tamepetmag.com. Quarterly for southwest Missouri pet lovers.

➢ **Teaching Canada's History:** www.historysociety.ca. New magazine from Canada's History Society. Aimed at teachers, it joins *The Beaver* and *Canada's History Magazine for Kids.*

➢ **TechKnow:** www.techknowmag.com. A Canadian online technology publication that debuted in August 2009.

➢ **Travel with Spirit:** www.travelwithspirit.com. Traveling for Christian families.

➢ **University Link:** www.ulmagazine.com. Fashion, music, sports, social issues for college students. Writers are primarily college journalism students.

➢ **Urban Farm:** www.hobbyfarms.com. A sustainable lifestyle and the local food movement, in the city and suburbs. Green products, gardening, recipes. Debuted September 2009. Companion magazine to *Hobby Farm,* and the Fancy Publications and Bowtie Magazines, such as *Dog Fancy, Cat Fancy.* Open to submissions.

➢ **Valley Faith:** www.valleyfaith.net. Online and annual print religious publication in the Red River Valley.

➢ **Vehicle:** www.vehicle-magazine.com. Quarterly contemporary narrative anthology stressing experimentation in story and art. Published in Canada.

➢ **Well Now:** www.wellnowmagazine.com. Health and fitness for mothers. Open to submissions.

➢ **West Valley Health & Living:** www.westvalleyhealthandliving.com. Phoenix, Arizona, health and lifestyle bimonthly.

➢ **WV Living:** www.wvlivingmagazine.com. West Virginia regional.

New Magazines

> **Women's Cycling:** http://womenscyclingmag.com. Women's bicycling, as sport and recreation. Has contributing writers.
> **TheWrap:** www.thewrap.com. Entertainment magazine. Uses freelance writers.
> **Xplor:** www.xplormo.org. A bimonthly nature magazine for Missouri children from the Missouri Department of Conservation. Not now using freelance, but anticipates accepting submissions in the future.
> **Your Teen:** www.yourteenmag.com. Quarterly print and Web publication for parents of teenagers.
> **Zone 4, Living in the High Country West:** www.zone4magazine.com. Gardening and outdoor living quarterly. Covers the Rocky Mountain states. Open to submissions.

> Martha Stewart Living Omnimedia made the news regularly last year, with high-profile editors coming and going, and its refusal to take lower revenues lightly. The flagship *Martha Stewart Living* is adding fashion, beauty, and travel to its editorial mix in hopes of attracting more advertisers. The company's health publication *Body + Soul* restructured and moved from Massachusetts to the corporate headquarters in New York.

> Forbes Media debuted *ForbesWoman* as a print quarterly and online. The launch was based on earlier, trial issues of *ForbesLife Executive Woman.* Coverage includes business, entrepreneurship, leadership, news, and luxury lifestyle.

> An innovative tack by *The Atlantic* was to divide an edition into regional quadrants centered on New York, Chicago, San Francisco, and Toronto. The monthly is now pursuing digital media, and its website has moved toward becoming a news aggregator.

> *The Wrap* launched. The Editor and Founder of the online entertainment magazine is Sharon Waxman, former Entertainment

Editor at the *New York Times.* Howard Schultz, the CEO of Starbucks, is one of the major investors. Given Starbucks' past history with expanding into various media, Schultz's investment is an interesting one.

➤ Bonnier Corporation appears to be doing well despite the economic climate. It acquired five magazines from Hachette Filipacchi Media: *American Photo, Popular Photography, Boating, Flying,* and *Sound & Vision.* In October, Bonnier also purchased *Conceive,* to add to its own *Parenting* and *Babytalk.* In November, the Transworld division named a new Editorial Director, Rob Campbell, who said the company expects to continue expanding "titles across new technologies."

➤ American Media, owner of the *National Inquirer,* returned the music publication *Country Magazine* to a weekly schedule, after publishing biweekly for a time. American Media also started selling *Country* on newsstands only, and ended its subscription base.

➤ *Life* never dies. The magazine has relaunched (again!), but publisher Time Inc. restructured and laid off hundreds of staff.

➤ Partnerships between publishers and other organizations and businesses could mean enriching the materials published for various media. In one example, *Nature Magazine,* from Macmillan's Nature Publishing Group, teamed with InnoCentive. The goal is to broaden "scientific collaboration and open innovation."

➤ Expanding its editorial content, *Southern Living* (Time, Inc.) now covers local artists, regional scenic drives, generational recipes, 30-minute entertaining, and decorating how-to's.

➤ Crain Communications' *Creativity* merged into *Advertising Age.*

➤ The Michigan-based *Spirituality & Health,* and the book review magazine *ForeWord,* looked to strengthen their business by teamwork and expansion. The two magazines joined to start a book publishing line. In 2009 Spirituality Health Media published *The Virtue of Wealth: Creating Life Success the Zenvesting Way* and

Carbonwise: An Average Midwestern Family's Search for a Responsible Standard of Living.

➤ In an interesting business experiment, in August, *ESPN, the Magazine* offered subscribers an annual renewal to its print version for one dollar, which included access to the paid website, *ESPN Insider*. The company saw the move not as much about *retention* as about aggressive pursuit of users who will last and resubscribe in future years.

➤ Even more dramatically, the print and digital music magazine *Paste* asked readers to help save it by contributing whatever they could. The magazine continues to publish.

➤ *Cowboys & Indians, the Premier Magazine of the West* continues to develop its brand through the glossy print version and a recent expansion and upgrade of its website.

➤ *Our Sunday Visitor* is the national weekly of the largest Roman Catholic publisher in the U.S. The 98-year-old company purchased Harcourt Religion Publishers, another large Catholic publisher. The acquisition strengthened Our Sunday Visitor's reach in Catholic education publications. Other OSV magazines are *Take Out: Family Faith on the Go; The Catholic Answer; My Daily Visitor;* and *Grace In Action*.

➤ Regional Down East Enterprises, publisher of *Down East Magazine*, sold its Performance Media to Anthem Media Group. The magazines include *Speedway Illustrated, NASCAR Insider,* and *Speedway Expo*.

➤ Great Lakes Publishing, which publishes a variety of regionals, acquired *Lake Erie Living* and *Over the Back Fence*.

On Hold or Gone

While magazines fade over the horizon in any economy, the number of substantial and small publications that have disappeared is somewhat disheartening. But behind some of the closed titles are healthy company consolidations, and the potential relaunches of other magazines.

➤ Wenner Media has put earlier plans for *US Style* on hold, but reportedly will try again to debut in the coming year.

➤ *Trump*, a Donald Trump vanity magazine, is no more. Publisher Ocean Drive Media took a new form, morphing into Niche Media.

➤ *Starlog*, a science fiction magazine, stopped publishing in print and moved fully online.

➤ *Mad* became a quarterly; *Mad Classics* and *Mad Kids* closed.

➤ No longer publishing are: *Accent Home & Garden; Arizona Woman; Bend Living* (former staffers opened *1859 Oregon's Magazine); Best Life; Blender; Breakaway, Brio,* and *Brio and Beyond* (from Focus on the Family); *The Church Herald; Cigar Report; CosmoGirl; Cotton & Quail Antiques Gazette; Country Home; Daughters; ExtremeTech; Jazz Times; KidZone; Launch; The Most; Open Air* (from *USA Today); Pray!; RN; Solano; Style Magazine (Las Vegas); Teen; Travel + Leisure; Washington Post* national weekly.

Book publishers reset their sights as much as magazine publishers this past year, through many of the same tactics: staff cuts, reigning in marketing and production costs, consolidating imprints or divisions, optimizing successful titles or strategies, and abandoning others. The book industry is also struggling with, and taking advantage of, the fast-paced digital revolution. The positives of the past year in book publishing are the still strong young adult market, and aligned with that, growth in the crossover publishing market among adult, teen, and children's books. Yet another important and still expanding crossover is the leap from print books to other media.

In the past, the technological trajectory of the book industry was somewhat slower than for magazines: People converted to online magazine and newspaper reading more quickly than they moved to electronic books. But the book publishing industry has now crossed a transformative threshold and it is embracing multiple media on all sides. Overall, the number of books published was up—with a *but* that must make publishers grateful for the technology of e-books. Numbers released by Bowker in mid-2009 indicated that, in the previous year:

> ➤ Total book output, print and electronic, was up by 38 percent.
> ➤ Nontraditional books—on-demand publishing— surpassed traditional print books for the very first time.
> ➤ Books produced by traditional print methods were down by 3 percent. Books produced by print on demand, one at a time or for short runs, were up by 132 percent.

Numbers from the different trade associations and media groups did not necessarily correlate, however, in a complicated financial year. The Book Industry Study Group (BISG) projected that overall book sales would grow by 1.8 percent by the end of 2009, and e-book sales would be up by 10 percent. Just for June, according to figures from the Association of American Publishers (AAP), e-book sales were higher by 150 percent over the same month in the preceding year, which meant an increase of $12 million.

Estimates from *Publishers Weekly (PW)* and the Institute for Publishing Research (IPR) are that, by the end of 2010, overall book sales would be down 0.5 percent. The projections are that trade book sales will be down or flat; paperback sales will decline less because consumers are turning to them for the lower cost. Education, professional, and standardized test publishing will be up overall, although reduced school and library budgets will impact sales. The *PW*/IPR study indicates that digital textbooks are a potentially huge area of growth. This study also predicted that after a small decline in 2009 (from $3.16 to $3.05 billion), children's book sales will be stable, at $3.05 billion, with paperbacks up slightly.

Year-to-date AAP figures released late in 2009 were:

> ➤ Adult hardcovers: down 12.2 percent
> ➤ Adult paperbacks: down 9.0 percent
> ➤ Adult mass-market: down 4.5 percent
> ➤ Children's/YA hardcovers: up 14.0 percent
> ➤ Children's/YA paperbacks: up 1.7 percent
> ➤ E-books: up 177.3 percent

Where the Good News Is: Teens Still Soar

The news of elevated numbers for children's and young adult book sales gets even better: *PW* reported that the largest teen category, which it labels fiction/fantasy/sci-fi, has grown 13 percent this year and that sales by 2013 will amount to a 30.6 percent increase over a five-year period.

Two publishers that recognized the continuing power of the teen market were Harlequin and Sourcebooks. In August, the well-known romance publisher launched Harlequin Teen. The company's Senior Editor, Natashya Wilson, said it was the perfect time to extend the brand to a new, growing, and strong audience. That's a difficult argument to refute in this year of the Twilight series phenomenon. Most of the Harlequin Teen titles will be trade paperbacks, but some will be e-books.

At Sourcebooks, the new YA imprint Fire will publish fiction across all genres; its first list had paranormal romance, a Civil War mystery, and a supernatural thriller. Editor Daniel Ehrenhaft said the imprint was named for those powerful moments of discovery that all teens experience. Discovering a favorite book, poem, or song as an adolescent is a moment that is burned into the memory.

Crossover publishing is undoubtedly one of the year's big success stories, and the book chains responded because they too are looking to teen and children's books for growth. Borders Group's CEO, Ron Marshall, said the company was counting on "kids and kitchens." Practically, that means those dwindling sections of the chain stores that once held CDs and DVDs are being used to extend the young readers (and cookbook) sections.

In July, Borders announced a distinct new teen section in its stores: Borders Ink. The Vice President of Merchandising/Trade Books, Kathryn Popoff, told the press, "We want this to be about more than the book." The section includes best-selling teen titles, and related merchandise (bookmarks, pencil cases, stationery, even action figures), plus other young adult titles, fantasy, manga, graphic novels, and some romance. Barnes & Noble stores have had teen reading sections for some time.

For publishers and booksellers alike, marketing is at the heart of the crossover—and marketing is changing dramatically in publishing. Is *Twilight* a teen or adult product? Both. Where is the line between trade books and mass-market? It's fuzzier all the time. Do Borders, Walmart, and that charming little shop around the corner sell different categories of books? Increasingly, no. As a result, publishers are changing how they deal with sales outlets. Where once they sent account representatives only to bookstores, the reps may now go to big box and other mass-market outlets too.

PW references PubTrack Consumer, a partnership of R. R. Bowker and Creative Byline, Inc., with these figures for children's books sold: 30 percent through chains; 18 percent, Internet; 12 percent, book clubs; 8 percent, other retail; 7 percent, mass-merchandisers; 5 percent, independent bookstores; 3 percent, warehouse clubs; 3 percent, book fairs; and 12 percent, all other.

The two big chains have also been duking it out for the tightening school and library market over the last year. Barnes & Noble increased the discount it offers teachers to 20 percent, and Borders went to 20 to 25 percent. Barnes & Noble brought out the big guns, though: It added the B&N@School website, to sell books and other educational products to teachers, librarians, and parents. Both online and in Barnes & Noble stores, it is now possible to search for a book by the widely used Lexile reading measure. The company has also increased its presence through book fairs, holding more than 10,000 of them in one year.

New Book Marketing Directions

Book marketing now goes well beyond bookstores. It also involves interactive websites, blogs, Facebook, Twitter, and more. Borders Ink has a Facebook page. Simon & Schuster launched Pulse It for teens. Pearson Education, which includes Penguin Books, launched Poptropica, a virtual world for children. (Turning the usual process on its head, the success of the Poptropica website has led to print books.) Penguin Group also launched From the Publisher's Office, an online network to help promote books and authors that are not getting big publicity.

Mitali Perkins, author of *First Daughter: White House Rules* (Dutton Books) came up with an innovative approach to promotion and started Twitter Book Birthday Parties. The idea is to hold a party via Twitter on the date of a book's release.

Publishers also are regularly thinking of multiple formats of a book across the media; of the increasing need for speed of publication; and reaching multiple audiences. That best-selling, high-quality picture book can be reformatted as a board book; the first of a series for older or younger readers; and, with new kinds of readers appearing all the time, it could be an e-book too. That science fiction or fantasy teen success may have adult interest (oh yes, those thirtysomethings reading the Twilight series), or be reworked for middle-graders. The list of books that can take the form of a graphic novel, reaching almost any age group, seems unending. Flux, the YA imprint of Llewellyn Worldwide, released its first graphic novel in September, *Black Is for Beginnings.* DC Comics had planned a graphic novel line for girls, Minx, that did not work out. Instead, in 2010 its Dark Horse imprint is publishing Jane Yolen's *The Last Dragon,* a graphic novel for teens. Papercutz is taking chapter books by Gail Carson Levine and creating graphic novels based on Disney Fairies, led by Tinker Bell. (For more on crossover markets, see the article, "Crossover: From Adult to Children's Writing & Back Again," page 103.)

The Big Guns: Struggles and Strategies

To be noticed by one of the big publishing guns has to be a dream of even the most literary of writers. But even if it is not, how the large publishing conglomerates of the world are faring, and what they are doing to be successful, impacts independent publishers, and ultimately every working writer. Highlights—or lowlights—of the year follow.

SIMON & SCHUSTER

Simon & Schuster has been innovative since its founding in the 1920s. It publishes literary books. It publishes popular books.

It started with a crossword book, which met with success because Richard Simon and Lincoln Schuster were good marketers. Despite big struggles, the publisher remains forward-thinking and true to its marketing roots. While its numbers were down at the beginning of the year, Simon & Schuster's sales increased 2.4 percent in the third quarter. In this instance, the adult division did better than the children's group, though it too had a small increase in sales. Over the past year, Simon & Schuster has restructured, revamped, replaced, and restarted. (For staffing changes generally, see the Book People Moving sidebar, starting on page 34.) Here is how:

➤ To take advantage of the strength of the young adult market, Simon & Schuster started Pulse It, a teen networking site named after the company's successful YA imprint (www.simonandschuster.com/pulseit). Targeting readers 14 to 18, it functions like other social networking sites, with profiles and friends. Like Goodreads (www.goodreads.com) and BookGlutton (www.bookglutton.com), Pulse It encourages reading and reviews of books, in this case Simon & Schuster titles. The site offers readers two books a month online for free.

➤ Another new site debuted earlier in the year to service elementary, middle school, high school, and college teachers and librarians: Simonandschuster.net.

➤ Traditional print galleys—the unbound pages of a book before it is published—are increasingly available online, as the digitized form of ARCs (advance reading copies). Simon & Schuster revealed in November that it would supplement its print galleys with Galley Grab (www.galleygrab.com), allowing galleys to be read on e-readers. (HarperCollins also distributed e-galleys at the summer publishing trade show, BookExpo.)

➤ The publisher came up with the innovative idea of selling

individual chapters from a best-selling health book series, You, beginning in November.

➤ Simon & Schuster joined with Vook, a new multimedia company, to create four *vooks*, a combination of video and book for the iPhone and iPod.

➤ In its various reorganizations, Simon & Schuster merged Pocket Books and Simon Spotlight Entertainment editors and publicity staff to create a new imprint called Gallery Books, in September. Pocket Books will return to mass-market paperback publishing. Early in the year Pocket Books took on the urban fantasy publisher Juno Books, to create Pocket Juno.

➤ The publisher combined the marketing departments of its children's and adult divisions.

HARPERCOLLINS

A subsidiary of Rubert Murdoch's News Corporation, Harper-Collins has its origins in New York City at the beginning of the nineteenth century. It claims today to be the first publisher "to digitize its content and create a global digital warehouse . . . ."

➤ In November, at the end of its first quarter and after a year of losses, HarperCollins announced a large increase in profits, although sales were slightly down. The children's and young adult group in particular did well, and e-book sales were solid in the first quarter.

➤ Earlier in the year, like other large publishers, HarperCollins had restructured. It closed the Collins division and the new children's imprint, Bowen Press; it also cut back Rayo, its Spanish-language imprint. A similar reorganization occurred in the U.K.

➤ HarperCollins released its first video book in February, *What Would Google Do?*

➤ At the summer BookExpo, HarperCollins distributed its

books primarily through e-galleys for the first time, for 9 children's books and 14 adult titles.

➤ The book publisher teamed with the magazine *Girls' Life* for a new tween series, Mackenzie Blue. Series promotions included an interactive website and music.

➤ Lauren Conrad's YA novel, *L.A. Candy,* made a big splash, in part because HarperCollins created viral mobile content, readable by scanning barcodes. In another endeavor, the Amanda Project website from HarperTeen promoted a YA mystery series.

HOUGHTON MIFFLIN HARCOURT
Houghton Mifflin Harcourt, founded in 1832, is one of the world's largest educational publishers. Its imprints and divisions include Harcourt School Publishers; Heinemann; Holt, Rinehart and Winston; Steck-Vaughn; and many others.

➤ Bruce Nichols became Publisher of adult trade and reference books in July.

➤ Houghton Mifflin Harcourt attempted to sell its trade division early in the year due to financial difficulties, but after various bids did not work out, the sale was stopped. Over the summer, a restructuring and refinancing of Education Media and Publishing Group (EMPG), Houghton Mifflin Harcourt's holding company, was underway; it was completed in September.

RANDOM HOUSE
The largest trade publisher in English, and publishing since 1927, Random House has been owned by the international media company Bertelsmann since 1998. It made frequent news since the recession hit, with all its comings and goings.

➤ Early in 2009, Random House Publishing Group changed its organizational structure, as did its Knopf Doubleday and Crown divisions. Bantam Dell and Dial Press came under the Random House aegis. By September, Steve Rubin, once the President and Publisher of Doubleday, was out after 25 years with Random House/Doubleday.

➤ Random House joined up with the social networking book club BookGlutton (www.bookglutton.com) to promote the publisher's books. Random House UK also started a book club-based social site, ReadersPlace, which joins AuthorsPlace.

➤ The publisher acquired San Francisco's Ten Speed Press and Tricycle Press, its children's imprint. They became part of the Crown Publishing Group.

SCHOLASTIC

After many layoffs and reassignments and faltering numbers last year, Scholastic saw an uptick in its first quarter for the 2010 fiscal year. Revenues rose by 14 percent overall. Children's book revenues rose 25 percent.

➤ Among the biggest news at Scholastic is that it has reorganized its book fairs, improving distribution through centralization. The company holds about 120,000 fairs at schools each academic year.

➤ Scholastic had some heat from teachers, however. Almost 1,300 signed a petition against using teachers to sell Scholastic's toy products to children.

➤ Environmental goals are important to Scholastic, which aims to increase the recycled paper it uses by 25 percent in 2010.

PEARSON/PENGUIN GROUP

Parent of Penguin Group, the British-based company Pearson

is now the world's largest publisher, according to the annual *Publishers Weekly/Livres Hebdo* ranking.

➤ Among Penguin's divisions is DK Publishing, which was restructured and reduced mid-year, largely because the reference market had softened. Early in the year, Pearson reported that its fiction and general nonfiction were holding their own, with reference and travel books weaker.

➤ In addition to launching the online sites Poptropica and From the Publisher's Office, Penguin Young Readers Group has another marketing effort directed at young readers. Called Point of View, the campaign focuses on challenging literary novels (www.pointofviewbooks.com).

➤ The textbook division provided digital texts when California Governor Arnold Schwarzenegger called for using e-books to help with the state budget. It was the first company to do so.

HACHETTE

Despite a difficult economy around the globe, the media giant Hachette reportedly is still looking to expand. The French-based company is now sixth largest in the world, on the *Publishers Weekly/Livres Hebdo* list.

➤ Hachette's sales, as reported in November, were up 15 percent in the U.S., in good measure owing to the Twilight books franchise and to Senator Edward Kennedy's memoirs.

➤ Hachette's commitment to digital media was reinforced with the November announcement of an arrangement with Tata Consultancy Services, to expand uses of the Web and other digital platforms. New product development growth is the clear message.

OTHER PUBLISHER NEWS

➤ When other publishers were down in early 2009, Blooms-bury USA sales were up about 36 percent. As the British publisher of the Harry Potter books, the company was actively looking to expand through other acquisitions.

➤ If it seems it could not be a worse time to develop a business, the still young novelty book publisher Just for Kids Press is beating the odds. In August, President Sean Sullivan reported that the company had tripled its sales over the preceding year. Just for Kids goes for unique, fun looks, and educational value.

➤ Hampton Roads Publishing signed a deal with Red Wheel/Weiser/Conari Press, which will distribute its books. It is also developing a list that will complement Red Wheel's.

➤ Lerner Publishing is now the U.S. distributor of the U.K.'s Andersen Press.

➤ Finney Company, an educational publisher and distributor, acquired Great Outdoors Publishing, which publishes books about Florida. The Great Outdoors list complements that of Finney's Windward Publishing.

➤ Turner Publishing bought the remaining inventory of Cumberland House, after Sourcebooks had first purchased about 90 of Cumberland's titles. Turner publishes adult and children's fiction and nonfiction. The flagship imprint specializes in regional history.

➤ Carson-Dellosa Publishing purchased School Specialty Publishing.

➤ Creating its own niche, the new, nonprofit Madras Press will publish fiction that has difficulty finding a home because it is too lengthy for magazines, but too short for a book. It publishes bound short stories and novellas.

➤ Amazon will be publishing reprints of books it deems interesting but forgotten or undervalued in its new imprint, Encore.

New Children's & YA Ventures

➤ **Alloy Entertainment Collaborative** was created early last year by Alloy Entertainment, publisher of the Gossip Girl series. Unlike the rest of the company, the Collaborative is open to submissions, with or without an agent. The dozen books on its list each year will primarily be women's fiction, and books for teens and children.

➤ At Britain's **Frances Lincoln Books**, Editorial Director **Janetta Otter-Barry** launched her own eponymous list.

➤ The San Francisco-based **MacAdam/Cage Publishing** debuted the Age Altertron, a new children's book series, with *The Calamitous Adventures of Rodney & Wayne, Cosmic Repairboys*. The publisher may be best known for its publication of *The Time Traveler's Wife*.

➤ The map company **Hammond Publishing** also moved into children's picture books with its first list in fall 2009. It had earlier launched a line of illustrated nonfiction for children and adults.

➤ Teaming up, **Capstone Publishers** and **Sports Illustrated Kids** debuted three lines of sports fiction and nonfiction for children.

➤ **Sterling Publishing** is working with the **American Museum of Natural History** to publish a series of science books, for adults and children.

➤ Growing primarily in children's books, as well as romance and fiction, **Sourcebooks** added a new imprint for young adults, **Fire**. It joins the three-year-old imprint **Jabberwocky**, which publishes picture books and middle-grade fiction.

➤ **Phoenix Books** is starting a children's and YA imprint, **Pickwick Press**.

➤ **I Am Hip Hop** is a new imprint from **PowerHouse Books,** a publisher that specializes in illustrated books on pop culture, fashion, celebrities, and fine art.

➤ A new nonfiction brand from **Lerner Publishing Group** is **Lightning Bolt Books,** for kindergarten to grade two.

Book People Moving

➤ Jon Anderson, formerly President of **Running Press,** replaced Rick Richter as President and Publisher of **Simon & Schuster Children's Books.** Richter was one of the founders of Candlewick Press.

➤ The Associate Publisher of **Aladdin**, Ellen Krieger, retired. She had been with Simon & Schuster for 25 years.

➤ Emma Dryden, former head of the **Atheneum** and **Margaret K. McElderry** imprints, left. Justin Chanda took over as Vice President and Publisher of Simon & Schuster Books for Young Readers.

➤ A Christian imprint now owned by Simon & Schuster, **Howard Books** has a new Vice President and Editor in Chief in Becky Nesbitt, formerly with **Tyndale House**.

➤ Formerly Editorial Director, Joe Rhatigan is no longer at **Lark Books,** a division of **Sterling Publishing**. He is now freelancing. Lark Books publishes arts and crafts, home decorating, gardening, and other books, and has a children's line. He was replaced by Paige Gilchrist.

➤ Also turning to freelancing, Liz Van Doren had been Editor in Chief of **Black Dog & Leventhal,** and before that, Editorial Director of **Harcourt** until it underwent a major reorganization.

➤ Jennifer Haller jumped from **Houghton Mifflin Harcourt** to **Penguin Young Readers Group,** as Vice President and Associate Publisher.

➤ Becky Saletan abruptly left Houghton Mifflin Harcourt and shortly after became Editorial Director of Penguin's **Riverhead Books.**

➤ Among its other layoffs, **Scholastic** let go Executive Editor Grace Maccarone, who had been with the company for 30 years. She became Executive Editor at **Wireless Generation**, an educational publisher.

➤ David Levithan became Vice President and Editorial Director of **Scholastic Trade Publishing**. He had been Executive Editorial Director of Scholastic Press Fiction, Multimedia Publishing, and PUSH.

➤ Debra Lande became Publisher at Scholastic's **Klutz** division. She had been at **Chronicle Books**.

➤ Editor Sheila Keenan left Scholastic, where she was part of the launch of the **Graphix** graphic novel imprint, to become Senior Editor

Book People Moving

at **Harry Abrams'** imprint, **ComicArts**.
➤ Luke Dempsey moved from Editor in Chief at **Hudson Street Press** to Editorial Director of Nonfiction at **Ballantine Books**.
➤ Theresa Howell left the **Cooper Square Publishing** imprint **Rising Moon**.
➤ Mary-Alice Moore became **Highlights for Children's** Executive Editor of New Product Development, to develop books and related products.
➤ The new Publishing Director of children's books at **Chronicle Books** is Josalyn Moran.
➤ Jim Joseph replaced Scott Watrous as President and Publisher of **Globe Pequot Press,** which publishes books on the outdoors and travel. Janice Goldklang came to Globe Pequot to oversee three of its imprints, Lyons Press, Skirt! Books, and Three Forms.
➤ After leaving her eponymous imprint at **HarperCollins**, Laura Geringer began editing books for **Egmont USA**.
➤ The new Vice President and Executive Editor of the **Random House** imprint is Andy Ward.

Alternative Routes

So many editors and other publishing personnel were laid off, or moved for other reasons over the past year, and so many companies restructured or tightened staffing, that many editors went in different career directions. A good number started their own enterprises. (See "The Dance of Change for Editors and Others," page 53.)
➤ Stephen Roxburgh, who founded Front Street and remained as its editor after the company was purchased by Highlights for Children, left to start a new venture, **namelos**. The consortium of publishing pros works with authors and artists creating children's books. Namelos also expanded into e-books and print on demand later in the year.
➤ Former HarperCollins Children's Books Editor Michael Stearns started **Upstart Crow Literary,** an agency.

Book People Moving

➤ After leaving her position as Scholastic Press Executive Editor, Kara LaReau started **Bluebird Works**, to work with authors and others on developing books.

➤ Sarah Shealy and Barbara Fisch launced **Blue Slip Media**, to provide publicity and marketing services for authors and publishers. Both had been publicity directors at Harcourt.

➤ Mark McVeigh left Simon & Schuster, where he had been Editorial Director of Aladdin. McVeigh opened up the **McVeigh Agency**, for children's and adult writers.

➤ Just as her eponymous children's imprint was about to debut, HarperCollins pulled the rug out from under Brenda Bowen (among the many others laid off). Bowen became a literary agent with **Sanford J. Greenburger Associates**.

More Publishing Technology News

➤ Scribd is a "social publishing site," where users can upload their own writing and other documents. The company has also made agreements with Random House, Simon & Schuster, Thomas Nelson, Workman, and others to publish and sell their books, or parts of them, online as well.

➤ Roaring Brook Press Executive Editor Nancy Mercado held a conversation via Twitter with author Nan Marino as a promotion for her middle-grade book, *Neil Armstrong Is My Uncle and Other Lies Muscle Man McGinty Told Me.*

➤ Hyperion Books, owned by Disney-ABC Television, experimented with a new e-imprint, Kernl, for releasing text and video. Its first Kernl concerned job hunting.

➤ Alexander Street Press, an e-publisher, and Arcadia Publishing, which specializes in local history books, teamed up to create a subscription research site, Local and Regional History Online:

A History of American Life in Images and Texts (http://asp6new. alexanderstreet.com/lrho/). It includes pictures and text on every state and parts of Canada.

➤ A new company, CellStories.net, is publishing short stories via cell phones, specifically the iPhone, as well as iPod Touch.

➤ Also using the iPhone is ScrollMotion, which brings books for adults, teens, and even picture books for children to the phone.

➤ E-publishing launched at Candlewick Press this year, starting with five books by Kate DiCamillo, including her latest release, *The Magician's Elephant.*

➤The President of Sterling Publishing, Marcus Leaver, told *Publishers Weekly* that he has decided on a new path for his business. Rather than spend most of his budget on trade shows and catalogues, he will be promoting Sterling's books singly, and primarily online.

Leaver's actions are likely a sign of the future. And they sum up the current and future state of book publishing: in flux, but moving ever closer to new forms, with high hopes of entering a newly expanding business climate for books.

Freelancing in Uncertain Times

By Mark Haverstock

C all it what you will: a recession, a downward correc-
tion, or a pause in recovery. The national economic
downturn has taken its toll on everyone, including
freelancers. Publications that have been around for decades
have cut back or closed their doors. "Print magazines and
newspapers are having a hard time right now," says writer
Donna Campbell Smith. "One editor told me her magazine has
been reduced by eight pages because of the recession. Some
others I've written for in the past are going online and reusing
articles I wrote for them in their print versions."

Assignments are tougher to find. "I work full-time for Clemson University, but have freelanced part-time since leaving the
newspaper biz eight years ago," says Ross Norton. "I was earning
between $600 and $700 monthly last year with two standing
freelance gigs. When Clemson started dealing with budget cuts,
I was glad to know that at least I could make my mortgage with
freelance income. But the same week I said that out loud, I lost

39

both freelance jobs as one of my outlets froze its freelance budget and the other closed *temporarily*. Of course, temporarily has now become permanent. I've done no freelance for a year and see none on the horizon for past clients."

The usual volume of customers that many freelancers have come to expect has also been diminishing. At the beginning of the recession, in the summer of 2008, sales of books and training materials on author B. J. Gallagher's website just about ground to a halt. "It was as if all of corporate America stopped buying anything. My phones fell silent and Web orders dried up. I was concerned about my ability to stay in business, as well as how to hold onto my house," she explains. "But, in the midst of my worry, I made a decision that transformed my fear into creative energy. I reminded myself that in every past recession, there have been people who made money—lots of money. I decided to be one of those people."

Marketing 101

Freelance writing is not for the fainthearted. It requires the wearing of many hats: writer, market developer, business manager. It also means learning to ride out tough financial times.

Freelancers are generally programmed to seek out new work periodically, but in a slow economy, we need to reprogram our patterns and accelerate our efforts if we expect to make a living. Freelance writers have the potential to do well because many publishers and companies still need things done but cannot afford to hire someone permanently or go through a high-priced agency. So how do you find these jobs?

Let everyone know you are looking. You really never know where work is going to come from. "To get the word out to potential clients, word of mouth is easiest and best," says author and writing coach Lisa Tener.

Do not overlook the obvious: the people who have hired you before. "You just need to let former clients and editors—people who already know and love your work—know that you are looking for referrals," says Tener. "Let them know what services you offer and what kind of clients you are looking for." Continue to cultivate these established relationships and see what else you can do for them.

> "I reminded myself that in every recession there are people who make money—lots of money. I decided to be one of those people."

Regularly seek new relationships with publishers. Learn how to query well, and then query like mad. "It's kind of like dating. Until you find the one you want to marry, you should keep all your options open and date lots of people," says Gallagher. "I'm always keeping an eye out for some cool publisher I haven't met yet and seeing if I have any ideas that would fit their publishing agenda."

Spend more time on self-promotion. Pass out your business cards. If you don't have a website already, get one. Network with other writing professionals and join professional or civic organizations. Blog, tweet, get LinkedIn, and blow your own horn.

Expand your reach. If you primarily write on one or two topics, start brainstorming articles in other niches. Do not overlook hidden markets like company newsletters or trade publications. While many industries are struggling right now, there are still plenty of opportunities to branch out and find new markets.

Keep Your Work in Circulation

Think of yourself as a circus juggler, but instead of keeping several balls in the air at once keep multiple manuscripts or proposals in circulation. You cannot sell unless your product is out there in the hands of potential clients, and the more work and ideas that are circulating, the better the odds. If one project comes back, get it off to another appropriate market as soon as possible. Do not drop the ball.

"I wrote a dozen book proposals and pitched them to various publishers, with great success," says Gallagher. "As a result, I have six new books published in the first six months of this year, including the perfect self-help book for these times, *It's Never Too Late to Be What You Might Have Been* (Viva Editions). Two more books will be published this fall. Eight books is an amazing number for any author in any year, much less in the midst of a recession, with the book business flat!"

Keep the projects coming on a regular basis. "I've got writing book proposals down to a science now. I can crank them out quite fast because I know what the formula is. It's no secret," Gallagher says. "Learn formats: book proposals, pitch letters, feature stories, opinion pieces, etc. There are formulas for all of them and once you've got the formula mastered, your work is much easier."

Diversify

Out of necessity, writers take on additional jobs to fill the gaps in income. This is especially important in times when writing assignments are few and far between. It might mean working retail or waiting tables. But frequently the best possibilities are ones connected, even peripherally, to the writing profession. Consider conducting writing workshops, seeking a teaching gig at a local community college or university, or writing

How Much Do I Charge?

It is a question that all freelancers ask at one time or another—and there is no single answer for all people or situations. You should be aware of some market practices, however, when pricing your work.

Periodicals. Most magazines and newspapers have standard rates determined by the word, page, or column inch. There is seldom room for significant negotiation, unless (1) you are a regular contributor; (2) significant expenses are involved in the research and production of the piece; or, (3) you are taking on a rush job, and the editor wants you to drop everything to write the piece ASAP.

Books. The bean counters at most publishing houses have payment down to a science. Typically, standard offers are made in the form of an advance plus royalties. Some companies may even offer to buy books outright, under a work-for-hire agreement where the writer gets a flat fee payment and retains no rights to the work. There is more wiggle room here than for periodicals, especially if you have an agent to negotiate for you, or you have a following among readers.

Other Writing Services. Here is where you have more opportunities to name your price, within reason. Whether you ghostwrite a book, write advertising copy, or provide website content, your rates will depend on your writing expertise, experience, and reputation. Some writers charge by the hour, others by the project. After doing enough assignments and working through quotes and offers, you will come up with baseline rates specific to you.

Writer's Market's "How Much Should I Charge" section, based on surveys of writers' and editors' organizations, is also helpful.

Online Rate Articles
➤ **Meryl.net:** Meryl K. Evans, www.meryl.net/2008/04/28/how-much-should-I-charge-for-writing
➤ **Writing-World:** Moira Allen, www.writing-world.com/rights/fees.shtml
➤ **Professional Writers Association of Canada:** www.writers.ca/whattopay.htm
➤ **The Write Direction:** Debra Jason, www.writedirection.com/rprt300e.htm

advertising copy for local businesses. Or try a new medium, such as the Web, to expand your reach.

T. Shawn Taylor is a professional writer who has been quite fortunate when it comes to finding work. "I got laid off from a newspaper in December 2005, but immediately started getting offers to write research reports, Web content, press releases, and commentary," she says. "Word of mouth has been terrific, but I know I cannot rely on that system forever. There are many journalists who have been set free over the last couple of years, and they're all out here looking for work. Freelance isn't my focus, because I've always viewed that as a quick way to starve."

Occasionally, Taylor writes for newspapers and magazines, but she has also learned to try new income opportunities. "I believe writers have to be more versatile, and be willing to take jobs they might have balked at a few years ago. Writing Web content and press releases isn't sexy, but it pays the bills. I do a lot of work for small businesses and nonprofits, and I can honestly say that it has been rewarding."

Taylor also started a writing and media consulting company called Treetop Consulting, which she believes has helped her establish credibility. Being a former editor and reporter for the *Chicago Tribune* did not hurt either. "Many writers don't realize the value they can bring to businesses and projects outside the industry," she says.

Julie Engelhardt, a freelancer who has written primarily for parenting, health, and travel publications, took a different tack to supplement her freelancing business in a down economy. "I began writing Santa Claus and Easter Bunny letters for children," she says. "It sounds a bit juvenile, but I was kept extremely busy crafting and sending these letters to kids."

Though the work is obviously seasonal, it helped Engelhardt improve her cash flow. It also fit in well with her writing style and schedule. "I'm a part-time writer, so this type of work was quite refreshing because it allowed me to be creative and continue to be my own boss," she says. Santa Julie does this all by herself, at least for now, but if business continues to grow as she anticipates, she may need to hire some elves.

Tener markets her skills as a writing coach to help others become more successful. "While there may be fewer well-paid writing opportunities, editing and writing coaching opportunities abound. People writing blogs, Web content, e-books, and self-published books need help learning how to articulate their messages." She finds editing extremely fun, "partly because you're not just correcting someone's writing, you're teaching them to write well. Poorly worded sentences or feebly constructed stories offer your creative mind lots of exercise in problem-solving."

Do More

Editors are working harder than ever because of staffing and budget cuts. "If you can help them visualize a well-rounded compelling package, where they don't have to do the legwork or imagining, you're going to work your way to the top of their list," says writer Kelly Bastone. Adding little extras to your pitches can make editors sit up and take notice.

There is also a need for diverse formats, according to Bastone. "It's not just print anymore. Can you provide a *call out* to a video on the Web? Can you provide photos?" she says. "For years, a lot of the magazines I worked for told me they didn't need me to take photos, that they would send a photographer."

Recently that scenario has changed. If a freelance writer can take decent photos and is already on location, then an editor does not have to pay travel and expenses for both a writer and photographer. "I've noticed much more editor interest in me packing a camera and taking the shots, to round out a print

Attention: Starving Writers

WANTED: Writers and aspiring writers needed for the Web.
Write as much as you want.
It's easy to get started and make money.

Ads everywhere recruit writers for Web content, on sites not generally associated with print magazines. Maybe you have gotten such e-mail solicitations or have seen the website ads. It seems simple enough: Register with the site, submit short articles on assigned topics or pitch your own topics, and wait for the money to roll into your PayPal account.

Sadly, you may end up working very hard for very little cash. Plans may pay based on *pay-per-click*—how many times a piece is viewed at the website. Or, they may make *upfront payments* in the form of a flat fee, which is basically the equivalent of payment upon publication in the traditional print market. Many sites buy all rights, meaning only they can resell the articles, and you cannot.

➤ Associated Content offers "upfront payments ranging from $1 to $20 for certain types of content. All of the content you publish can earn you money via Performance Payments, which currently pays a baseline PPM™ rate of $1.50 for every one thousand page views it receives," according to its website.

➤ Demand Studios offers writing, editing, and video work. The homepage at the time of this writing said there were 65,221 freelance jobs available, paying $559,834.71. That works out to an average of $8.58 per job if you do the math. Blog posts from writers who have worked for Demand Studios indicate its flat fees average about $15.

➤ Examiner.com's workings were reviewed by Angela Hoy, Editor of *WritersWeekly.com* e-zine ("How Much Are Examiner.com Writers

Attention: Starving Writers

Really Earning?" May 13, 2009). She asked her readers to share their experiences doing work for the site. She changed the names of writers to protect their privacy, but determined that Penny earned $526.17 for 229 articles, averaging $2.30 per article. This was the highest per piece mentioned in the article. At the low end, Mario earned 21¢ for 3 articles, or 7¢ an article. One respondent, Marianne, went through the Examiner.com application process but eventually declined to work for them because, she said, "I just don't understand why writers are willing to give away their time and work." From another perspective, Barbie agreed that the pay is poor but used the site "as a platform builder and for self promotion."

Put things in perspective when you consider Web content offers. At the low end of the print market, regional parenting publications generally pay from $20 to $100 for a short article, and it is standard practice that the author can resell such articles at any time in a noncompeting market. That is, if you sell an article to *Fort Worth Child* on the movement to increase elementary school recess time, you can probably sell it the next month to *Western New York Family*. Religious publications such as *Guide* pay 6¢ to 12¢ a word, while high-profile periodicals like *Rolling Stone* pay $1 a word. I recently sold a 500-word piece to a little-known website for $35, and the editor even apologized that she could not offer more out of her limited budget.

If you write well—and are very prolific—you might make enough from Web content sites to help pay the bills. But can you really make a living? You decide.

version [of an article], but also for the Web," says Bastone. Pictures do not have to be as technically perfect for the Web as they do for print, and many new digital still cameras can take video that is adequate for display on websites.

"I'm a contributing editor for *Backpacker*. As part of its Web development, the magazine wanted to incorporate more video and interactive elements, and the editors asked if I'd be willing to start shooting video for some of the stories I did for them," Bastone says. "Not only was I willing, but I also thought it was a lot of fun." The success of these article add-ons depends on learning some basic video and photography techniques, as well as developing an artistic eye. "Study a magazine's photography like you study their articles," says Bastone. "What do the photos have in common? What kind of angles do the photographers use?"

With many magazines developing a Web presence, article add-ons are likely to become more important. Look at print and Web editions of a magazine. Is there any additional content on the Web version that does not appear in print? If so, it might be worth pitching website content as part of your proposal.

Brand and Network

Freelancers may find more competition and fewer traditional writing jobs, but the up side is the expanding number of non-traditional possibilities. To compete in a diverse multimedia world, you cannot just go by your freelance job description or be identified by the occasional articles you published in *Boys' Life*, *Car and Driver*, *Guideposts,* or your regional newspaper. You need to establish a platform, or brand, for yourself, based on your reputation, expertise, skills, and interests. Become your own marketer for Me, Inc.

"In the latter half of a bygone century, successful freelancers gained prestige and were assured of a healthier income by creating alliances with book and periodical publishers and their editors," says literary agent Robin Mizell. "A writer who could consistently deliver professional copy on a deadline was an editor's dream, and those writers' professional identities became closely aligned with their publishers' brands. A talented colleague might have been defined primarily by his or her work for a well-known periodical. Writers who did not have an inside track with mainstream publishers, or identified opportunities outside of the mainstream, ventured into new media: websites, blogs, forums, podcasts, self-published e-books, and online social networks. Gradually, the best of these freelancers attracted recognition, acquired followers and clientele, and became their own brands."

Today, brands are everything: They distinguish the Cokes, Nikes, and Starbucks of the world. So how do you distinguish yourself? Identify the qualities that make you different from other freelancers. What is it about your writing that makes it different? Your brand is the service that is unique to you—one that cannot easily be duplicated by the writer down the street.

Becoming a known source is vital to any author—freelance, staff, member of a stable, book or magazine—who wants to develop a successful career. Just like the big corporations promoting a brand, you need to do a little advertising of your own. Take advantage of social networking sites on the Web, blogs, tweets, and special interest sites frequented by those in the writing business. "A freelancer's best advertisements have always been satisfied clients and recently published work, which can be showcased with a website or blog that includes the writer's brief biography, areas of expertise, and current contact information," says Mizell. "Over time, the effort a writer invests in building and maintaining an online platform can pay off in assignment opportunities that would otherwise be missed."

Job Searching on the Web

Among the questionable sites that periodically pop up on the Web, there are also bona fide job sites for writers that are worth checking for job leads. Although most of these sites have generally good reputations, exercise some caution when replying to specific ads. Insist on seeing a publication and submission guidelines before agreeing to take any job or submitting a manuscript. Here is a review of some of the job sites.

➢ <u>Craigslist</u>. Despite its at least partly undeserved reputation, Craigslist can still be a good source for writing-related jobs. The site does try to stay on top of scams. Many writers' jobs posted on other sites come from Craigslist, which tends to be up to date. www.craigslist.org

➢ <u>Elance</u>. On this selective site, all new providers must take and pass a basic admissions test before placing proposals and having their profiles listed in search results. Elance charges freelancers to use its services and bid for projects. www.elance.com

➢ <u>JournalismJobs</u>. JournalismJobs.com is the largest and most visited resource for journalism jobs. You can search its job database, or post your résumé. www.journalismjobs.com

➢ <u>Online Writing Jobs</u>. This is a compilation of job ads for writers, and it's quite helpful in terms of finding specific types of writing, like journalism, creative, ghost writing, etc. www.online-writing-jobs.com

➢ <u>Writing-World</u>. This site features a long list of writing and editing job board links. www.writing-world.com/links/jobs.shtml

Writer and equestrian guru Donna C. Smith tries to get as much exposure online as possible. "Right now my best networking medium is HubPages.com," she says. HubPages calls itself "the leading online publishing ecosystem," and consists of publishing tools and an author community, with the goal of helping members earn income. Smith explains, "I've had some assignments, both writing and photography, come my way as a result of editors finding their way to one of my Hub articles." The articles also include links to her books on Amazon.com.

Smith has been a member of Writer's BBS (http://writersbbs.com), an international writers community, for at least 15 years and met the current publisher of her young adult historical fiction books through the forums there. "Facebook.com is also a good networking website; Writers and Friends (www.writersandfriends.org) is another one of my favorite hangouts."

Persistence Pays

Experienced freelancers are almost perpetually in job-seeking mode; it becomes second nature. "Writers have always worked hard, often at multiple projects, to earn a living. They're a collegial bunch, quick to offer each other assistance and encouragement, and modest about their own achievements," says Mizell. "These traits help them adapt to rapid technological developments and make it through tough times."

Smith suggests that in these lean times we have to pull from our creative selves to come up with new ways to market our writing, while keeping up with the changes in the industry. "I think we just have to hang in there, work hard at marketing our writing, and keep our name circulating," she says, "and don't quit the day job if you're blessed enough to have one."

Finally, work hard to keep your attitude positive, optimistic, and upbeat. "The most important thing I did to thrive in this recession is that I managed my emotions, attention, and attitude at all times. I focused on what I can do, not what I can't do," says Gallagher. "I took more risks, not fewer risks. I geared up rather than hunkering down. I brought more new products to market, not fewer new products. I swam upstream, ignoring people in retreat all around me. I ignored the chorus of *ain't it awful* that was being sung by newspapers, TV pundits, and people on the street. Recessions don't last forever and by staying positive, I figured I was doing my little bit to help turn it around faster."

Branding

➤ "Personal Branding Becomes a Necessity in Digital Age," Mark Glaser, *Mediashift* (July 16, 2009).
www.pbs.org/mediashift/2009/07/personal-branding-becomes-a-necessity-in-digital-age197.html
➤ See "Business Cards to Blogs, Creating a Marketing Platform," page 171 of this *Writer's Guide to 2010.*

The Dance of Change for Editors & Others

By Judy Bradbury

The publishing business is constantly in motion, though the tempo changes with the times. Publishing staff fox-trot *(slow-slow-quick-quick)* from house to house. Companies merge, diverge, and divest *(cha-cha-cha)*. Assistants waltz up the street to become editors, while editors high-step it to executive offices, and executives tap dance on tables when a *Twilight* hits, or shuffle off when the balance sheet rhythm falters.

The latest dance consists of editors and others leaving publishing houses altogether, for literary agencies or to form their own—sometimes unique—businesses. It is no wonder authors get dizzy trying to follow along. Nevertheless, being in the writing business means keeping apace of changes. To that end, here is news on some of the moves over the last year. Tap to the beat at your desk, and perhaps contemplate a new dancing partner of your own.

Blue Slip Quality

Barbara Fisch and Sarah Shealy have two-stepped for more than 15 years. They began their collaboration at Harcourt Brace Jovanovich (HBJ) in the marketing department. They job-shared the senior publicist position, the first such arrangement in the company. In 2002 they were promoted to Associate Directors of Publicity and survived three company mergers, "all the while doing the work that we love—talking about books we adore, calling an author to schedule an interview, coming up with the perfect pitch for a new title, and sharing a laugh with a reviewer," says Shealy. "We finish each other's sentences and truly can't imagine not talking about children's books every day."

When Houghton Mifflin bought Harcourt and this duo eventually lost their position, they decided to choreograph their own steps with Blue Slip Media (www.blueslipmedia.com), a publicity and marketing service for the children's trade book industry. Fisch explains how she and Shealy came up with the name for their joint venture: "At one time, supervisors at HBJ placed *blue slips* in employees' personnel files when they did something extraordinary. As HBJ transitioned to Harcourt Brace & Company and then to Harcourt, the blue slip system fell by the wayside, but we continued to use the phrase as a metaphor for a job well done."

Fisch and Shealy sustain a high level of service to their clients. "In a business climate where major publishing houses are stretched thin, we offer expertise in crafting effective press releases; targeted mailing lists; and niche and local market outreach and event planning—to create comprehensive campaigns for print and online media," says Shealy. Fisch adds, "The work is very similar to what we've always done. We look at books and try to assess where audiences might be and how to reach them. It's a different piece of the puzzle now in that we look at how we can complement the marketing being planned by the publishing house." With each partner having more than 20 years of experience in the industry, they know the market well; their successful track record proves they are effective working in tandem with authors, artists, and publishers to maximize a book's reach.

Fisch and Shealy offer a variety of services to authors in addition to the press releases, mailing lists, and niche marketing. They help develop pitch letters, author bios, and background materials; target pitches to media, from local to regional to national, in print, online, and broadcast formats; package and mail books and press materials; coordinate bookstore appearances and tours; plan and execute online publicity campaigns, including blog tours; create supplemental materials, such as discussion guides, curriculum guides, and event kits; and offer manuscript marketing evaluations for Society of Children's Book Writers and Illustrators (SCBWI) members.

"Authors have learned they need to be more savvy; smarter," says Shealy, "and we can help them as they become more hands-on. We have the freedom to think outside the box." Fisch finishes the thought: "Things have changed so much. There's more demand but fewer people and fewer marketing dollars at publishing houses. There will always be more that can be done, and that's where we come in. It's a rewarding, positive place to be."

Creative Consulting

Kara LaReau is finding the place where she has landed to be rewarding as well. For more than ten years, LaReau edited award-winning books for young readers, first at Candlewick Press and more recently at Scholastic Press. She tangoed with such authors as Rosemary Wells, Paul B. Janeczko, and Alison

McGhee. Kate DiCamillo calls LaReau an "intuitive, exacting, and truly outstanding" editor. When LaReau's position at Scholastic was eliminated, she explains, "I decided to spread my wings and offer my creative consulting services through my own company." She named that business Bluebird Works (www.bluebirdworks.com).

"So far," LaReau is happy to report, "the transition has been surprisingly smooth. I have a really nice list of clients now, and I'm working on a range of amazing projects, from very young picture books to young adult novels." She finds this new venture a blend of tried and true practice, and stretching herself in new directions. "In many ways, I'm doing exactly what I was doing

Book Launching Tips

Sarah Shealy and Barbara Fisch of Blue Slip Media offer these suggestions for launching your book.

➤ Provide your publisher with a list of contacts you know well who should see the book. (To ensure timely delivery, include complete addresses.) Send personal notes to go along with each book so that all the publicist needs to do is pack and ship to those addresses.

➤ Include all pertinent information to optimize those contacts—your neighborhood, for local papers; the year you graduated and your major, for your college alumni magazine; and so on.

➤ If you are hoping to garner sales in nontraditional book markets, be sure any printed materials you develop include accurate ordering information and a contact in your publisher's sales office.

➤ Keep timing in mind. It is best to ask your publisher for promotion and publicity when your book is new. Do not wait until it is a backlist title.

➤ Take your local bookseller or librarian to lunch.

before—developing manuscripts and cultivating new and established talent—but now I'm doing it on my own rather than for a publisher. There is a certain freedom I enjoy, and I'm no longer exposed to the politics and anxieties that can be a part of publishing, especially these days. But being in business for myself also means that I am the one responsible for making sure I get a paycheck each week. It's a bit stressful, but it's also exhilarating."

Despite dancing to a new tune, LaReau's professional goals remain the same. "I've always had two objectives in my work: to nurture talented artists and create great books. Through Bluebird Works, I'm fully dedicating myself to these pursuits, in delivering singular editorial and copywriting services for projects, reviewing and developing manuscripts, and offering all levels of creative advice and support."

As a published author, LaReau appreciates the demands of the writing process. "I enjoy collaborating with artists who are passionate about their work and about writing in general; who understand and appreciate the role of revision in the bookmaking process; and who possess an open mind, a good sense of humor, and a willingness to take risks." At Bluebird Works, LaReau keeps these attributes firmly in mind. "The market is clearly changing, but I don't think any of us are quite sure what's going to happen next. All we can do is try to stay flexible. The downsizing of so many publishers means that there are fewer editors on staff, which means fewer acquisitions and a longer response time for manuscripts, so authors need to have a bit more patience and fortitude, and they need to make sure their work is at its very best when it goes out. That's where I come in. I'm on hand to help in getting manuscripts in optimum condition for submission, and I'm on hand to offer whatever support and advice I can."

Bluebird Works offers three tiers of editorial service. *Preliminary evaluation* includes the review and consideration of a full manuscript, a detailed editorial letter outlining project strengths and weaknesses, and a follow-up telephone conversation. *Revision service* is the equivalent of one in-depth round of editorial revision, including a review of the full manuscript, a detailed editorial letter outlining macro issues, detailed line editing of the manuscript, a follow-up phone conversation, and, if and when ready, preparation of the manuscript for submission to a publisher or agency. *Additional revision* is available when necessary, ranging from another in-depth round to light copyediting and polishing.

Heard But Not Seen

Namelos (www.namelos.com) has taken the floor with some new and original steps. Composed of a team of publishing professionals with decades of combined experience in editing, design, art direction, subsidiary rights, sales, and marketing, namelos is an agency that provides services to authors, agents, and publishers. The concept began with Stephen Roxburgh, who was formerly President and Publisher of Front Street, the small independent press he founded. Most recently he was Publisher at Boyds Mills Press, which acquired Front Street in 2004. Roxburgh says, "In these difficult times, publishers are reducing staff, laying off editors, art directors, designers, and support staff. Increasingly, resources are devoted to the sales and marketing end of the process. Development is time-consuming and expensive. But publishers still need books. Namelos is a source for books, and for support with just about every piece of the publishing process."

The company title (pronounced *nam-a-lohs*) means *nameless*, and comes from a medieval German poem, *Valentin und Namelos*. The philosophy behind the choice is made clear on website: "We believe that we should be heard (by the author) and not seen (by the public). What goes on between an author and an editor in their work on a project is intimate and private." Roxburgh offers details. "We work with writers and artists on the development of projects we think are publishable. Our primary service is editorial development: evaluating and developing projects to enable writers to place them with an agent or publisher. We guide efforts and offer support on every level, from design and art direction to marketing, publicity, promotion, and subsidiary rights. We do everything a publisher does except manufacture, warehouse, and distribute books." Roxburgh considers his team a bridge from an author who has a project that needs work to "that same author [but] with a publishable project ready to be handled by an agent or sold to a publisher."

The process takes time and diligence. "The first step is an evaluation that enables namelos to determine if the project has merit," explains Roxburgh. "If we feel it's not yet viable, we'll suggest ways the writer might improve it, though we won't continue to work with the author on that project. If the project has merit, however, we'll offer suggestions for how to develop it. Further services are incremental and range from a phone conversation to an in-depth editorial assessment of a full draft of a novel, much the same as what an author under contract receives from an editor."

Roxburgh says namelos "won't move to the next step unless we feel the previous level was successfully achieved. It is not our intention to work on projects we feel don't have potential for publication, or to work beyond a substantially productive point. When a project is, in our opinion, publishable, we suggest guidelines for presenting it to agents and/or editors. If we feel a project is right for a particular agent or a specific editor, we will make the introduction."

The namelos dance card includes other options. Once a book is published, it must garner attention. "Marketing is like making omelets: It's best done one book at a time," reflects Roxburgh. "Large publishing houses have many books to promote, with limited resources. Not all of the books get equal attention. In addition, some books benefit from niche marketing, which requires going beyond the blanket efforts provided by the publisher. We can get books into the hands of the right people. We also help authors promote themselves: We can build low-cost websites and explain to authors how to maintain them, compose press releases and promotional pieces, manage targeted mailings, and more." Still evolving, namelos will expand and modify its services.

Encore

Other editors moving to a new beat are Brenda Bowen, Mark McVeigh, and Joe Monti.

Bowen, whose eponymous imprint at HarperCollins was a victim of the economic downturn just as she was about to launch her debut list, left the company in early 2009. Midyear she announced her decision to take a position as a literary agent with Sanford J. Greenburger Associates (SJGA). Bowen represents authors and illustrators of children's books for all ages from preschool to young adult, as well as select adult titles. She plans to build her client list gradually, and also to package books for publishers. "It's great to be an independent agent within an established firm," says Bowen. "I get the benefit of my colleagues' experience, the stability of SJGA's steady backlist, and the latitude to sign a wide range of authors and illustrators." Bowen brings considerable experience in the field of children's books. In addition to her recent stint at HarperCollins, in nearly three decades of service in the industry Bowen has collaborated with a stellar list of authors and illustrators at Disney, Simon & Schuster, and Scholastic Press.

Mark McVeigh's meteoric rise in children's publishing included positions at "virtually every major publishing house" over the course of an 11-year career. Most recently Editorial Director at Aladdin, McVeigh decided last year "to take the leap and open

> "The only limit I place on my list is that my clients' books must take me somewhere I've never been before."

my own literary agency." His *boutique*, the McVeigh Agency (www.themcveighagency.com), represents adult and children's authors, graphic novelists, photographers, and illustrators. "My clients create everything from literary fiction and nonfiction for adults and children to graphic novels, photographic books, and picture books. The only limit I place on my list," states McVeigh, "is that my clients' books must take me somewhere I've never been before."

Joe Monti, formerly Director of Paperbacks at Little, Brown Books for Young Readers, also took the leap to agenting last year, joining Barry Goldblatt Literary (www.bgliterary.com). Monti describes this switch as one that "combines what I'm good at with what I love about working in publishing: tracking and encouraging trends and discovering and encouraging writers and artists." Monti is focusing on children's and teen literature as well as adult genre fiction, particularly fantasy and science fiction, and he hopes to work with "writer-artists of graphic works." Cultural diversity and books for boys are of big interest to Monti. "Guys will read if they have a range of material that interests and speaks to them," believes this former children's fiction book buyer for Barnes & Noble, a position he held for over ten years.

The magical melody, the underlying chords, the three-part harmony of author-editor-reader ring true in publishing. Although dancers may twirl and dip to a new tune with a new twist, one thing never changes in the switch-of-the-hat dance of publishing: the bow to the book at the end.

What Women & Girls Read & Why

By Jan Czech

W riters often hear the assertion that boys only read books about boys while girls read everything they can get their hands on. The logical conclusion is that boys limit themselves, while girls are open and allow themselves a much wider range of choices. Do girls read more than boys, and does the behavior extend into adulthood? Do women read more, and more widely, than men?

A few years ago, award-winning author Ian McEwan (*Atonement, Saturday, On Chesil Beach*) put this possibility to the test when he passed out books from his own library in a London park. He found that women were more likely to accept a free book, and be excited about it. Most men kept their distance and did not take up McEwan on his generosity. Tongue in cheek, the author published his findings in the *Guardian*, saying, "When women stop reading, the novel will be dead."

Publish or Perish

Steven Chudney, founder of the Chudney Agency, knows McEwan's statement is an exaggeration, yet says, "I would hate to think that might be even close to the truth, but he does have a point. Publishers need to explore and figure out the buying patterns of men and see what more they can do to attract more men readers."

A publishing industry veteran, Chudney held various sales and marketing positions at Viking; Penguin; Farrar, Straus and Giroux; Simon & Schuster; and Winslow Press before opening his agency in 2002. He sold and marketed every imaginable type of book—adult and juvenile, hardcovers, paperbacks, and pop-up books—to wholesalers, independent bookstores, and chain stores. He attended countless acquisitions meetings, which gave him a bird's eye view of what publishers were looking for. While Chudney would like to believe that a good book is a good book, whomever the intended audience, he admits, "One can discern that there are some editors and publishers actively looking for women's fiction. We do know that many publishers believe that women buy more books than men. Even on the kids/YA side, there are many more books published for girls."

Peggy Tierney, owner and publisher of Tanglewood Press, comes at McEwan's statement from another angle. "I happen to be a big fan of Ian McEwan, but this statement surprises me. I'm sure that more women than men read novels. But James Patterson, for instance, wouldn't be a mega-selling author if there weren't men out there looking for a novel that interests them." She concedes that a bookstore or library section would not be the same without novels written for females. "It would be much, much smaller."

As the owner of a small children's press, Tierney is very

selective about the books she publishes, and from the perspective of acquisitions she has to think about readers in terms of gender. "Considering the audience is central to considering a manuscript; gender plays a large role. We really need more authors who know how to write for boys, something that sounds authentic and appealing."

Some books do appeal to both genders. Tierney hit upon the happy medium with the Blackbeard Quartet, by the *New York Times* best-selling author of *The Kissing Hand,* Audrey Penn. With their pirate theme, the Blackbeard titles would seem natural for marketing more to boys than girls. But Tierney says, "Actually, one of the things I love about the Blackbeard books is that they are equally appealing to boys and girls. The strongest character is a girl, Stephanie, and interestingly enough, when I've talked to classes of kids about this book, even the boys say that she is their favorite character."

Real Men Don't Read Romance Novels

Women read more books than men in all categories except history and biography. They especially out-read their male counterparts when it comes to fiction. According to surveys conducted in the United States, Canada, and Britain, men account for only 20 percent of the fiction market.

It should come as no surprise that more women than men read romance novels: 38 percent to 3 percent to be exact. On its website, the Romance Writers of America makes the claim, "Of those who read books in 2007, one in five read romance novels." Those readers, mainly women, accounted for $1.375 billion in estimated romance fiction revenue in 2007, the last statistics available to date.

These numbers are not a revelation to author Cheryl Zach, who, under the pseudonym Nicole Byrd, has published 11 historical romantic adventures in the Applegate Sisters/Sinclair Family Saga. She is a member of the Romance Writers Hall of Fame. Under her own name, Zach has published 25 young adult novels, 12 middle-grade novels, and one children's nonfiction book.

Zach believes that women's attraction to romance novels is mainly emotional. "Supposedly, women often read for emotional satisfaction and like the rush of a happy ending, which men are less invested in. Men can be sated with the puzzle of a mystery, the gadgets in a techno thriller, the futuristic projections of science fiction, the blood and gore of a violent thriller, and so on."

Is Zach onto something? According to studies done by cognitive psychologists, women are more empathetic than men and possess a greater emotional range, attributes that make fiction more appealing to them. Louann Brizendine, author of *The Female Brain* (Broadway Books), explains that this pattern emerges in childhood. "At a young age, girls can sit still for much longer periods of time than boys," she says. "Girls have an easier time with reading or written work, and it's not a stretch to extrapolate that to adult life."

So, girls and women may have a built-in capability for appreciating reading, especially fiction. But what exactly is women's fiction? On her *Publishers Weekly* blog, "Beyond Her Book," Barbara Vey poses that question. The answers are as varied as the people who post them. In her first blog she reports asking people in a variety of places what they think women's fiction is.

> The answers ranged from intimate issues, family, and mysteries to just books written by women. And while there was no runaway winner, the main ingredient was romance. . . .

To make it more interesting I included men, but when I mentioned women's fiction their eyes tended to glaze over. "Women's fiction? You mean like relationship stuff?" They were clearly not comfortable with the question. My favorite was the 18-year-old high school student who said, "Books about women in the 1950s" and she was serious. . . . Her 17-year-old male friend suggested women's fiction is "a book with people kissing on the cover."

One comment on this first blog focused on relationships—not just in romance, but with mothers, sisters, friends—and how more men, like Nicholas Sparks, are writing "women's" novels.
But perhaps Katherine Coble, author of the blog "Just Another Pretty Farce," said it best on her blog, cited by Vey:

Now as for what fiction is most appealing to women . . . I think it depends on the time, the life circumstance, and the desires and experiences of each individual woman.

It's whatever makes us think, laugh, and understand. It's whatever makes us feel better about the world and our place in it.

There is a lot of fiction out there. I think of Women's

Defining What Women Read

➤ Barbara Vey, "Beyond Her Book, What Is Women's Fiction?" blog, www.publishersweekly.com/blog/880000288/post/830045283.html, (March 14, 2007, first blog); www.publishersweekly.com/blog/880000288/post/830045283.html (June 4, 2009)

➤ Katherine Coble, "Just Another Pretty Farce," blog, http://mycropht.wordpress.com/?s=women%27s+fiction

The Numbers Do Not Lie

➤ According to an online Harris Poll, 44 percent of women read more than 10 books a year, compared to 29 percent of men. Thirty-two percent of women are likely to have bought more than 10 books in a year, compared to 22 percent of men. A breakdown of some of the genres or categories by gender reading preference is:

- *History:* women, 27 percent; men, 44 percent
- *Mysteries:* women, 57 percent; men, 38 percent
- *Political:* women, 9 percent; men, 22 percent
- *Religious:* women, 32 percent; men, 24 percent
- *Romance:* women, 38 percent; men, 3 percent
- *Science fiction:* women, 18 percent; men, 34 percent

Information about the poll can be found at http://harrisinteractive. com/harris_poll/printerfriend/index.asp?PID=891.

➤ *Publishers Weekly* discusses a Bowker annual report, released in 2009, that confirms that women buy more books than men. It found that females purchase a whopping 65 percent of all trade books. Consumer habits differ by gender in another way. While women are bigger buyers of print and audiobooks, men buy 57 percent of e-books. See www.publishersweekly.com/article/CA6671785.html.

➤ A 2009 survey conducted in the United Kingdom found that of the 2,000 adults who took part, 48 percent of women were considered to be avid readers, compared to 26 percent of men. Twice as many men as women admitted that they often do not finish a book soon after starting it, and that they have many titles on their shelves that they never read. See www.telegraph.co.uk/culture/culturenews /5033672/Women-more-avid-readers-of-books-than-men-survey-says.html.

Fiction as that which, like women, nurtures and gives care. It can be sexy or funny or full of lusty descriptions of delicious foods. It can be about fashion—if you're into that, and I'm so hopelessly lost when it comes to that—or family.

Good Women's Fiction is like your best self on your best day. It's beautiful, confident, has good taste, and is fun to be around.

Yes, Virginia, Women Do Read Nonfiction

The same studies and polls that point to women out-reading men in fiction categories are unanimous in their findings that men read more nonfiction than women, but not by much. According to the Harris Poll, men outnumber women as readers of nonfiction by 84 to 79 percent. Is this the trend with children too? Do boys read more nonfiction than girls?

Peggy Thomas, author of more than 15 nonfiction books for children and teenagers, including *Forensic Anthropology: The Growing Science of Talking Bones* (Facts on File) and the Science of Saving Animals series (Twenty-First Century Books/Lerner Publishing), does not consciously target boys over girls or vice versa. She says, "My focus is the subject itself. One topic may be more interesting to boys rather than girls, but I don't write with that in mind." While Thomas says it is hard to tell if she signs more books for boys than girls at book signings and festivals, "when my conservation books first came out I did notice that boys would wander around the book festival with a glazed look in their eyes until they saw the alligator on the cover of *Reptile Rescue* (Savings Animal series). Even though it was a hardcover parents seemed willing to pay the price because it was the only book their son was interested in."

Thomas is also a librarian and in that role she has seen that boys "would definitely check out the nonfiction for enjoyment more often. They usually had a passion for one subject like dinosaurs, big trucks, sharks. But, when it came to checking out nonfiction for school projects, it was even"—girls and boys took out books in similar numbers.

One type of nonfiction read more by women than men is self-help, especially in the category of relationships and family. According to book consumer trends tracker R. R. Bowker, in 2008, women bought 74 percent of relationship and family self-help books.

Thomas is a woman who is an avid nonfiction reader, and says most of the books she read and purchased in the preceding year were nonfiction. She disagrees with McEwan's assessment that women single-handedly hold the future of the novel in their hands. "I don't think that is true. I know a lot of guys who enjoy a good novel, even ones with female protagonists. I just think that women like to share their reading experiences more. They are more vocal about what they like and don't like."

Thomas's thoughts may go a long way to explaining why book groups are primarily female. To many, the term *book group* conjures up the picture of a group of women gathered in a member's living room, cup of coffee or glass of wine in hand, debating topics like the importance of Dante's *Inferno* or Jodi Picoult's novel *The Tenth Circle* (Washington Square Press/ Simon & Schuster) or the theme of people's attitudes toward the disabled in Kim Edwards's *The Memory Keeper's Daughter* (Penguin). But the book group has evolved from the neighborhood club to Internet groups with legions of members. The most famous of these was surely the brainchild of Oprah Winfrey, whose online book club has upwards of 2 million readers.

What Does the Future Hold?

According to statistics, girls read less than women. Anastasia

Goldstein, author of *Totally Wired: What Teens & Tweens Are Really Doing Online* (St. Martin's Press), asserts that today's young people were born into a digital society and are used to almost instant gratification on all levels, so they take their cues from social networking sites like Facebook and YouTube rather than more traditional media, like books.

There is hope. Books like Stephenie Meyer's Twilight series (Little, Brown) spread through the tween and teen female population faster than a vampire can drain his victim of blood. When the third book in the series, *Eclipse*, was released, it bumped the final Harry Potter book off the top spot on some bestseller lists. After the release of the paperback of *Harry Potter and the Half-Blood Prince*, Scholastic reported that slightly more boys than girls had read the series (57 to 51 percent). Be that as it may, in the end, the girls trumped wizards with vampires.

"Girl books are being bought strongly at the moment and paranormal and supernatural books are very hot," says Chudney. Contemporary fiction rules the day at his agency.

JoAnn Ross, one of the founding authors and first board members of Novelists Inc. (NINC, and formerly Women's Fiction Writers), may say it best: "It's been said that women readers are more eclectic than male readers and I do believe that's true as a rule. Which is why if you use the definition *what women read*, then you're going to have to say *everything*."

Writing for the Sake of Writing: Literary Magazines

By Katherine Swarts

L iterary writing seems to be one of those things people either love or hate. The haters may see it as so very serious, even heavy, or too artsy and ultimately dull. The lovers may see it as a fascinating journey into the depths of human nature, with explorations of style, character, and/or form, and at its best barrier-breaking and fascinating.

One thing everyone agrees on is that not all writing is literary. Stories intended for pure fun rarely need apply.

"Literary fiction goes beyond entertainment," says Paulette Licitra, Publisher of *Alimentum: The Literature of Food.* "Writers dig deeper, find sources more closely tied to who they are."

"I think the *literary* concept comes down to the importance of language and characters," says Peter A. Balaskas, Editor of the annual *Silent Voices: A Creative Mosaic of Fiction.* "Quality *popular* or *genre* fiction stems from the characters; plot comes right after that. Literary fiction focuses more on the author's narrative voice and how a character evolves—or devolves—in the world."

73

"Literary fiction sets itself apart because its focus is style and depth rather than commercialized," says Desirae Aguirre, Editor of *RiverSedge*, "of which the typical literary magazine reader is appreciative."

For a Select Crowd

Who is this typical literary magazine reader?

"Literary fiction appeals to cult audiences, or small audiences," says Steve Hussy, Co-Editor of *The Savage Kick* magazine. "Literary is the home for stories wacky enough that the mainstream won't take them, or for new writers who have yet to establish an audience. The same ethos runs through to the readers. *Litmag* readers are dedicated enough to search for new stories, or young enough to be having *outside* thoughts and searching for something different."

Perhaps surprisingly, litmag fans come in all demographic sizes and shapes. What they have in common is a mindset perhaps best described as more serious than average, or as more analytical or intellectual than average. "Our subscriber base is equally divided between men and women, from their twenties to their early nineties!" says Susan Burmeister-Brown, Co-Editor of *Glimmer Train*. "They are all people who think about life."

"I would describe the typical literary magazine reader as not typical," says Licitra. "It's anyone who can slow down long enough to read, not just fan through glossy magazine pages. Someone who got in on the secret that thoughtful writing is great fertilizer for the soul. Readers who get this grab litmags like candy."

While Licitra notes that people with that sweet tooth "seem to be getting scarcer" in the high-speed modern age, deep reading is far from dead. What are changing are the forms of media where it appears. Balaskas believes that the popularity of literary magazines in print has decreased. "However, literary magazines in general have increased in popularity, mainly online. There are also more independent publishing companies. I ought to know; I own one: www.exmachinapress.com. With more publishing companies come more opportunities for authors to get published."

Hussy presents a less optimistic picture: "Before desktop publishing and cheap printing, it was harder to create and distribute a literary magazine. On the flipside, the paying market now is largely killed by the Internet. It's easy to get stories for free on an online *zine*, but the writers suffer, wanting their work out there but facing the cold fact of making enough income to survive." Because anyone "can send out something and get 'published'" on many websites, he continues, "young writers have no pressure to succeed, no impetus to improve. Older writers had to survive sending to unreceptive editors." The financial and professional realities of being a writer may be especially resonant in literary markets: True-to-life issues are the soul of literary writing itself.

Too Young for Literary Fiction?

Because literary fiction is generally considered deep, people often do not think of children's stories as falling into the category. Yet many fiction-heavy juvenile magazines call themselves literary. Their audiences can be surprisingly young. The Cricket Magazine Group's *Babybug* and *Ladybug* are specifically designed for pre-readers and call themselves literary magazines.

Does children's literary fiction differ from adult literary fiction? Somewhat, in that endings tend to be happier and the line between literary and genre stories is thinner. Yet there are strong similarities. Literary magazines do not include popular, commercial fiction for adults or children.

Deep Stories for Hard Times

For all the difficulty in getting decent pay for literary stories, many editors believe that the overall economic decline for the past few years has helped, or at least not hurt, the literary magazine market.

"Established knowledge and TV news pound into everyone's head that people have less money to spend today," says Steve Hussy, Co-Editor of *The Savage Kick*. "But in the litmag market, I think [money] evens out; our sales have remained solid. After all, litmags tackle feelings of being on the outside. If you're feeling like hell, why not read a story that deals with the issue?"

"Until recently," says Susan Burmeister-Brown, Editor of *Glimmer Train*, "the Internet tended to overwhelm people's time and attention. We have experienced a surge in subscriptions since the decline of the economy. I think people are taking more time to reflect."

"The creation of art does seem to rise during hard times," says Paulette Licitra, Publisher of *Alimentum: The Literature of Food,* "so let's hope we have at least that perk!"

Not all editors are as sanguine about the current state of literary magazines: "I think publishing houses are trying to cut costs," says Peter A. Balaskas, Editor of the annual *Silent Voices: A Creative Mosaic of Fiction.* "Many privately owned houses are closing up completely. But one thing about the arts and Americans: We have a tenacity and innovation that surpasses many international companies."

"I would define literary fiction as energetically embracing and relating complex themes, experiences, and characters through thoughtful, imaginative, even poetic prose," says Jenny Gillespie, Associate Editor at *Babybug* and *Ladybug.* "A salient plot and page-turner effect are not as important, though good literary fiction still exhibits a conflict and a strong narrative pull; the reader cares about what happens to the characters. With our magazines, we try to exercise the same judgment we hold for adult literature in terms of quality of language and pull of story. The only differences are the use of art in our magazines, and that we must be judicious in the maturity level of what we accept."

"I think of literary fiction as being more reflective and poetic than other types of fiction," says Editor Kalen Marquis of *Creative Connections* (formerly *Mr. Marquis' Museletter*), a small Canadian literary periodical for all ages. "Emphasis is upon the evocation of thought and feeling. Words or phrases are chosen for their multiple layers of meaning and effect. Literary fiction is

> "Literary fiction energetically embraces and relates complex themes, experiences, and characters through thoughtful, imaginative, even poetic prose."

often less plot-driven and more discerning with language, inviting readers to savor the poetry, the prose, or even the poetry within the prose."

Many magazines encourage children not only to read literary fiction, but to write it. "All our authors are under 14," says Gerry Mandel, Editor of *Stone Soup* magazine. "We call ourselves a literary magazine because we publish stories and poetry, everything from personal narratives to fantasy to sports." As for the economy's effect on sales, "*Stone Soup* has been in publication for 37 years, and it is no less popular than 25 years ago. We are actively developing online resources, including teacher blogs and digital subscriptions, as a way to stay current and maintain strong sales. The current economy has probably hurt magazines

Recommended Reading

➤ **Peter A. Balaskas, *Silent Voices*:** "In *Silent Voices*, Volume Four, we published two stories we nominated for the Pushcart Prize: 'Cathedral,' by Damian Newton, and 'The Rule of Law,' by Edward Belfar."

➤ **Susan Burmeister-Brown, *Glimmer Train*:** "'Monkeys of the Sea,' in our Spring 2010 issue, won our Short Story Award for New Writers."

➤ **Paulette Licitra, *Alimentum*:** "'Sacrifice in Fukuoka,' by Paul Silverman; 'Front Yard Fruit,' by Ellen Price Estilai; 'Something Like Anger,' by Scott Cheshire; 'Urban Planning #6,' by Tim Horvath; and the poems by Gaylord Brewer and Sam Feigenbaum in our Issue Eight."

➤ **Gerry Mandel, *Stone Soup*:** "Akash Viswanath Mehta's 'Love—A Cursed Blessing' (www.stonesoup.com/writing/949), about how his parents' divorce affected his life; Eden Marish Roehr's poem 'Ocean Memories' (www.stonesoup.com/writing/958); and Alison Buick's 'To Be a Swan' (www.stonesoup.com/writing/922), about a girl who dreams of dancing in *Swan Lake*."

that rely on advertising dollars more than those that do not. *Stone Soup,* like most literary magazines, does not carry advertising."

Gillespie thinks otherwise: "People aren't willing to spend as much now on a specialty product" such as a literary magazine subscription. Nonetheless, she says, "There are more children's literary magazines now. In the late 1990s and the years immediately following, there was an influx of new kids' magazines around the world, including the Bayard Jeunesse group in France, which also owns the Owl Magazine Group in Canada. Such magazines have maintained the same entry point from when I was growing up, in the sense that parents have to make the effort to make the magazines a part of children's lives. Most children aren't going to seek them out."

Some children's literary magazines are adopting a classic approach. Online magazine *Sparrow Tree Square,* for example, publishes only older, public-domain works. Says Editor Megan Friel, "Our primary mission is to show middle-schoolers and young adults that classic literature can be fun and accessible, and to introduce kids and parents to forgotten poems and stories. Classic literature is as new and different to children as something written today. I also hope that our magazine inspires parents to sit down and actually read with their children, an activity that seems to be going to the wayside in this age of computers, television, and video games. Children are introduced to literature primarily through the adults in their lives."

Classic literature and literary writing differ from modern *stuff* in various ways. "Literature from both eras has its good and bad points," says Friel. "Early twentieth-century children's literature can be very didactic, with overt moral messages. I try to avoid this kind of literature, because I want children to enjoy reading. Today, writers are encouraged to create stories that show children overcoming obstacles and experiencing personal growth. It's an improvement over didacticism, but reading is supposed to be fun. Not every situation in life spurs growth or change, and it's okay to let children read stories that show this."

When classic stories are not didactic, says Friel, "Children benefit in many ways from being introduced to older works. Older literature, even stories and poems specifically for children, is often at a higher reading level than today. For example, Frances Hodgson Burnett's 1905 book *A Little Princess* is on about a sixth-grade reading level, even though the main character is only seven when the book starts. This discrepancy in complexity and character age is particularly useful when dealing with gifted children, who may be ready for more difficult

Literary Publishers

➤ *Alimentum:* P.O. Box 210028, Nashville, TN 37221.
www.alimentumjournal.com

➤ *Creative Connections:* P.O. Box 98037, 135 Davie St., Vancouver,
British Columbia V6Z 2YO Canada.
http://creative-connections.spaces.live.com

➤ **Cricket Magazine Group:** 70 E. Lake St., Suite 300, Chicago, IL 60601.
www.cobblestonepub.com, www.babybugmagkids.com,
www.ladybugmagkids.com

➤ *Glimmer Train:* 1211 NW Glisan St., Suite 207, Portland, OR 97209.
www.glimmertrain.org

➤ *RiverSedge:* The University of Texas-Pan American Press, 1201 West
University Dr., Lamar Building, Room 9A, Edinburg, TX 78539.
http://utpress.utpa.edu

➤ *The Savage Kick:* Murder Slim Press, 129 Trafalgar Road West, Great
Yarmouth, Norfolk NR31 8AD, United Kingdom.
www.murderslim.com/savagekick.html

➤ *Silent Voices:* Ex Machina Press, P.O. Box 11180, Glendale, CA 91226.
www.exmachinapress.com

➤ *Sparrow Tree Square:* www.sparrowtreesquare.com

➤ *Stone Soup:* P.O. Box 83, Santa Cruz, CA 95063.
www.stonesoup.com

See also, "The Short Story Form," page 143 of this *Writer's Guide*.

reading material but not the emotional content of books with
older protagonists. Introducing children to classic literature is
also a good way to teach them about history. *Little Women* can
be a starting point for learning about the Civil War, and E.
Nesbit's 1906 novel *The Railway Children* has connections to the
Dreyfus Affair, a political scandal of the late nineteenth century."

What Lasts?

Many famous writers of generations past got their first publishing credits from literary magazines for adults, too. "There is great writing in all generations," says Licitra, although "style shifts and changes. *New Yorker* stories from the 1930s, 40s, and 50s were wonderful, but a large percentage of them would feel out of place now. Readers hear the style of their own age better."

But perhaps one more quality that makes a story literary is an inherent timelessness rarely seen in mass-produced paper-

> "Litmags aren't looking to crowd-please. We're looking for great writing of any style, from writers with any or no credentials or platforms. Great writing lives here."

backs. "The best, most enduring works," says Friel, "are those that we can read over and over without tiring of them. I think classic children's literature appeals to adults as well as children for this reason; there is something eternally enjoyable about it. If a story is fresh and different in its own time, it may be read for years without losing any of its charm."

Trendiness counts for almost nothing in literary writing. What does count are the core elements, "good writing and a good story to tell," says Hussy. "The best stuff comes from stories people have to tell to get out of their heads."

Marquis says, "I would remind all aspiring writers of literary fiction of two quotations featured prominently in my writing space: 'Writing is the art of a listening heart' (Julia Cameron) and 'It is only well with me when I have a chisel in my hand' (Michelangelo)."

Licitra sums up the independent nature of literary magazines: "Here's the place that takes no demands from the marketplace. Litmags are not looking to crowd-please. We're looking for great writing of any style, from writers with any or no credentials and platforms. Great writing lives here."

Writing Science Fiction Today

By Mary Rosenblum

S*cience fiction* is the technology end of the *speculative fiction* spectrum, although it blurs into *fantasy* to some degree. As technology dominates the media more and more, with news of genetically engineered crops, cloning, and the renewed interest in space exploration and lunar landings, science fiction has enjoyed increased attention, particularly by Hollywood. It is gaining a more mainstream readership at all age levels.

Adult science fiction is no more a one-size-fits-all genre than is mystery. Like mystery, it has a number of subgenres, although the divisions are less clear-cut and many books cross lines. The adult subgenres include:

➤ Hard science fiction
➤ Space opera
➤ Near future science fiction
➤ Military science fiction

Hard science fiction depends on a technological conflict and resolution. It may be a lunar landing crash, the need to terraform a planet, or the consequences of a biological experiment gone wrong, but the technological conflict carries the story. This particular subgenre is less character-dependent than some of the others, and plausible science is an absolute must. The readers often have PhDs in physics. Research is critical; real science must be accurate. *Analog Science Fiction and Fact*, a magazine edited by Stanley Schmidt, is the premier market for hard science fiction short stories and an excellent window into the genre. All the major book publishers publish hard science fiction and it generally sells well. The readers tend to be male. Tor Books and Warner Aspect are frequent publishers of hard science fiction.

Space opera is the classical spaceships and aliens part of the genre. Think *Star Wars* (the books are published by Random House) and *Star Trek* (Simon & Schuster). In space opera books, adventure and imaginative alien worlds are key. Readers want to journey to a new planet and meet interesting aliens. Often, galactic warfare or politics are involved, but the plot is not focused on military strategy. The central conflict tends to carry the book, although strong and vivid characters are important. More women readers enjoy this subgenre than others, and romance is often a strong subplot, although very rarely the central plot. Here, although the technology is very far future and largely made up, it is important that it be plausible. A common weakness in a novice submission is a failure to evolve today's technology into the future. Cell phones on a faster-than-light spaceship will not work, and why hasn't high blood pressure been cured two thousand years in the future? All the major publishers offer space operas, including Bantam Spectra, DAW Books, Del Rey, and Tor. A number of shared worlds, such as the *Star Trek* and *Star Wars* universes, are open for work-for-hire submissions.

Near future science fiction tends to be the most character-driven of the subgenres. It stays close to the present, often looking at the consequences of today's technological changes and sociopolitical trends. Examples are *Beggars in Spain*, by Nancy Kress (Eos); *Darwin's Radio,* by Greg Bear (Del Rey); and *Water Rites,* by Mary Rosenblum (Fairwood Press). Often the technological conflict is equal in weight to the character conflicts, and both drive the story. Romance may play a key role, although it does not dominate the plot. Readers are a mix of men and women. These books tend to get good critical attention from reviewers, as they tackle today's real world issues extrapolated into the future. There is some crossover into the mainstream with books such as Margaret Atwood's *Handmaid's Tale* and *Oryx and Crake* (Random House/Anchor), which were marketed primarily to the literary mainstream reader. Tor Books is a major publisher of near future science fiction. In the short fiction market, *Asimov's Magazine* and *The Magazine of Fantasy and Science Fiction* are the top entry points into the genre and illlustrate what readers expect.

Military science fiction focuses on military conflict and strategy, set in space or on alien planets for the most part. Imaginative military technology is a must, as are realistic military details. The readership here is mainly males, especially those with a sound knowledge of military procedure and protocol. Ace (Penguin) and Baen Books are two major publishers of military science fiction. This is the one subgenre in the category that regularly publishes series.

Cutting Edge

Science fiction readers are sophisticated. The most common mistake a writer makes is to write science fiction without understanding the genre as it works today. David Hartwell, Senior

Editor of Tor Books, the top publisher in the field, says that any aspiring science fiction writer, professional or novice, "should be widely read in contemporary science fiction and in the classics of science fiction, so as not to reinvent the wheel."

The cutting edge of today's science fiction tends to be found in the top short fiction markets: *Asimov's, Analog,* and *The Magazine of Fantasy and Science Fiction.* Reading a number of recent back issues of these three magazines will give an aspiring science fiction writer a clear sense of the current hot topics in the genre. They will also provide insight into the level of explanation needed for science fiction readers.

It is nearly impossible to write marketable science fiction if you do not read the genre and understand reader expectations and levels of sophistication. The audience is not interested in that reinvented wheel, unless the author can put an entirely new spin on it. A writer who does not read science fiction simply does not know the trends, fads, and what has become passé. *Locus Magazine's* editor and author blogs are excellent resources for ascertaining current trends, but always in addition to firsthand reading.

Most important, science fiction demands imagination. Readers want new and richly realistic alien worlds to explore. They want details of spaceflight and technology that transcend episodes of *Star Trek* or *Battlestar Galactica.* When asked about his most common reason for rejecting professional manuscripts, Hartwell cites inadequate setting and the use of off-the-shelf science fiction worlds. Good writing is simply not enough. Hollywood is not a good resource. Readers recognize recycled series, sets, and technology. Off-the-shelf settings do not fly.

Characters matter in today's science fiction. For many years, the science plot carried the story and characters were mere puppets to move that plot along. That scenario has changed, and in all the subgenres, including hard science fiction and military science fiction, strong and complex characters richly portrayed can mean the difference between a sale and a rejection. The cool idea is very important, but it is no longer the only thing that matters. However, the science fiction idea does need to be integral. If the story can take place without that science fictional setting, then it is not a science fiction story.

"The most common reason for rejection," says Gardner Dozois, winner of many awards as Editor of *Asimov's*, "is that the story is dull. The best advice is usually to start with the people. If you can immediately introduce an interesting person with an interesting problem that they must solve, especially in an interesting setting, then the natural instinct is to turn the page and see what happens to that person next. This is practically hardwired into us, and is as true today as it was when we were Ice Age hunters sitting around a campfire telling stories to get through the long night."

Young Readers on Mars

Science fiction for young adults and children is not divided into subgenres in quite the same way as adult science fiction is. In both YA and children's science fiction, plots relate to issues appropriate to the age group. The science fictional elements tend to serve more as the background than as the central focus of the story. The story may be a classic coming-of-age plot for young adult readers, but it takes place on Mars rather than in a Louisiana bayou. This is even more true in science fiction for children, although authors like acclaimed children's science fiction writer Bruce Coville often deftly incorporate educational elements into the characters' adventures.

As with adult science fiction, science accuracy is critical. The level of technology is much less complex than is required for

Science Fiction Publishers

Magazines

➢ *Analog Science Fiction and Fact:* Stanley Schmidt, Editor. 267 Broadway, New York, NY 10007. E-mail: analog@dellmagazines.com. Guidelines, www.analogsf.com/information/submissions.shtml.

➢ *Asimov's Science Fiction:* Sheila Williams, Editor. 267 Broadway, New York, NY 10007. E-mail: asimovs@dellmagazines.com. Guidelines, www.asimovs.com/info/guidelines.shtml.

➢ *Interzone:* Andy Cox, Editor. TTA Press, 5 Martins Lane, Witcham, Ely, Cambs CB6 2LB UK. Britain's "longest running science fiction and fantasy magazine." Guidelines, http://ttapress.com/interzone/guidelines.

➢ *Locus Magazine:* P.O. Box 13305, Oakland, CA 94661. www.locusmag.com. About science fiction publishing.

➢ *The Magazine of Fantasy and Science Fiction:* Gordon Van Gelder, Editor. P.O. Box 3447, Hoboken, NJ 07030. Guidelines, www.sfsite.com/fsf/glines.htm.

➢ *Talebones, A Magazine of Science Fiction and Dark Fantasy:* Patrick Swenson, Editor. 21528 104th St., Ct E, Bonney Lake, WA 98391. www.talebones.com. Calls itself a "semi-pro" magazine. Not accepting submissions at *Writer's Guide* presstime.

Books

➢ **Ace, Roc:** Penguin Group USA, 375 Hudson St., New York, NY 10014. Guidelines, http://us.penguingroup.com/static/pages/special-interests/scifi/submission.html. E-mail query and 10 pages in body of message to sff@us.penguingroup.com, or send, by regular mail, a query, synopsis, and first 50 pages.

➢ **Baen Books:** P.O. Box 1403, Riverdale, NY 10471. Guidelines, www.baen.com/FAQS.htm#Manuscript Submission Guidelines. Accepts complete manuscripts.

➢ **Bantam Spectra:** Random House, 1745 Broadway, New York, NY 10019. www.randomhouse.com/bantamdell/spectra. Agented only.

Science Fiction Publishers

➤ **DAW Books:** Penguin Group USA, 375 Hudson St., New York, NY 10014. Guidelines, http://us.penguingroup.com/static/pages/daw/submissions.html. Accepts complete manuscripts.

➤ **Del Rey:** Random House, 1745 Broadway, New York, NY 10019. www.randomhouse.com/delrey. Agented only.

➤ **Fairwood Press, Darkwood Press:** 21528 104th St., Ct E, Bonney Lake, WA 98391. www.fairwoodpress.com. Not accepting submissions at *Writer's Guide* presstime. Book publishing arm of *Talebones*.

➤ **Nightshade Books:** 1423 33rd Ave., San Francisco, CA 94122. www.nightshadebooks.com. Agented only.

➤ **Pyr Books:** Prometheus Books, 59 John Glenn Dr., Amherst, NY 14228. www.pyrsf.com. Agented only.

➤ **Tachyon Publications:** 1459 18th Street #139, San Francisco, CA 94107. www.tachyonpublications.com. Not accepting submissions at *Writer's Guide* presstime.

➤ **Tor Books, Starscape, Tor Teen Books:** Macmillan, 175 Fifth Ave., New York, NY 10010. www.tor-forge.com. Guidelines, http://us.macmillan.com/Content.aspx?publisher=torforge&id=255. Has an open submissions policy.

E-Zines

➤ *Orson Scott Card's Intergalactic Medicine Show:* Guidelines, www.intergalacticmedicineshow.com/cgi-bin/mag.cgi?do=content&article=submissions. Open to submissions.

➤ *SF Crowsnest:* Guidelines, www.sfcrowsnest.com/contribute.php.

➤ *Strange Horizons:* Guidelines, www.strangehorizons.com/Guidelines.shtml. Open to articles, fiction, poetry, reviews.

adult science fiction, however, and the science tends to be in the background rather than a central plot element. Even when it is central, the protagonist is young and the description of the science fits him or her. "I think the biggest error I see when I am reading science fiction manuscripts at a conference," says Coville, "is a failure to think through all the implications of whatever has been set up. *A* will imply not only *B*, but also *C, D, E,* and *F*. Failing to think past *B*, or skipping *D* and *E* means you lose credibility with the reader. Once that is lost, there is no getting it back."

Coville also says that the critical element of writing science fiction for younger readers is "a sense of fun and adventure. Kids come to this kind of reading to enjoy themselves. Hopefully, they learn some things, have their sense of the world expanded, see new possibilities. All good. But they come to the books first and foremost hoping to have a good time." Once upon a time, science fiction for children was aimed almost entirely at boys. Now, Coville believes that more and more girls are reading it.

Finding an Entry

The YA and children's markets have not been hit as hard by the faltering economy as have adult print publishers. Dozois feels that YA is still a strong and vigorous market for science fiction. "I think it's actually growing right now," Coville agrees, "but not necessarily in terms of old-fashioned, nuts-and-bolts, hard science fiction. The lines between fantasy and science fiction have become ever more smudged. A lot of things that are pretty much science fiction are being packaged in ways that are meant to invite in the non-science fiction reader. Some really cool science fiction is coming in under the radar." All the major New York publishing houses have YA and children's imprints that include science fiction, and agents are encouraging their clients to submit. Top YA editor Sharyn November's website is full of useful links and information (www.sharyn.org/children.html).

The major adult publishers of nearly all genres are struggling in this era of print industry upheaval. It is increasingly difficult to sell to the major companies if you have no established name in the genre. A good route to publishing a science fiction novel is

> YA is still a strong and vigorous market for science fiction, even as the lines between fantasy and science fiction have become more smudged.

first to publish short fiction in magazines whose stories are regularly reviewed by *Locus*, *Kirkus*, the *New York Times Review of Books,* or *Library Journal.* For any author interested in becoming established in the adult or YA science fiction genre, *Locus* is a valuable asset; it lists books sold and includes reviews and articles on market trends. It does not, however, report regularly on the children's book market.

An agent is critical if you wish to sell novels to the traditional publishers, for any age group. Even though some of the major adult science fiction imprints still accept over-the-transom submissions, this route is unwise. Response time can be one to two years, and submissions through agents are enormous, almost unassailable, competition for unsolicited submissions. When looking at agencies, be sure that the agent handles a significant number of speculative fiction clients. In this rather small genre, business is done on a face-to-face basis, at the

Of SF Interest

➢ **Biology in Science Fiction**: A blog on the biological sciences in science fiction writing. http://sciencefictionbiology.blogspot.com

➢ **The British Science Fiction Association**: An international forum for authors, publishers, booksellers, and fans of science fiction. Publishes *Matrix*, a magazine with news and reviews. www.bsfa.co.uk

➢ **Science Fiction and Fantasy World**: Books, movies, blogs, and more, including opportunities for authors and publishers. www.sffworld.com

➢ **Science Fiction & Fantasy Writers of America**: Professional author membership organization. www.sfwa.org. Information on its Nebula Awards and more about the genre can be found at www.nebulaawards.com.

➢ **Science Fiction Research Association**: Calls itself "the oldest professional organization for the study of science fiction and fantasy literature and film." Its mission is to improve education and research in the field. www.sfra.org

➢ **SFF Net**: Speculative fiction community, with discussion groups, chat rooms, news feeds, information on writing and publishing workshops, and more. www.sff.net

➢ **SFReader.com**: Speculative fiction book reviews. www.sfreader.com

➢ **SFScope**: News about speculative fiction. http://sfscope.com

➢ **The SF Site**: Reviews, opinion, reading lists, author and fan sites, writer resources, and more. www.sfsite.com

➢ **Speculative Literature Foundation**: Begun in 2004 to "create a comprehensive website which serves as a hub for information of use to speculative fiction readers, writers, editors, and publishers." www.speculativeliterature.org

➢ **Tachyon Publications Blog**: See the piece on how to go about getting science fiction published. www.tachyonpublications.com/zblog/2006/12/so-you-want-to-publish-your-sf-fantasy.html?Session_ID=new

larger science fiction conventions or in Manhattan. Agents who are not familiar with the genre will not have personal connections to editors. An agent who is not familiar with the various editors will be much less effective at placing a manuscript than one who knows what a particular editor is looking for.

A number of small presses have become well established, and offer new writers a slightly wider entry than do the major houses. They include Pyr Books, Tachyon, and Nightshade. Even at these companies, however, agented submissions have now become the preference. Such reputable small houses may still pay out less, but their books get reviewed by major reviewers and they have a solid distribution system in place. They serve as a stepping stone to a major publishing house. Jay Lake published his early work with Nightshade before being picked up by Tor Books. Sales, of course, count. Poor sales in the small press marketplace will not arouse interest from the major publishers.

The e-book market is growing, and expected to continue growing in the future as e-readers like Amazon's Kindle become more popular and the reading public shifts from print to electronic books. A host of very small e-publishers exist. Some research will reveal whether a publisher's books are reviewed by major reviewers and whether they publish established authors in the field or first-time authors new to the field only. If an author's goal is to be listed by a traditional company or to achieve reasonably large sales, it is critical to choose the right small press or e-book publisher. Only a handful receive mainstream reviews or see significant sales numbers—the factors that count for editors at traditional houses who are searching for promising new authors.

The science fiction genre is always open to new voices and new authors, but it can be a difficult genre to crack unless you read science fiction. Imagination, research, real characters, and ultimately, good writing are a must, backed by a sound knowledge of the genre itself.

Looking Back: Writing History Fact & Fiction

By Susan Taylor Brown

The past is alive with thousands of stories waiting to be told. True stories about historic events, biographies about people well known and little known, and historical fiction are popular across a continuum of readers. Serious articles and texts delving deep into the causes and effects of an age or impact of a figure fascinate many—but so do page-turning historical novels, some serious literature and some lighter but entrancing. The writer interested in history literally has countless worlds to explore.

"History is so much more than names and dates," says author Elaine Marie Alphin. "It is the story of individuals and of the constraints and possibilities of the times they lived in. Writers who feel passionate about history can see themselves in print by entering into the times and lives of those individuals, and illuminating them for editors and readers alike."

"Everything has a history," says Christine Schwerin, who was Associate Editor for *Michigan History Magazine* and is now with the Michigan Department of Natural Resources. "Topics do not need to be limited to politics, economics, and war. Think outside the realm of traditional history; go beyond the facts and reach the meaning. When you research, let it sink in. Give yourself time. Mull it over. Get it all over you."

Give Me Liberty?

History or historical fiction: "They are both about communicating historical truth," says Joyce Moyer Hostetter, author of the middle-grade historical novels *Blue, Healing Water,* and *Comfort* (all from Calkins Creek), "but to write about history is to retell or maybe interpret some historical event. Writing historical fiction (which is what I do) is the art of weaving historical truth into a fictional tale. My novels typically center around some noteworthy but relatively unknown event or situation. They usually even have a few real life characters, but for the most part my characters are fictional. I use the facts I find in my research to tell a story that could have taken place. To me, good historical fiction is truth at an emotional level. But it's also accurate in its probability."

"Writing about history requires a great deal of research and attention to historical accuracy," says Schwerin. "*Michigan History Magazine* relies on old newspaper articles, documents tucked away in various archives, dissertations on microfilm, and of course, reputable websites. In writing historical fiction, writers use these references as well. However, with fiction, the writer can take the liberty to develop their characters' thoughts, feelings, and actions in whatever way works with the story. There is no guessing about what the person thought, or why they did the things they did. The author can make them up. In writing history, it is difficult to determine what a person thought unless that person left a diary or we can otherwise find direct quotes. We have to piece together the information that we find to understand that person's identity."

"The articles in both magazines that I edit," says Rosalie Baker, Editor of Cobblestone Publishing's *Calliope* and *Dig*, "are basically nonfiction. We do sometimes include fiction, and of course, all myth-related articles are fiction. While we qualify that these latter are fiction, we try as much as possible to have them follow the historical record, being as historically accurate

> "History is the story of individuals and of the constraints and possibilities of their times. Passionate writers can enter into those times and lives, and illuminate them for readers."

in their text as possible. For me, historical fiction varies greatly, according to the author and market. I prefer stories that are based on the historical and archaeological record, with fictional characters and dialogue inserted to complement that historical and archaeological record."

Best-selling historical novelist Elizabeth Chadwick says, "When writing history, you have to study primary sources and stick to the physical facts. You can interpret the facts in certain ways, but your argument has to be empirical and rank speculation is out. A novelist, on the other hand, has the leeway to speculate. They can explore the emotional lives of the characters and the what-ifs that writing pure history doesn't allow. For example, the great William Marshal may or may not have had an affair with the wife of his young lord. There is evidence both for and against such a happening. The historian has to state the facts and may voice an opinion based on those facts. A novelist can take the incident, decide what they believe happened, and then craft an imagined scene to portray it to the reader, complete with emotional input."

Chadwick continues, "The key words are *historical fiction*, i.e., it's a story set in the past, and the imagination plays its part to a far greater extent. Both historians and historical fiction writers need insight, and both need to do their research. Just because a work is fiction doesn't mean that the author should skimp on the background research, because even if it doesn't go into the novel, it will underpin the novel's foundations. The more research a historical novelist does behind the scenes, the better the eventual book written." Chadwick's novel about Marshal is *The Greatest Knight: The Unsung Story of the Queen's Champion*, published by Time Warner UK.

Seamless Balance

Writing about historic events brings challenges. First among them, says Kensington Publishing Assistant Editor Megan Records, is to find a path between a strong and excessive use of details. "If you don't get them right, readers will make sure you know about it. At some point, however, you have to stop obsessing about every tiny thing," Records says. "Some details are more important than others. We once got a letter from a fan about a contemporary romance. It informed us that on page such-and-such, the heroine was said to be driving a particular vehicle in the color green. Apparently, that particular make and model of car did not come in green that year. A detail like this is so minute that most readers would not be aware of the mistake. It is usually not worth the author's time to go over such a detail."

To know how much is enough, Records suggests a yardstick:

"Does the detail affect the believability of the character or situation? Is the detail one that a good portion of readers are familiar with? Are you trying to introduce your readers to a new facet of the time period? Accuracy is very important, but so is sanity."

The opposite problem is not being able to find enough details to compose a fully rounded scene, event, or person. Authors who want to write for true history magazines often struggle to find enough legitimate facts to piece together the story they want to tell. Schwerin says, "In many cases, the events we cover happened anywhere from a few decades ago to several hundred years ago. Frequently we must rely on information that others left behind as opposed to interviewing someone who witnessed the event. It is difficult to use descriptive language because so many sources do not note what the weather was like, how the air smelled, or any of those seemingly insignificant details that give the reader a sense of atmosphere."

Ultimately, the purpose of the details is to support the story, whether it is fictional or real life. They can even be the impetus for the story or its angle. It's not enough just to report a true event or plop a modern-day character in, say, the Old West. "I look for the seamless balance between research and story," says Carolyn Yoder, Editor at Calkins Creek Books and Senior Editor, History, at *Highlights for Children*. "You're going to find your story in those rich details in the research. Don't be afraid. Many people don't trust their research. You've gone on this journey. Use the research to fuel your story."

"After accuracy," says Baker, "I look at the approach an author takes. An article needs to have an interesting angle, and text that makes you want to keep reading and to learn more by going beyond what you are reading."

An important step in fiction is "balancing all that lovely detail with an actual plot. You could be the best researcher in the world, but if all that detail slows down the plot too much, the book will be dead in the water," says Records. "Being successful in the historical market means you have to find a story that hasn't been told. Sometimes this means finding a new point of view for an old story, sometimes this means finding a completely new story altogether. It's not easy to spot the compelling stories that are hiding between the dry facts of research."

Shana Drehs, Senior Editor at Sourcebooks, wants to see "a strong voice and characters I can identify with even through the years. I love reading about some character who only figures in the background in history books, but who gets to shine in a novel. It can be hard to write a new story about figures that readers already think that they know. We've heard the story of Henry VIII's life several times. Writers have to contend with the real facts that readers will bring to the table, facts from academic scholarship and works of history. In addition, popular historic time periods often attract crowds of writers, which makes finding a unique untold angle a challenge."

David A. Simmons, Editor of *Timeline*, agrees. "Finding the right written sources or where the appropriate archives are located is always a challenge. *Presentism* is a major problem. Too many writers assume that because something is a problem now, it always was."

Digging Deep

Today's find-it-fast way of thinking sends many writers racing to the Internet for answers. The Web is best used, however, for beginning the research process.

"The Internet is wonderful for finding *where* you can do research," says Elaine Marie Alphin. "When I was working on *An Unspeakable Crime* (Carolrhoda), about the 1913 Leo Frank case, I found out which libraries and public records collections had what letters, papers, or newspaper archival material, so I could plan my research trip to Atlanta. The Internet may also contain information that isn't available elsewhere: The identities of the men who lynched Leo Frank were originally posted on an Internet site, before appearing in print in books. But the Internet can also be unreliable because, unlike a published book, Internet articles are not vetted or fact-checked. I found numerous sites that completely misrepresented the facts of the Leo Frank case by only quoting excerpts from archival material, slanted to support the author's opinion. But I also found very useful sites that posted scanned newspaper articles and scanned documents. For me, the rule is that if it's scanned archival material, or if it's contact information for actual archives, I'll use Internet information and be grateful for it. If it's anything else, I take it with more than a few grains of salt."

Schwerin agrees. "The Internet can be a tremendous resource if used wisely. There is much more to researching topics online than simply typing keywords into a search engine and looking at Web pages. Dig deeper. Many different libraries and archives around the world are digitizing their collections and putting them online, or at least putting their finding aids online. There are literally thousands of journals online, with articles written by experts in their field. These journals are searchable through libraries and universities and many are available online as full-text documents."

"The Internet is a fabulous thing," says Drehs. "It gives authors a breadth of knowledge that would be hard to get elsewhere. But there's no substitute for primary research—visiting the areas you're writing about, reviewing documents, and getting an overall sense of place."

Yoder, a history author as well as an editor, says the Internet

"is really great for locating sources—people, places, and reposi-tories. I Google a particular subject and find the right museums, special collections, and experts. Then I can go to those websites because I know they are respected sources."

Baker cautions authors to "be very careful when they use the Internet. It is a great place to begin research and to find the creditable sources for a historical piece, but once the creditable sources have been found, they should be heavily consulted. Reliance on non-creditable Internet analysis should be at an absolute minimum. It is good to know all that is out there about the topic on which you are working, but for historical nonfiction and fiction, sources that are creditable and accurate lead to the best follow-through."

Readers of history are passionate about their history books. Authors need to be willing to immerse themselves in their chosen topic so they can bring their passion for the subject to the page.

Most all, says Yoder, "You need that commitment to the believable past. If you don't have that, I don't know why you're writing about history. You have to really love to find the truth."

Crossover: From Adult to Children's Writing & Back Again

By Sharelle Byars Moranville

I f you are an established writer of adult fantasy and you decide to write a picture book, do you have to start wearing fuzzy bunny slippers while you work? Access a different part of your brain? Will you be offered a smaller advance when you sell your project?

Or, if you are a successful children's writer and you decide to tackle a project for adults, should you write under a pseudonym and get a new agent? Only one of these changes is likely to be necessary, according to successful crossover writers and the agents who represent them.

Laura Langlie, who has an eponymous agency, says, "It's a fairly new situation to have a good many agents who represent authors of both children's and adult books." She attributes the change to the explosion in young adult book sales. Explaining how she crossed over to include children's writers as clients, Langlie says, "I ended up working with authors of young adult fiction when one of my clients, Meg Cabot, who had been writing historical romances, gave me *The Princess Diaries* to read. I loved it, realized it was young adult, and began marketing the manuscript to YA editors. Because of that series' success, I now represent quite a few authors of children's and young adult fiction."

Susan Cohen, of Writers House, agrees that more and more agents find themselves with both adult and children's writers on their client lists. She says there are not "substantive differences" in how an agent goes about selling an adult project versus a children's. "Perhaps more adult books are submitted simultaneously. For the most part, with some notable exceptions,

> The increase in crossover writers—children's to adult and back—may stem from the explosion in young adult sales.

bigger deals are made for adult books. And from my perspective, they have a bit more *politics* in terms of personal relationships between editors and agents."

The similarities extend to contracts, Cohen says, although dollar amounts vary. "With obvious exceptions, *big* and more midlist adult books still get somewhat bigger bucks. But standard base royalty rates are the same (with the exception of picture books, where the pie is split between author and illustrator), although the escalations might differ."

Langlie concurs. "The terms in children's publishing are traditionally lower than for adult books, as children's books have a lower price point. Thus, often the advances and royalty structure are less than what an author might receive for an adult book."

Institutional Snobbery?

Recent years have seen a rash of celebrities (Madonna, Jamie Lee Curtis, Jay Leno) writing books for children, as well as famous adult authors, such as James Patterson, whose Maximum Ride series (Little, Brown) crossed over to aim at children 11 and up. With the exception of famous authors, Cohen says, "credits in one domain won't necessarily bridge to success in the other. In fact, children's authors may not be taken as seriously when they try to cross over. By the same token, children's editors may feel that an adult, non-celebrity author doesn't *get* a younger audience and should stick to the adult market."

Poet Laurel Snyder, a graduate of the Iowa Writers' Workshop and the author of two volumes of adult poetry (*Daphne and Jim: A Choose-Your-Own-Adventure Biography in Verse* and *The Myth of the Simple Machines*), admits that she was worried people might not take her seriously as a poet after she became a children's author. (Her credits include two picture books from Tricycle Books, *Inside the Slidy Diner* and *Baxter the Kosher Pig*; and two middle-grade novels from Random House, *Up and Down the Scratchy Mountains* and *Any Which Wall.*) But her fears have not come true.

"This is one of those times when you realize that your own insecurity is your biggest stumbling block," says Snyder. "I was at the Dey House [the Writers' Workshop building at the University of Iowa] recently, and they seemed very pleased and excited to see me, saying, 'Oh! We want copies of all your books for the library!' I was surprised that they'd include kid lit in the library, but maybe I'm the only one who is thinking these silly things. Because sometimes there's an institutional snobbery of sorts. A certain esteemed writers' colony told me that if I wanted to apply, I'd need to apply in poetry, and not mention my work for kids, since they aren't allowed to fund it."

The good news is that writing for children has given Snyder a way of earning income that is compatible with her lifestyle. "A poet really needs to be an academic if they don't want to wait tables or sell real estate. Children's authors have a shot (not a promise but a shot) at earning from their books, and then supplementing with school visits and freelance work and so forth. As a stay-at-home-mom, writing children's books has been a lifesaver. Before I published kid lit, I was trying to work as an adjunct professor and stay in the academic landscape. I'm not anymore. I miss teaching a lot, the actual classroom and kids, and hope to teach again someday—but on my own terms."

So, while advances and royalty structures may be lower for children's writers, money to pay the bills can be had from the opportunities that go along with writing for children.

Carol Gorman, author of the hugely successful Dork series and the YA novel *Games* (all from HarperCollins) and a frequent speaker for librarians and teachers, maintains a busy school visit schedule. She says, "I think that writers of children's books have, in general, more opportunities to meet large numbers of readers. Schools and libraries invite writers to visit and talk about writing and publishing, and they pay the authors for their time and expertise. One editor told me this was the fastest way to build a career in children's books."

Which Voice Do You Hear?

Although she is very successful as a children's author, Gorman is now writing a novel for adults that she describes as mainstream women's fiction—a genre she has always loved reading. Some authors, however, accidentally make the crossover from one audience to the other.

Sarah Prineas was preparing for a career in academia, working on her doctoral dissertation, and writing adult fantasy and science fiction stories as a hobby. After she sold several stories in high-profile genre venues, she became inspired by writers who had begun with short stories and then graduated to adult novels published by major houses. Hoping to do this herself, Prineas wrote the Magic Thief series (HarperCollins), which rocketed to success, with two books out and four more coming. The manuscript was an outgrowth of a story Prineas had written for *Cricket*. "But the funny thing is, once I finished the book," she confesses, "I somehow didn't realize it was a children's book. I got an agent and expected her to send it to one of the major genre publishers—Tor, Del Rey, or DAW. But she told me it was a children's book, and she was going to send it to HarperCollins and Simon & Schuster and Scholastic. I had never thought of myself as a children's writer, just as a fantasy writer! Finding out I'd been writing for children was a revelation. But really, I had discovered my voice at last."

Some writers do not really think about the audience as they work on their projects. Renaissance woman Deborah Noyes (Candlewick editor, photographer for the publisher's *African Acrostics: A Word in Edgeways*, and author of many books ranging from adult fiction to picture books) is such a person. She admits, "I'm selfish and almost never think about audience while I'm drafting, but go wherever the story and characters take me and revise my way into a format if need be. I couldn't afford to take this attitude, of course, were I writing genre fare or series books, where you have to meet the expectations of your publisher and fan base (hence the day job!). But if you're not writing straight to category, *audience* is a Sales and Marketing Department concern, something to consider after a book is written, not before."

Like Noyes, Rebecca Janni also writes for a broad span of readers. Janni's first picture book, *Every Cowgirl Needs a Horse* (Dutton Books), has a spring 2010 publishing date, and she already sold its sequel, *Every Cowgirl Needs Dancing Boots.* A third picture book, *Jammy Dance*, is under contract with another publisher. For several years, Janni has also freelanced nonfiction for major publishers. She says she loves an integrated career. "Right now, I have half a dozen projects on my desktop, including a handful of picture books, one middle-grade novel, one

> One author loves an integrated career—some children's books, some adult, some journalism. "Each project stretches me; each one brings its own kind of joy."

adult novel, and the freelance job of the hour. Each one stretches me; each one brings its own kind of joy. The freelance jobs are more journalistic, and they put me in touch with fascinating people all over the world and present the challenge of writing on assignment. I'm given the prompt, the purpose, the audience, and a new opportunity to play with words. The other projects—my picture books and novels—I write because I need to, the way some people need to run."

The Skill Set

Writers seem to agree that it does not necessarily take a different set of skills to write for one audience or the other. Greg Van Eekhout, author of many short stories, published his first adult novel, *Norse Code* (Bantam Dell) last year, and his first middle-grade novel, *Kid vs. Squid,* is on Bloomsbury USA's spring list.

"The tools are the same no matter the age of the audience, from sentence-level prose, to world-building, to shaping a character over the course of a story," Van Eekhout says. "Whether I'm writing fiction for adults or fiction for children, I'm using both the kid side of my brain and the grown-up side. The kid side comes up with the sense of wonder and the neat stuff. The adult pays attention to psychological realism and responsible acknowledgment of complexity, ambiguity, and diversity. Good fiction requires both these components, no matter the age of the reader, and writing is a never-ending quest to get the kid side of the brain and the adult side working in concert, and expressing the thoughts they come up with gracefully and skillfully."

As a writer who made a radical shift from poetry to the novel form, Snyder points out differences she has encountered. Speaking of her novels, she says, "It was hard for me to learn how to throw hundreds of words at the page all at once. Poetry teaches you a wonderful and weird economy of language, and I had to unlearn that to write long-form fiction."

Even the shift from poetry to picture books produced a wonderful difference. "You have this amazing gift of the pictures to come. It's a poet's dream, really—the idea that you can take out even more words than you might otherwise, because a picture will show up and fill in all the blanks. You can kill adjectives, slaughter facial expressions. It's wonderfully freeing to revise a picture book with the sketches in hand."

Gorman speaks of writing novels for children, in contrast to writing novels for adults: "Content and its treatment are the most important differences. I feel a responsibility to younger readers to provide characters who can eventually discover (or

stumble upon) effective ways of dealing with difficult situations, so my readers can benefit as well. I do love the freedom of writing for adults, being able to include a transgendered character when the point isn't about being trans, or allowing a mature character to have sex without the experience becoming a defining moment in her life."

Noyes confesses to wanting to write a graphic novel someday and admits to having worked in almost every genre already: picture books, young adult (both fiction and creative nonfiction), anthologies, and adult historical fiction. She says, "I get something different from each. What I'd love to figure out is where I can best give back, where my real strengths lie, but until I do, I'll enjoy the journey."

If you wake up some morning and decide to write a children's book for a change—or discover you accidentally did it without realizing—you don't have to start wearing fuzzy bunny slippers and you probably don't have to use a different part of your brain. You likely will, however, receive a smaller advance for your manuscript when you sell it. But school visits can both pay well and be lots of fun, and take you to some surprising places around the world (last year Gorman went to Warsaw, Poland).

If you are writing for a younger audience and want to cross over to an adult audience, there is no need to take a pseudonym or find a new agent. Many agents now represent both. And many writers (Neil Gaiman, Stephenie Meyer, Meg Cabot) have shown that crossover writers can find great marketplace success.

Those Cunning Companions

Narrative Nonfiction & Journalism

By Carmen Goldthwaite

Storytelling the news started in the distant past and continues to this day. In the 1920s, E. B. White—journalist, *New Yorker* writer and editor, and later children's author—advised writers, "Don't tell a story about man, tell a story about one man." Today, journalists often follow that maxim while braiding modern journalism techniques, expectations, and requirements through the story.

By Any Other Name

Whether called *narrative nonfiction, literary nonfiction, creative nonfiction, long-form narrative news*, or any other label, a nonfiction article or commentary often tells its factual truth by means of storytelling techniques. This combination of reporting and storytelling differentiates narrative nonfiction from the classic journalism technique: an inverted pyramid structure in which the most important, solid, news-making facts are straightforwardly placed at the beginning of an article, which

A Short History of the Newspaper

News has been conveyed through story from time immemorial. Think of such events (or stories) as the Greek runner who came to report victory in the Battle of Marathon, or the accounts by surviving Native Americans of the Battle of Greasy Grass Creek (otherwise known as the Battle of Little Big Horn or Custer's Last Stand).

Forms of newspapers circulated in ancient Rome and China. Newspapers and magazines unfolded in the sixteenth and seventeenth centuries. Among the first printed in Britain was a report based on eyewitness accounts of the 1513 Battle of Flodden. In America, the *Boston News-letter* ran weekly in 1704; by 1732 John Peter Zenger had fought for freedom of the press and won. In magazines, some of Britain's premier writers (Steele, Addison, Swift) produced or contributed to *Tatler* and *Spectator*. Technology allowed for the rapid expansion of publications throughout the nineteenth century, and the journalism as we know it today began to unfold.

It wasn't until the twentieth century that the concept of journalism took firm hold, and not without vigorous ongoing debate. The late nineteenth century saw the dramas of yellow journalism, with lurid emphasis on scandals and tragedies and limited concern for accuracy. But after these excesses, journalism began to become a more respected profession. Joseph Pulitzer endowed the first journalism graduate program at Columbia University in 1912. The field continued to be dynamic, when in mid-century, established publications were challenged by alternative papers like the *Village Voice*. Other media—radio and television—increasingly had an impact on reporting.

The standards and ethics of factual reporting—sources, objectivity, accuracy, forms of writing—today are like a living organism, healthy but often challenged, and usually strengthened by the challenges. For every James Frey and Stephen Glass, journalism can counter with names like John Hersey, H. L. Mencken, Damon Runyon, John Reed, Edward R. Murrow, Rachel Carson, I. F. Stone, Gay Talese, Joan Didion, John McPhee, Martha Gellhorn, and . . . today's best? That is a matter of opinion, and checking your sources.

then progresses toward less important facts. These news pieces traditionally offer the *who, what, where, when,* and *why.*

But narrative journalism can be of more appeal, and use, to an audience. "Serving the readers is the whole purpose of the press and what we're supposed to do. It doesn't do any good to do wonderful, powerful, investigative reporting if you can't

> "Long-form narrative journalism lets people go into worlds they wouldn't otherwise see, takes them for a ride."

write it in a way that people can read it," Ken Wells says. He speaks from his roles as former Page One Editor of the *Wall Street Journal* and a writer of narrative nonfiction. He has also written four Louisiana-based mystery novels.

In narrative nonfiction, writers often focus on a single individual, so as to tell the story through "the narrative of someone's eyes," says Sonia Nazario, a former feature writer with the *Los Angeles Times* who won a Pulitzer in 2003. "Long-form narrative journalism is a wonderful way to get people to go into worlds they wouldn't otherwise see, take them for a ride, educate them to things they'd never see." A perspective that Nazario "came to in middle age" is "the idea of newspaper writing being like a novel, a story with a beginning, middle, and end."

To reach the reader in today's fast-paced society, Nazario says, "You need some sort of lead that draws you in. Once you've gotten beyond a certain point, you've got a question you want answered, so that keeps you reading to the end to find out what happens." Departing from the inverted pyramid story and

adapting the five *w's* of traditional journalism, long-form narrative journalism embraces "the *who, how,* and *why*," she says.

Like the New Journalists of the 1950s and 1960s, which included Truman Capote, Joan Didion, Norman Mailer, Gay Talese, and Tom Wolfe, Nazario and many of her contemporaries in the late twentieth and early twenty-first centuries are moving from writing long narrative nonfiction pieces in newspapers and magazines to writing books. Nazario turned her *Los Angeles Times* series about a boy immigrating to the U.S. into the fuller story of *Enrique's Journey* (Random House).

Nazario continues to migrate toward books, a decision that in part reflects the current newspaper economy. At the same time the *Los Angeles Times* was scaling back long-form narrative stories, "Random House wanted me to write a second book," she says. "I like to write about social issues, big issues. I looked three years down the road and realized, 'This newspaper won't do want what I to do'" again very easily. The costs were too high in personnel (editors, designers, photographers), time, and space. Nazario wanted the newer challenge of books, and realized at the newspaper she "would likely have to go back to doing stories of the scope and length that I was doing 15 years ago." But she does believe newspapers will figure out a new business model and bounce back.

Cream on the Milk

The *New Yorker, Vanity Fair,* the *Atlantic,* the *Sunday New York Times Magazine,* and *Bloomberg News Wire* continue to draw writers and readers of narrative journalism.

Wells moved from the *Wall Street Journal* to *Bloomberg* to find a home for the news stories he likes to write and edit. The goal of engaging a reader in major news is "why story is so important," he says. The task is "to take these wonderful reported stories and make them interesting." He insists that long-form narrative journalists must "satisfy standards of fairness and accuracy yet write in an interesting way."

Wells's recent work includes a narrative nonfiction book about shrimpers, *The Good Pirates of the Forgotten Bayous: Fighting to Save a Way of Life in the Wake of Hurricane Katrina* (Yale University Press). It won the Harry Chapin Media Award and a Pulitzer nomination. Yet he worries about the future of long-form narrative journalism as newspapers cut costs, peo-

> "Good narrative reporting is investigative reporting humanized."

ple, and pages. "It's getting harder and harder to keep the tradition as vigorous as it was," he says, lamenting the decline of the long narrative story at his former paper, the *Wall Street Journal.*

Other journalists take a different perspective. Bob Rivard, Editor and Executive Vice President of News for the *San Antonio Express,* a Hearst newspaper, says, "Even the best newspapers are going to be overwhelmingly devoting space to stories that they need and want. Storytelling is the cream on the milk," he says. "Good narrative reporting is investigative reporting humanized." He broadens the form to include features—in-depth pieces that are not necessarily tied to a news story, and which might even include an opinion or perspective. "Sometimes a profile can relive a guy's life through his memories. That won't be investigative, but it will be a good story."

Rivard has also taken a swing at nonfiction book writing with

 Style 115

Trail of Feathers: Searching for Philip True (PublicAffairs/Perseus Books). In it he reported on his efforts as the Editor of the *San Antonio Express* to locate a missing reporter, later found to have been murdered in Mexico, and to bring the murderers to justice.

Adamant about the effectiveness of narrative nonfiction stories in the world of journalism, Rivard believes they fit into the spectrum of what newspapers do and how they function. "There's a certain daily rhythm, weekly rhythm, seasonal rhythm," he says. "Sunday is the engine that pulls the whole train with its greater news hole. People have more time and can be more reflective, so we can add value on Sundays in a series of stories, and more dimension in multimedia online. We look for the best possible story for the day's drama—weather, a standoff, a rescue."

As an editor in Hearst publishing group, which has 15 Texas newspapers, Rivard explains how things work: "Texas papers are collaborating more in the investigating of the story—digging up lots of numbers, trends, and then we'll each find examples in our markets." He calls this reporting and investigating the "architecture of the story." The papers then share the jointly discovered facts, and each paper develops the story—puts a face on it—for their respective markets, perhaps with a local individual who exemplifies that story.

No Blurred Lines

"It's really smart for people writing nonfiction to look at fiction," Rivard says, "yet we have to remain absolutely truthful, no blurring of lines for the truth. That's not acceptable now, though it may have been in the earlier days of new journalism."

"Sticking to the truth, absolutely," appears to be a mantra for literary journalists, including Kevin Fedarko, former Senior Editor of *Outside Magazine* and now a freelance adventure writer for

that magazine and others while he works on his first book, *Dorys of the Grand Canyon*. "I see myself as a journalist. I write as a reporter first. The first and last objective is to not get the facts wrong. Everything else has to subordinate itself to that [accuracy]," says Fedarko, who got his start as a fact checker for *Time*. He credits *Outside* with being a place "where the tools and techniques of long-form narrative story writing were being applied to a subculture—adventure."

> "The act of pitch writing is one of the most essential."

Magazines like *Parade, Men's Journal,* and *Skiing* also call on him to write assigned stories on outdoor adventure, but he prefers to develop and pitch his own ideas. "The act of pitch writing is one of the most essential. It forces you to do minimal research and create a mini story of 300 to 1,500 words, a microcosm of the story you want to go out and tell," Fedarko says. "It's a delicate balance when you're a freelancer spending time on research to know when to stop, yet on the other hand not be so shoddy in research that you develop pitches that fall apart."

Tension Between Journalism Forms

Bill Marvel, a newspaperman since the 1960s, who worked most recently at the *Dallas Morning News*, applies story techniques to feature stories. "Writers have always used techniques of fiction to write nonfiction," he says. He finds regional and special interest magazine markets—*D Magazine* in Dallas, Denver's *5280 Magazine,* and *American Heritage*—receptive to his narrative stories.

But he talks about the tension that still exists among older

Style 117

editors and long-form narrative journalists: Older editors "were impatient—always the nut graf [nutshell paragraph], always the inverted pyramid. Writers wanted to move beyond that old journalistic style engraved in a stone structure, to have character, conflict, and setting, for the reader to have an experience, a scene." Yet the editors would say, "Don't fancy it up, just give me the facts." Today, Marvel's former editor at the *Dallas Morning News* encourages narrative nonfiction stories to the point that during staff reductions one department has remained uncut—long-form narrative journalists, or project writers.

But as with other writers, books beckoned. Marvel's *The Rock Island Line* is a corporate history written as a story. His Voyageur Press editor remarked, "This will be readable for a change," instead of the normally dry discussion of a corporation's past. Viking Press will publish Marvel's other book, *Islands of the Damned,* the story of his co-author, a World War II Marine.

A Golden Age

Marvel believes the Golden Age of narrative nonfiction is now, "because so much of it is being done and so much of it is really good, by so many good writers—and the Mayborn is a prime example."

The Mayborn, or the Mayborn Literary Nonfiction Conference, began five years ago. It is headed by former *Wall Street Journal* bureau chief George Getschow, who is now the University of North Texas's writer-in-residence. The school of journalism wanted a conference and Getschow shepherded the focus to literary nonfiction.

"Long-form storytelling in journalism, with all the elements of fiction, has been around for years," Getschow says. "The style harks back to Jack London, Mark Twain, and Ernest Hemingway. It's not unique to American journalists. The stories are all based in fact, well-researched, often with a subjective point of view; they have a beginning, middle, and end. They have well-developed characters, characters who make choices. There's tension and conflict and a sense of place.

"A large body of the work exists today despite the new platforms of the Internet—the blogosphere and Twitter. There's still a deep-seated craving for stories, stories that get under our skin, make us think, expand our knowledge and understanding." Getschow points to *Texas Monthly* as a prime example.

> "Many newspapers are waking up, delivering stories out of their communities that they haven't had time or space for before."

"Many newspapers," he says, "are rediscovering what great newspapers used to deliver: deeply felt stories. More and more newspapers are waking up to that, delivering stories out of their communities that they haven't had time or space for before." He calls this an experiment in staying meaningful and profitable. It is a "return-to-the-roots experiment, [undertaken] so that papers will be seen as indispensable by delivering stories that are unforgettable, stories that can't be obtained anywhere else, and that engage their readers on an emotional level." Getschow also notes the growing presence of long-form narrative journalism on the Web, particularly at *Lost Magazine*, founded by John Parsley, a New York book editor. The *Lost* website explains,

> Many topics on which *Lost* seeks to publish are bittersweet; all are worth remembering, and many are

worth celebrating. *Lost* is a magazine for people who think about lost landscapes, lost albums, lost letters, lost loves, lost elections, lost cultures, lost faith, and lost time. *Lost* is a magazine for readers who care for how much life exists in what's left and left behind.

While not currently a paying market, *Lost* regularly looks for submissions and says "it provides unique publicity through the site and its events." It is open to established and "emerging" writers.

"America's greatest writers," Getschow says, "came out of the newspaper field." He calls it a literary tradition where the "writerly imagination" produced "the kind of stories where you would sit back and read breathtaking pieces that unfolded deep below the substrata of the story."

True Commitment

The problem for newspapers and journalism today is the cost of people, time, and space. Those costs multiply when narrative nonfiction takes the form of *immersion journalism*, in which the writer lives with and participates in the lives of the people being written about. Nazario spent two years with Enrique from the beginning of reporting to publication of *Enrique's Journey*. Fedarko worked months as an apprentice river guide in the Grand Canyon to tell the history of the canyon dory guides, and Rivard spent six years searching for the missing reporter and bringing his killers to justice. These in-depth reporting experiences command long stories that fill a sizeable news hole. Writing and publishing them "takes commitment, institutional commitment," says Wells.

Long-form narrative journalism is leaping from paper to monitor, according to Michele Weldon, author of *Everyman*

Narrative Nonfiction Markets

In addition to newspapers and general interest magazines, many literary journals publish creative nonfiction, a few of which are listed below. Some special interest or niche publications also use creative nonfiction.

➤ *AGNI:* A literary journal. www.bu.edu/agni

➤ *Alaska Quarterly Review:* A literary journal. www.uaa.alaska.edu/aqr

➤ *Alimentum:* Food-related literature. www.alimentumjournal.com

➤ *Bellingham Review:* A literary journal. www.wwu.edu/bhreview

➤ *Canoe & Kayak:* www.canoekayak.com

➤ *Catholic Digest:* www.catholicdigest.com

➤ *Christian Science Monitor:* www.csmonitor.com

➤ *Civil War Historian:* www.civilwarhistorian.com

➤ *Columbia:* A literary journal. www.columbiajournal.org

➤ *Creative Nonfiction:* www.creativenonfiction.org

➤ *Cross Currents:* Scholarly nonfiction on faith, social issues, religious diversity. www.crosscurrents.org

➤ *Hadassah:* Jewish women's organization. www.hadassah.org/magazine

➤ *Harper's:* www.harpers.org

➤ *Horizon Air:* In-flight magazine. www.horizonairmagazine.com

➤ *The Iowa Review:* A literary journal. www.iowareview.org

➤ *Irish Connections:* www.irish-connectionsmag.com

➤ *Latina:* www.latina.com

➤ *Lighthouse Digest:* www.lighthousedigest.com

➤ *More:* Women 45 to 64. www.more.com

➤ *North American Review:* A literary journal. www.webdelsol.com/NorthAm-Review/NAR/NAR/Home.html

➤ *The Paris Review:* www.theparisreview.org

➤ *Sport Diver:* www.sportdiver.com

➤ *Sports Spectrum:* Sports and faith. www.sportsspectrum.com

News: The Changing American Front Page (University of Missouri Press). A Chicago journalist and Assistant Professor of Journalism at Northwestern University Medill School of Journalism, Weldon says that "more investigative work, enterprise work" will be needed from serious writers "to differentiate themselves from citizen journalists" in online media. "There is a lot of opinion in the blogosphere, so more reporting—hard reporting that differentiates professional journalists from amateurs"—is the avenue of distinction.

"People are looking for great storytelling in text or multimedia to connect to the individual. The character is the portal into the journalism," Weldon says. "Professional writers owe it to their audience to deliver a product that has more context, more thoughtful review, more insight, [and] a way to formulate trends and events into a well-crafted and determined story." Like Marvel, Rivard, and Getschow, Weldon believes that *now* is the golden age of literary journalism. Writers have great opportunities to "show the reader the back story, to offer a quilt of information that is not available elsewhere."

The platforms for writers are more varied today than at any other time in history, and perhaps White's maxim about telling one man's story is more potently true than ever before. Even more necessary today too, despite borrowings from narrative or fictional forms, is the journalist's mandate for getting the story absolutely straight. The storyteller's gift of entertaining joins with the newsprint writers' skills to forge a strong vessel in today's uncertain waters.

A Mosaic of Images

Writing with Clarity & Power

By Cindy Rogers

I've come back from the colorless world of despair by forcing myself to look hard, for a long time, at a single glorious thing: a flame of red geranium outside my bedroom window. And then another: my daughter in a yellow dress. And another: the perfect outline of a full, dark sphere behind the crescent moon. Until I learned to be in love with my life again. Like a stroke victim retraining new parts of the brain to grasp lost skills, I have taught myself joy, over and over again.

— *Barbara Kingsolver, "High Tide in Tucson"*

Novelist Barbara Kingsolver finds joy after despair by studying single glorious things. When I am in a snit about my writing or when I am wandering the dry desert of feeling unable to write, I find inspiration by reading a single piece—a short story, an essay, a poem. Making these readings a daily practice provides regular doses of inspiration. "Like a stroke victim retraining new parts of the brain to grasp lost skills," good writing has taught

123

me to write, over and over again.

An interesting, apt analogy is an invaluable device for writers, offering up a clear comparative image that gets to the heart of a matter. Images matter. Rhetorical tools overall, matter greatly. They not only provide clarity, they boost the quality of the writing into something memorable, and they can even motivate.

Good writings that have inspired me many mornings come from a collection of essays with the unimaginative title of *Touchstone Anthology of Contemporary Creative Nonfiction: Work from 1970 to the Present*, which includes the Kingsolver essay. Here I will present to you a few gems from that single glorious essay collection. My hope is that they inspire you, as they did me, to write with more imagery and clarity, and that they infuse you with new vision. Whether you are a writer of fiction or nonfiction, whether you write for adults or children, rubies like these essays remind us that polished phrasing, memorable imagery, and interesting writing styles are exactly what our manuscripts need.

Wants and Needs and Going Aloft

Pause on that word *need*, and listen again to Kingsolver, from the same essay:

> Want is a thing that unfurls unbidden like fungus, opening large upon itself, stopless, filling the sky. But needs, from one day to the next, are few enough to fit in a bucket, with room enough left to rattle like brittlebush in a dry wind.

What the author is saying to me is that the books that rattle around in my must-read bucket are all I need during a dry writing spell. They are the nourishment that will push my writing from nonexistence to reality, from commonplace to memorable— much more than all those hopes, wishes, and despairing, fungus-like moments that clutter my mind.

The rattling brittlebush reminds me of the dry Midwestern prairie where I grew up. Fungus that grows and grows reminds me of mushrooms popping up all over my lush, green lawn after two days of rain. The author has compared two disparate images in order to distinguish two words that are often used interchangeably: *wants* and *needs*. That is also the definition of metaphor: comparing two dissimilar things or actions that share some common quality to achieve a clearer picture.

Annie Dillard discusses need—necessity—in her essay in the *Touchstone Anthology*, "Living Like Weasels":

> I think it would be well, and proper, and obedient, and pure, to grasp your one necessity and not let it go, to dangle from it limp wherever it takes you. . . . Seize it and let it seize you up aloft even, till your eyes burn out and drop; let your musky flesh fall off in shreds, and let your very bones unhinge and scatter, loosened over fields, over fields and woods, lightly, thoughtless, from any height at all, from as high as eagles.

This fabulous bit of writing appears after Dillard has talked about a hunter who, upon examining a dead eagle, discovers the dry skull of a weasel fixed by the jaws to the eagle's throat.

Can you picture this image? Can you conceive of the weasel's tenacity, or the eagle's? The author took that image of tenacity and ran with it right into her own world, where she explores the idea of holding onto something that matters and being

 Style 125

unwilling to let it go—not for anything, even death. Most days, that is how I feel about reading and writing. I will never give them up; I will let them take me wherever they want, until my eyes burn out, until my flesh falls off in shreds, until my bones unhinge and scatter. A powerful image like Dillard's makes a cliché like *until I die* sound incredibly dull.

The sky is a subject writers use often in images, but many of the images are composed without much thought and therefore little gripping power. In "Flight," Barry Lopez details the sky in an unusual, memorable way:

> I pictured the skies as a landscape of winds—West Africa's harmattan, Greece's damp Apeliotes, California's Santa Ana, Japan's Daiboufu ("the wind that knocks horses down").

Later, Lopez extends his wind landscape:

> . . . Now far to the south a ribbon of sunlit cumulus towers, fumaroles and haystacks, great pompadour waves of clouds. . . . a vast sheet of wool-nap cumulus . . . a rice-paper layer of cirrostratus . . . .

What fun it must have been for the author to come up with a vista of winds. He traveled around the world to name them, something a little research would allow any of us to do. And he wielded a paintbrush of known images to illustrate the clouds. The marriage of clouds with sunlit towers, fumaroles, haystacks, pompadour waves, wool-nap sheets, and rice paper is stunning.

Lists

Like Lopez, I love lists. I especially love those that show the passage of time. Rather than spend long paragraphs reporting what happens between two characters over an afternoon, a writer can offer a revealing list, one that grows in intensity. Bill Roorbach's "Shitdiggers, Mudflats, and the Worm Men of Maine" supplies an example:

> Between ten-packs, she gives a small shrug, a
> smile, talks a snippet of politics, a bit of worm theory,
> tells a quick story, offers a confession.

Here's how Cheryl Strayed wades through years of romance in "The Love of My Life." Her creativity could jumpstart your own list of, say, jobs or friends or pets or monsters under the bed.

> The people I messed around with did not have
> names; they had titles: the Prematurely Graying
> Wilderness Guide, the Technically Still a Virgin Mexi-
> can Teenager, the Formerly Gay Organic Farmer, the
> Quietly Perverse Poet, the Failing but Still Trying
> Massage Therapist, the Terribly Large Texas Bull
> Rider, the Recently Unemployed Graduate of Julliard,
> the Actually Pretty Famous Drummer Guy.

In "Mastering the Art of French Cooking," E. J. Levy nudges her reader through a listing of her favorite foods. Plump, oily avocados. The dainty lavender-sheathed teeth of garlic. Ginger. Tonic and Tanqueray gin. Green olives. Blood oranges. Pungent Italian cheese. Can't you see, smell, taste, feel these lovelies? With sensual detail, Levy offers up bowl after bowl of imagery.

 Style 127

Earlier in this same piece, she uses wordplay and metaphor to describe her mother:

My mother cooked with a vengeance in those years, or perhaps I should say she cooked for revenge. In her hands, cuisine became a martial art.

Don't you want to hear more about this mother? You have probably remembered that Levy gave her essay the same title as Julia Child's famous cookbook. The author turns it into a double

> Writers bring together disparate parts and artfully create a new whole. The world needs art.

entendre, hinting that she is trying to understand this mother who spoke French, admired Julia Child, and used the chef's cookbook to tatters (conveyed through the martial arts metaphor).

At the end of the essay, Levy again makes use of double entendre and metaphor when she writes that she wants to "bring together disparate elements and mix them—artfully, beautifully—and make of them some new and marvelous whole." She is no longer talking about recipes, or even her mother's history, but about her own art—writing. Writers all want to bring in the disparate elements that interest us (no matter if we're working toward a picture book, a novel, or a memoir) and make of them a new and marvelous whole. The world does not need another report; the world needs art. At least that's how I see it.

That is how Mark Doty sees it, too, as he says in "Return to Sender":

Like any artist, when I've made something I believe to be beautiful, what is one to do with it but give it to someone? If there is a meaning to be taken from this, it is that art cannot be counted on to mend the rifts within or without. Its work is to take us to the brink of clarity.

Clarity is what we are after. Clarity is not bees buzzing around a water hole. Clarity is bees humming "at the edge of the water hole, nosing up to the water, their abdomens pulsing like tiny hydraulic pumps; by late afternoon they rimmed the pool completely, a collar of busy lace" (Kingsolver, "High Tide in Tucson"). In many years of reading, writing, and research I have seen—over and over—that imagery creates clarity. And imagery can be had in the variety of ways seen here—metaphor, simile, analogy, lists, modifiers, double entendre, sensual detail, even anecdote, as in Wendell Berry's "Getting Along with Nature":

> I knew a barber once who refused to give a discount to a bald client, explaining that his artistry consisted, not in the cutting off, but in the knowing when to stop. He spoke, I think, as a true artist and an individual.

Ah, that business of knowing when to stop. Our story, novel, essay, memoir, picture book, chapter book is finite. At a certain point, we have to figure out where and when best to stop.

I want to tell you how Brian Doyle ended "Leap," his nonfiction piece about the day the Twin Towers went down. But first, let me tell you that he began the two-page essay with one incredible image:

A couple leaped from the south tower, hand in
hand. They reached for each other and their hands
met and they jumped.
Jennifer Brickhouse saw them falling, hand in hand.

At the essay's midpoint, after giving name to many people who
saw the falling, the somersaulting, the author repeats that
image of a hand-holding leap. He compares the leap to an elo-
quent, graceful, powerful prayer. And then he ends the piece
with: "Jennifer Brickhouse saw them holding hands, and Stuart
DeHann saw them holding hands, and I hold on to that."

In one very short essay, the author sears the image into the
reader's brain. Doyle takes it one final beat, telling the reader
how much that visual meant to him, that that image somehow
mitigates the horror of that day, helping him "to believe that
some unimaginable essence of who we are persists past the
dissolution of what we were." Because of a memorable image
and because the author knew when to stop, this work is nothing less than a piece of art.

Over and over, observant writers use what shows up in their
world as material for their writing. Whatever the subject, we
must—we need—to make the most of it, until the image becomes on paper what it is in life: alive. Kingsolver began my
mosaic of writers' clear and brilliant images, and she will bring
it to a close, for she speaks eloquently of what each of us must
do with the bits and pieces that come our way:

If you ask me, when something extraordinary shows
up in your life in the middle of the night, you give it a
name and make it the best home you can.

She is talking specifically about a hermit crab that appeared on the coffee table in her living room. Figuratively, she is talking about making art. I met my hermit crab in the form of an anthology, a book that inspired me to create the best home I knew how to make for it—a mosaic of images that I have now given to you.

The Essays

> All the cited essays are reprinted in the *Touchstone Anthology of Contemporary Creative Nonfiction: Work from 1970 to the Present* (edited by Lex Williford and Mark Martone, Touchstone Books, 2007).

All About Us: Personal Experience Sells

By Sue Bradford Edwards

Experience. You live it. Ideally, you learn from it. You can also use it to fuel your writing even if you don't live life in the fast lane.

"The obstacle I come across constantly in my [writing] classes is people saying, 'I don't think my life is very interesting,'" says John Patrick Grace, author and Editor of *The Life Writing Class,* published by his company, Publishers Place. "Almost everyone's life has something that can translate into an interesting book."

The interest comes not so much from the event itself as how you experience it and what you learn from it. "A good writer can make a trip to the local grocery store (Eudora Welty's 'The Little Store') or the zoo (E. B. White's 'Zoo Revisited') as exciting as visiting Paris for the first time or swimming with dolphins," says teacher and author Sheila Bender.

Learn to connect with readers through personal essays, memoir, nostalgia, and fiction, even if you are simply the girl or boy next door.

Personal Essays

The personal essay is perhaps the most versatile literary form your life experiences can take. An essay is a short piece of prose written to persuade, explain, or describe something. A personal essay does so from the writer's experience.

Topics vary widely. In "Sharpening the Pointy Hat" (*Chicken Soup for the Soul: All in the Family*), Ali Monroe compares her urban lifestyle with her mother-in-law's rural wisdom. Hyla Sabesin Finn explores whether a house leads to happiness in "Perfect House? Perfect Life" (*Christian Science Monitor*, October 19, 2009). Personal essays can be argumentative, explore cause and effect, or even be nostalgic.

Even with this variety, personal essays share certain traits. "Readers won't connect with general details and proclamations. They want the writer's truth and experience in specific detail," says author Barbara Abercrombie. A personal essay is rich in detail, so dig deep.

"What makes the writing appealing to an audience is the extent to which the writing allows the reader to enter into the process of thinking and exploring as if it were their own story, as well as the writer's," says Bender. "A good personal essay shows the mind working to find some answers to the human questions about longing, mortality, grief, joy, sorrow, love, and compassion." These emotions provide the link readers need to connect with the personal experience.

Discovering the emotional connection requires having processed the event deeply. "One thing that doesn't work in a personal essay is the voice of the victim," says author and teacher Laurie Wagner. "Lots of people have stories of bad things that have happened to them. That's not to say we don't write about them; we do. Stories where we ask ourselves, 'How does this happen?' not, 'Who did this to me?' are interesting."

Explaining how and why enables you to bring a larger truth home to the reader. Pooja Makhijani's young adult piece "The First Time" (*Cicada*, November/December 2003) is more than a description of learning to wear a sari. It tells about how this garment connects her to the courage and strength of a long line of Indian women.

To see how writers shape their experiences into the variety of forms personal essays can take, read widely. "Read every day for at least an hour or two, just about anything you can get your hands on, but especially essays of the type you hope to produce: Give yourself a tutorial. Follow one author to another, and one group of authors to another," advises author Bill Roorbach. "Read stuff you never thought you'd be interested in, even stuff you imagine you're inclined to hate. Purposefully and aggressively stretch your horizons. React to what you read in a notebook or journal."

On Personal Essays

➤ Barbara Abercrombie. *Courage and Craft* (New World Library).
➤ Robert Atwan and Adam Gopnik, editors. *The Best American Essays* (Mariner Books).
➤ Sheila Bender. *Writing and Publishing Personal Essays* (Silver Threads).
➤ John Patrick Grace. *The Life Writing Class* (Publisher's Place).
➤ Phillip Lopate. *The Art of the Personal Essay* (Anchor).
➤ Brenda Miller and Suzanne Paola. *Tell It Slant* (McGraw Hill).
➤ Bill Roorbach. *Writing Life Stories* (Writer's Digest Books).
➤ Sue William Silverman. *Fearless Confessions: A Writer's Guide to Memoir* (University of Georgia Press).

Memoir

Your particular life story may not fit the short essay form. If this is the case, consider writing something longer, such as a memoir.

The difference between a memoir and a personal essay may be length alone. "My memoir, *A New Theology: Turning to Poetry in a Time of Grief* (Imago Press), was constructed from personal essays that I knit together into a narrative," says Bender. She refers to Sue William Silverman's *Fearless Confessions: A Writer's Guide to Memoir* (University of Georgia Press). "Silverman considers the personal essay a kind of memoir writing, so perhaps the differences are not that big except that a memoir is usually book length."

Memoir also has much in common with the autobiography, but does not cover the writer's life from birth to the present. More a slice of life, a memoir contains selected events that shed light on a topic or theme. In *Waking: A Memoir of Trauma and Transcendence* (Rodale), Matthew Sanford explores what it is to be whole after an accident in which his father and sister died and he was left paralyzed at age 13. But he leaves out many events that occurred between the time of the accident and the end of the story. He chooses certain events and deepens the whole by writing on a theme.

Bender advises, "Be aware of the ways that writers focus their books to tell about a particular chapter in their lives or the gathering of particular knowledge."

"Lots of fabulous experiences can make a great story but you have to find out what the glue is, what is underneath, and go deeper. Experiences can entertain. They can inform. They can dazzle," says author and teacher Anya Achtenberg. "But to make a full memoir, there has to be a voice that goes further."

Young adult memoirs often present an edgy story. When Jack

Gantos, author of the Rotten Ralph and Joey Pigza books, penned *Hole in My Life* (Farrar, Straus and Giroux), he wrote about how he became involved in a get-rich-quick drug scheme, and about the resulting time he spent in a medium security prison. Teens appreciate memoir for its honesty and an author's willingness to give them an inside look into his or her world.

That said, memoirs don't have to be edgy. They can be revealing and innovative in other ways. *To Dance: A Ballerina's Graphic Novel* (Atheneum), by Siena Cherson Siegel, combines a story of life experience with the popular graphic novel form.

What stops many writers from trying memoir is the dialogue they cannot recall word for word. That need not be an impediment if the writing remains true to your real life. "Create dialogue that represents the way people talked. You know how they talked and the kinds of things they said," says Grace. "As long as the event was real, you can't expect a writer to recall dialogue word for word that took place 25 years ago."

5 Tips on Memoirs

➤ "Don't consciously elaborate beyond the event," says author John Patrick Grace. "Then you're fictionalizing."
➤ "Interview family and friends," says Grace. "They'll remember things you've forgotten."
➤ Don't worry about writing scenes in chronological order. Write them as you recall them. Put them in order later.
➤ Be ruthless. Cut every scene not related to your theme.
➤ Your theme may not be clear from the start, but it must be clear before you finish.

Nostalgia

Worried your story is not memoir gritty? Try nostalgia.

Maybe your taffy pull story doesn't teach a lesson, but it evokes a feeling—a glow, a warmth, a yearning. This is sometimes called nostalgia writing.

This form of personal nonfiction lets you reminisce about the past while capturing the "good old days." Nostalgia often focuses on childhood memories, good times, family, and home. In "Simply Skating," author Stephanie Prentiss tells about her grandmother's love of roller skating and how it transformed her life (*Nostalgia Magazine*, October 2007). There is a message of change, but stronger is the yearning for simpler times.

Nostalgia does not have to take place in the distant past. In a piece that could have occurred anytime in the last decade, the joy of fresh produce and family dinners infuses "Bob's Allotment," by Charlotte Paton (*Best of British Magazine*, October 2008).

It isn't the time period that is as vital as is the emotion. Even when nostalgia makes you laugh out loud as Garrison Keillor does in his tales of Lake Wobegon, nostalgia always makes us smile.

4 Tips on Nostalgia

➤ Don't tell people how the story should make them feel. Just lead them to it.

➤ Select details that elicit the feelings you intend to provoke.

➤ Remember that smell and taste have strong links to memory. Use them whenever you can.

➤ Be sure also to choose details that bring the past alive. Make it feel as immediate as yesterday.

Nearly True

If nonfiction will not do your story justice, try what Grace calls "close-to-true-life fiction." Some fiction based on personal experience is very much like what actually happened. Other pieces are less so.

Character, plot, scene, and dialogue can come in part or in whole from your life. The story "can be close to one's life. Or it can be something you wouldn't think was autobiographical. It could take place in a different place, a different country," says Achtenberg. It may not even be called autobiographical fiction when it is published, but [the author has written "a close examination of who they are and their connections to certain types of experiences. Alex Sillitoe wrote a story called 'Sunday Morning.' You don't know if this is about him or a kid he knows, but you know there is a depth of connection to *this* family, *this* block, and folks living *this* way. It is a great use of the autobiographical."

At Publishers Place, Grace published the novel *Father's Trouble$*, by Carter Taylor Seaton, based on the life of the author's grandfather, an Appalachian wildcatter in the 1920s who rises and falls. The book contains much that is nonfiction. Grace says

4 Tips on Life-Based Fiction

➤ Draw on your own life story a little or a lot.
➤ "That's how it happened" is not a legitimate reason for a story that does not work.
➤ Combine characters, alter scenes, and create dialogue as needed to create strong fiction.
➤ Do whatever it takes to make the story work, even as you use it to explore reality.

that Seaton "wrote about herself discovering the story. She wove in real letters from the state banking commission and the Treasury Department. She used the Q&A from his trial."

But those factual pieces were not enough for the story. "She invented the dialogue," says Grace. "The letters from the family, she made up." These additions yielded a complete story close to life but fiction nonetheless, but it worked because Seaton made changes as necessary to write good fiction.

Focus on Craft

When you write from personal experience, your story may not immediately gel. That's not a problem if you keep writing. "Throw away the censor button. Give yourself permission to say anything on the page. Know that what you start with is very rarely what you will end up with," says teacher and author Gretchen Clark. "View writing as an archaeological dig— eventually you're going to come upon something precious, but you're going to have to be willing to sift through a lot of dirt to get to it."

This means reworking each piece repeatedly. "After years of teaching I saw too many people who thought writing something once and then cleaning it up would be enough, but most of writing is rewriting, like six drafts maybe," says Wagner. "I know some stunning writers who write for the *New York Times* and other big publications. I've seen their first, second, and third drafts. Many of these great writers start with very messy pieces. Each draft gets better and better, but it's the sticking with the process that is so crucial."

This may mean starting a piece as an essay, trying it again as memoir, and only later discovering it works best as fiction. Not a problem. "Write your story without regard for labels, make it as true as you can, and be a good storyteller—that's what's

Personal Experience Markets

- *AIM:* www.aimmagazine.org
- *Best of British:* www.bestofbritishmag.co.uk
- *Body & Soul:* www.bodyandsoulmag.com
- *Capper's:* www.cappers.com
- *Chicken Soup for the Soul Magazine:* www.chickensoup.com
- *Cicada:* www.cicadamag.com
- *Creations:* www.creationsmagazine.com
- *Creative Nonfiction:* www.creativenonfiction.org
- *Essence:* www.essence.com
- *Good Old Days:* www.goodolddaysonline.com
- *Granta:* www.granta.com
- *Grit Magazine:* www.grit.com
- *Latina:* www.latina.com
- *Mature Living:* www.lifeway.com
- *Maxim:* www.maximonline.com
- *Memoir:* http://memoirjournal.squarespace.com
- *Ms.:* www.msmagazine.com, "Guest Room" is the back page essay.
- *Native Peoples:* www.nativepeoples.com
- *Naval History:* www.usni.org
- *Newsweek:* www.newsweek.com, My Turn column
- *Ocean:* www.theoceanmag.com
- *Orion:* www.orionmagazine.org
- *Parenting:* www.parenting.com
- *Reminisce:* www.reminisce.com
- *Skipping Stones:* www.skippingstones.org
- *Smith Magazine:* www.smithmag.net

important," says Roorbach. Make your story the best that it can be, giving yourself the freedom to write and develop. Find the truth within, then look for a market. Editors are hungry for well written personal experience, both fiction and nonfiction.

The Short Story Form

By Christina Hamlett

When teachers and editors tell writers to try their hand at short stories before leaping into the challenge of writing a 90,000-word epic, the assumption is often made that composing a short story is easier. The reality is that delivering a condensed tale in 900 words is much tougher than writing a rambling tale with 100 times the words.

Whether a short story's plot is a reworking of true events or an idea born entirely of your imagination, the same rules of structure, character development, dialogue, setting, and pacing apply as if you were writing a full-fledged novel. The only difference is a turbo-charged approach of three Gs: Get in. Get going. Get out.

Into the Woods

What do fairy tales, Greek myths, folklore, and religious parables have in common? Not only do they all embrace the concept of short-form storytelling, but they also have a proven shelf life that exceeds whatever paperback you were reading at the beach last summer. Even if it has been eons since you heard the names Cinderella, Hansel and Gretel, and the Frog Prince, or the titles "The Fox and the Grapes," or "The Hare and the Tortoise," you can recall their stories off the top of your head because their simplistic plots are indelibly inked in your brain.

The intent of these early tales was to teach lessons about choices and consequences. How the characters are rewarded or punished as a result of their decisions correlates with a reader's

> We do not care whether the three bears had nice neighbors, or why Rumpelstiltskin did not have his own kingdom considering he was an ace at the gold-spinning gig.

openness to transformation and ability to reflect on what he or she might have done under similar circumstances.

These stories may revolve around a single, inciting incident that represents a stand-alone episode of a much larger (but from the point of structure, irrelevant) tableau. We do not care, for instance, whether the three bears had nice neighbors, that Red Riding Hood's ancestors were homesteaders who raised carrots, or why Rumpelstiltskin did not have his own kingdom considering he was such an ace at the gold-spinning gig. All we care about is the *now* and what is to be done about it.

In a nutshell, characters in short stories—your own included—act quickly not only because they do not have the time not to, but also because they only have one problem they are required to solve. Whether you are starting a new story or are going

back and reading one you have already written, answer the
following questions:

> What is my protagonist's problem?
> Is the problem introduced as early as possible?
> Does the problem have sufficient obstacles?
> What's at stake if my protagonist fails?
> What's to gain if my protagonist wins?
> What do I want my readers to come away with?

A-Lines, B-Lines, and Pacing Yourself

There are two sides—or, rather, two lines—to every story,
regardless of its length or genre. The A-line is the external threat
or quest affecting the protagonist's status quo and provoking a
call for action. Readers are continually reminded of the A-line's
existence throughout the plot, often in conjunction with a deadline (ticking clock) over which the protagonist has no control.

The B-line is the internal, psychological makeup of the protagonist and is associated with the *character arc*. Because of the
challenges that force a protagonist to take risks or confront
longstanding fears, he or she evolves (or degenerates) over the
course of the story. An easy way to remember the coexistence
of these two symbiotic threads is that conflict grows out of
character (the A-line) and character grows out of conflict (the
B-line).

To put this in the context of traditional three-tiered structure
of beginning, middle, and end, A-line and B-line developments
and revelations are treated as beats along the continuum of the
unfolding story. Just as a musical beat is a rhythmic accent
defining the tempo of the piece being played, a story beat refers
to accented scenes that move the action from start to finish and
keep the pacing snappy. The same approach can be taken in a

 Style 145

book, but the beats will fall in much different places.

Let's say you are writing a 1,000-word story. On the surface, the easiest thing to do would be to divide the total number of words by three and allocate the resulting number to each of the sections—beginning, middle, end. Unfortunately, this strategy does not guarantee either the right focus on the central problem or adequate time to develop enough substance for a plausible story arc.

A better way is to diagram a short story plot in the following fashion, with the numbers one to seven representing your beats:

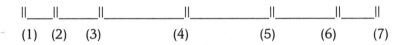

|| ___|| _____|| _____|| _____|| _____|| ____||
(1)   (2)   (3)   (4)   (5)   (6)   (7)

> Beat 1 is the set-up that introduces your main player (A-line).

> Beat 2 is the inciting incident that affects the main player's status quo (A-line) and reveals his weakness (B-line).

> Beat 3 is the protagonist's first major obstacle (A-line) that makes him question his worthiness or ability to succeed (B-line).

> Beat 4 is the point of no return (A-line); the main player realizes that in spite of his weaknesses (B-line), he has more to lose if he does nothing.

> Beat 5 is the second major fly in the ointment (A-line).

> Beat 6 is the complication (A-line) that threatens to cost the hero everything unless he confronts his demons (B-line) and risks all to win.

> Beat 7 is the resolution of both the conflict (A-line) and the character angst (B-line).

In a 1,000-word story, the beats would occur at the following word-count intervals:

➢ Beats 1 and 2: by the first 100 words
➢ Beat 3: by 250
➢ Beat 4: by 500 (the halfway point of the story)
➢ Beat 5: by 750
➢ Beat 6: by 900
➢ Beat 7: by 975

These benchmarks can be adjusted up or down depending on the length of the story. They are an excellent tool for making sure that you are maintaining a tight focus and making every word count.

Characters Wanted

Readers of any age want two things from characters in short stories. The first is someone they can relate to. Since they are not going to spend that much time with the characters in a short story, readers need to be given enough information from the get-go to decide whether they should be for the characters or against them. Unlike novels, which often employ a huge cast of participants, a short story uses only a handful at most and puts them front and center against a backdrop of just one or two settings.

The second thing readers want are characters who care deeply about something. Caring manifests in five different levels that, in turn, relate to the character arc.

➢ At the lowest level are characters who only care about themselves and getting everything they want. In fairy tales and fables, these are individuals who are greedy for treasure or prestige and will do just about anything to get it.

 Style 147

➤ The second level of caring is the bond that exists between siblings, friends, and lovers; it often takes on the theme of "you and me against the world."

➤ Next comes the family unit, whether a family defined by biology or by membership in an exclusive club, such as a fraternity, sports team, or squadron.

➤ At the fourth level are characters who feel a strong kinship with their social or political community and take actions that will be to the group's benefit.

➤ At the top of the list are the humanitarians who engage in selfless, spiritual activities without thought to their own needs, desires, or safety.

For the heroes in your short story to experience an arc, they need to move up at least one level from where they start out. As an example, you could have a shy character whose life revolves tightly around his family but who is forced to become an activist when he learns that his community is in jeopardy at the hands of a corporation polluting its water supply. Not surprisingly, villains usually stay at the same level throughout.

Character Checklist

➤ What does my main character want?
➤ What does my main character need?
➤ Who or what does my main character care about?
➤ What is my main character afraid of?
➤ Why is this character best suited to be the star of my story?

Plotting Techniques

For most writers, the hardest part of the craft is coming up with a plot that is sustainable. For short story authors, the hardest part is finding a plot that also fits the parameters of a petite package. Whether your approach is to start with your characters and build a plot around them, or begin with a crisis scenario and determine the people who will react to it, exercises or techniques should become a regular part of your short story writing routine.

➤ The first step is to get yourself a journal in which you can scribble every idea, phrase, joke, title, image, or character trait that could lend itself to a story. This is also the place to jot down anecdotes you hear from other people; stories you read in newspapers or magazines; or conversations you overhear at the grocery store, in restaurants, or while riding public transportation. Although you may not have a plot in mind when you first jot down these observations, they are still going to percolate in your subconscious and eventually evolve into an idea you cannot wait to develop.

➤ Take a fairy tale you are familiar with and rewrite it from the first-person point of view of every character in the story. This technique will not only assist with developing vocal variety for your character, but also help you determine which character is the most intriguing, and likely to be the lead (or possibly the villain).

➤ Experiment with three alternative endings for every short story you write.

➤ Picture your characters in different settings and eras. Explore how the context of their environment and the mores of the society they inhabit influence the choices they make. What might be very easy for a twenty-first century teen to do, for instance, would be fraught with obstacles if she lived in a time period where female freedom was limited. These obstacles will make for a more compelling story.

Short Story Markets

➤ *American Letters and Commentary:* Experimental fiction under ten pages. www.amletters.org

➤ *American Short Fiction:* Literary fiction. www.americanshortfiction.org

➤ *Analog Science Fiction and Fact:* Science fiction only; no fantasy. www.analogsf.com

➤ *Antioch Review:* Compelling, high-quality fiction for a general readership; no science fiction or fantasy. http://antiochcollege.org/antioch_review.html

➤ *Asimov's Science Fiction:* Science fiction, and some fantasy; no sword and sorcery, sex, or violence. www.asimovs.com

➤ *The Atlantic:* Special newsstand fiction issue. www.theatlantic.com

➤ *Boys' Life:* Adventure, mystery, science fiction, sports, YA, for boys 6 to 18. www.boyslife.org

➤ *Calliope, Cobblestone, Cicada:* The magazines of the Cricket Magazine Group and Carus Publishing publish short children's fiction. www.cricketmag.com. www.cobblestonepub.com

➤ *Capper's:* Adventure, historical, mystery, romance, western; all the fiction is homey and upbeat. www.cappers.com

➤ *Carolina Woman:* Adventure, historical, mainstream, mystery, slice-of-life. www.carolinawoman.com

➤ *Country Woman:* Protagonist must be a rural woman. www.countrywomanmagazine.com

➤ *Dogzplot:* Experimental, literary. www.dogzplot.com

➤ *Esquire:* Literary excellence. www.esquire.com

➤ *Gargoyle:* Experimental, magic realism, surrealism. www.gargoylemagazine.com

➤ *Glimmer Train Stories:* Literary stories. www.glimmertrain.org

➤ *Hardboiled:* Crime fiction, private-eye stories. Search the catalogue at www.gryphonbooks.com for *Hardboiled Magazine*.

Short Story Markets

➤ **Hemispheres:** In-flight magazine; adventure, contemporary, ethnic, historical, mystery. www.hemispheresmagazine.com

➤ **Highlights for Children:** Ages 2 to 12. www.highlights.com

➤ **Alfred Hitchcock Mystery Magazine, Ellery Queen Mystery Magazine:** Mysteries. www.themysteryplace.com

➤ **The Hudson Review:** Literary fiction. www.hudsonreview.com

➤ **Ladies' Home Journal:** Stories must be submitted via an agent. www.lhj.com

➤ **Liguorian:** Religious, senior. www.liguorian.org

➤ **Literary Mama:** Fiction for mothers. www.literarymama.com

➤ **The Magazine of Fantasy & Science Fiction:** Fantasy, science fiction, horror. www.fandsf.com

➤ **MindFlights:** Christian fiction akin to C. S. Lewis and J. R. R. Tolkien's writings. www.mindflights.com

➤ **Neon:** Genre fiction, especially experimental, science fiction, suspense, horror; UK-based. www.neonmagazine.co.uk

➤ **One Story:** Publishes one short story every three weeks; nonprofit. www.one-story.com

➤ **On Spec:** Speculative fiction. www.onspec.ca

➤ **The Pedestal:** Website; genre fiction, literary fiction. www.thepedestalmagazine.com

➤ **Ploughshares:** Mainstream and literary fiction, no pop or commercial fiction. www.pshares.org

➤ **Prairie Schooner:** Realistic and experimental, mainstream and literary. http://prairieschooner.unl.edu

➤ **The Saturday Evening Post:** Prefers light, humorous touch. www.saturdayeveningpost.com

➤ **The Sewanee Review:** Literary fiction. www.sewanee.edu/sewanee_review

➤ The next time you have Chinese food, incorporate the fortune from your cookie as either a line of dialogue or the first line of your story.

➤ Visit Hatch's Plot Bank (www.angelfire.com/nc/tcrpress/plotbank.html). This is an innovative website that contains several thousand one-liner prompts. To get your creative juices flowing, pick a number between 1 and 2,000 before you go to the site. Look at the prompt that corresponds to the number you chose. Spend 15 minutes coming up with a short story plot that uses the prompt. For ideas you really like, be sure to record them in your journal for future development.

➤ Reverse engineer your story by deciding the outcome first, then work backwards to set up the circumstances in which this outcome could plausibly come to fruition.

➤ Add books to your library, such as Ronald Tobias's *20 Master Plots and How to Build Them*; Lou Willett Stanek's *Story Starters*; Tom Sawyer's *Plots Unlimited: A Creative Source for Generating a Virtually Limitless Number and Variety of Story Plots and Outlines*; and the Brothers Heimberg's completely silly *The Official Movie Plot Generator: Hilarious Movie Plot Combinations*. Another fun tool to assist with plotting is the Story Spinner (available at www.bonnie-neubauer.com/storyspinner.shtml), a handheld writing wheel in which you select settings, starters, and words to spin the recipe for a new story.

Last but not least, listen to whatever your characters are trying to tell you. After all, who knows this story better than they do? You may not always follow down the paths unfolding characters want to tread, but it is still essential you keep your eyes and ears open to possibilities.

From Gossip Girls to Princess Diaries: Must Today's Settings Glitter?

By Sue Bradford Edwards

Bookstore shelves glitter with novels set in glamorous Manhattan, trendy Hollywood, and ritzy British boarding schools. These settings draw readers in, and it is not hard to imagine why.

"They are such a great escape from mundane, ordinary life. I love to escape to a ballroom and wear a beautiful gown, if only in my imagination," says author Julia London, "particularly on really hot days when I am wearing shorts and flip-flops."

Dial Editor Alisha Niehaus agrees: "Everybody loves a little glamour—fiction, after all, is about living lives that aren't ours—and seeing how the glitzy half lives is an easy kind of wish fulfillment. Buying Gossip Girl costs a lot less, both money and time-wise, than buying a private helicopter or becoming an insane, work-around-the-clock banker to afford said private helicopter." These settings give readers a chance to see the life of someone they would like to be.

This does not mean that a glamorous setting is enough to

sell your novel. Authors who successfully create larger-than-life settings know when to say *enough*. They also know how to use these settings to ratchet up tension and to shape compelling characters.

Character Set-up

One way to pull readers in is to create a character with whom they can identify. Tyne O'Connell does this in the teen series, the Calypso Chronicles (Bloomsbury USA), set in an elite boarding school in Britain. "My protagonist Calypso is from L.A. and her parents, though well off, live comparatively humbly, sans pool, private jet, and stately home or castle. This gives Calypso the perspective of an outsider observing and ultimately fitting into a world that a girl of her background could only read about in glossy magazines. As she is the narrator of my books, the reader gets to live and move around in this glamorous world with her," says O'Connell.

Calypso's classmates give her, and the readers who follow her adventures, a window on a variety of glamorous worlds. "Pupils in boarding school often come from extreme wealth and privilege, and often from exclusive backgrounds; worlds with closed doors. Their parents may be captains of industry, glamorous stars, or royalty, so my characters come into contact with people from a vast array of backgrounds," says O'Connell. "Princesses like Indie rub shoulders with daughters of rock stars like Star." Her main character learns to navigate this privileged world, opening it up to the scrutiny of the reader.

O'Connell's boarding school setting works in another way that appeals to the target teen audience. "I chose to write about boarding school life as it is a unique world within a world," she says. "Teens at boarding school in the U.K. have to become very independent from a young age. They cannot escape school at the end of the day or ask for parental assistance in dealing with their daily struggles." Calypso's freedom from parental authority immediately appeals to the target readership.

Settings can be used to the utmost, if the writer goes beyond putting characters in expected places. Think of the character traits setting could reveal.

"What kind of house do they live in? Large yard for large dog? Apartment? No yard for kids? Condo? Penthouse? Trailer? Each helps to show the personality of the character," says agent Kelly Mortimer. "But don't stop at *where* they live; show *how* they live. They may bunk in a seedy part of town, but their house and yard are immaculate. They may lounge in a beautiful mansion, but empty champagne flutes sit, leaving rings on the table from the liquid on the stems. What about piles of dirty but expensive clothing strewn all over the floor? There are many ways to use setting to bring your characters to life."

As your character moves through palace or penthouse, think about what the location and furnishings tell your reader about her. Adjust the place, objects, and surroundings here and there until they reveal as much as possible. Then look to see how the setting functions within the plot itself.

Tension and Drama

Just as talented writers use settings to reveal facets of their characters' personalities, they also use them to create and heighten the tension needed to pull readers through a story. Some settings make this job easier than others.

"The Elizabethan Court is glamorous, but it was equally a place of intrigue, and intrigue—wherever people gather to seek power—makes for conflict," says author Jacqueline Kolosov, whose books include the young adult title, *A Sweet Disorder* (Hyperion). "Conflict sells."

Grit & Grime & Middle-Class

Glamorous settings may sell, but they are not all that sells. "There's a basic intrigue with people who are worse off than you are, with anything that seems like a train wreck (think James Frey), or involves eating food from a dumpster. That sounds crass, but you get the idea," says Dial Editor Alisha Niehaus. "I can think of a ton of books that offer such splendid rubbernecking—*Waiting for Normal, Penderwicks,* and *Are U 4 Real*? They sell to readers and editors. Always have, always will."

Sometimes less glamorous settings are a must, depending on the genre. "Right now, the inspirational publishers I deal with like small-town settings over big, elaborate city ones. For contemporary fiction, my editors are sticking with the smaller towns, in the USA," says agent Kelly Mortimer. "For historicals, I've seen a couple of requests for different foreign settings, but most want the sure thing: That would be England and Scotland, or nineteenth-century America."

Other genres demand glamour. "Historical romance settings are almost always more elegant than real life, and they play into the fantasy of being wooed and seduced by a dark, dangerously sexy, and wealthy man," says author Julia London.

At yet other times, specific, vibrant settings just don't work. "It's not important when you're trying to have an everyperson, everykid kind of place. I think of middle-grade school settings this way; they can be non-specific because the idea is to show kids that most teens are suffering through the same thing in the same kind of place," says Niehaus. "That sounds kind of imperialist when I think about it, and all kids experience this differently based on class, race, where they live in town, etc. But those experiences can be spoken to in a general way if you want that. Some authors do this on purpose, to focus on universality."

Posh, penniless, or plain: No matter what setting you use, work it deep into your story. That is when the whole will catch an editor's attention.

Another advantage of O'Connell's boarding school setting is that it is also a world ready-made for conflict. "Teens in boarding school must endure the constant company of boys or girls they might not get on with," she says. "To some extent pupils in day school can escape girls or boys they find disagreeable or clash with, whereas in boarding school you simply must fit in and rub along with others, as my narrator Calypso discovers."

> "The setting is the chessboard on which writers move their pieces. Every nook and cranny must provide possibilities for character and plot to develop."

O'Connell uses individual scene settings to heighten the tension. "The setting is the chessboard on which writers move their pieces. Every nook and cranny must provide possibilities for character and plot to develop. I create the place and then I see the things that could occur in that place," says O'Connell. "I created the Head Mistress's office as a place for girls to feel uncomfortable and guilty. I used a large looming desk behind which Sister Constance meted out her justice. Above her, a statue of Christ on the cross shadowed over the guilty girls as they were asked to reflect on their crimes. Even the smells resonated with the situation." Specific details can relax or terrify, humor or annoy. Use them to heighten the emotion vital to the scene in question.

Carefully chosen settings can also heighten a character's inner tension. "For Miranda, an upper class but impoverished girl in *A Sweet Disorder*, moving to the Countess of Turbury's

spartan home was difficult. She found the austerity of the place in conflict with her character, one drawn to music, color, and sensuousness, as in flowers, paintings, tapestries. Miranda has to find a way to make a life for herself here, and this means clashing with her new guardian, the Countess," says Kolosov. "If there is advice here for another writer, it is to see how setting can bring the character's situation—her desires, her fears—to the forefront of the story. How can her interaction with place help her to grow?"

Does your story need to be set on the yacht or country club or other location you have selected? If not, you have some work to do. Rewrite your novel until it could not take place anywhere else.

Lighten Up

Even when the setting for your story is the most dazzling place anyone could possibly imagine, approach it with a light hand. "The details of setting as they relate to the main story are what matters. It's great that you've got a book set in a medieval castle, but it is not necessary to describe the castle down to the garderobe," says London. "A writer must give a sense of place and time, but the sense should be relayed as part of the story itself, not laid out in a lengthy description. Descriptions should be woven into the story to keep the attention. With a few such sentences the writer can set the place and scene, and the reader's imagination will do the rest."

This balance can be especially tricky when writing historical fiction. "For the Elizabethan period, it is perhaps more difficult to imagine daily life. For example, the floors would often be strewn with rushes for the purposes of hygiene," says Kolosov. She keeps even such unusual specifics to a minimum. "I don't think I've included this detail more than once, if that, though I

From Glam to the
Wrong Side of the Tracks

➤ Candace Bushnell. *One Fifth Avenue* (Voice): Manhattan.
➤ Melissa de la Cruz. *Masquerade: A Blue Bloods Novel* (Hyperion):
Wealthy New York City and Italy.
➤ Neil Gaiman. *The Graveyard Book* (HarperCollins): Set in a decaying
cemetery.
➤ K. L. Going. *King of the Screwups* (Houghton Mifflin Harcourt): A
trailer park.
➤ Amanda Goldberg and Ruthanna Khalighi Hopper. *Celebutantes*
(St. Martin's Press): Hollywood, the week before the Oscars.
➤ Erick S. Gray, Anthony Whyte, Mark Anthony, and Kíwan Foye.
Streets of New York, Volume 2 (Augustus Publishing): New York City
gang culture.
➤ Philippa Gregory. *The White Queen* (Simon & Schuster): The Court
of the Plantagenets.
➤ Kim Gruenenfelder. *Misery Loves Cabernet* (St. Martin's Press):
Hollywood and Los Angeles.
➤ Elin Hilderbrand. *A Summer Affair* (Back Bay Books): Summer at a
Nantucket Island beach.
➤ Jeanne Kalogridis. *The Devil's Queen: A Novel of Catherine de
Medici* (St. Martin's Press): French Royal court in the sixteenth century.
➤ Katie Kitamura. *Long Shot* (Simon & Schuster): A fight ring in
Mexico.
➤ Roland Merullo. *Breakfast with Buddha* (Algonquin Books): North
Dakota, including a diner, a bowling alley, and the family farm.
➤ Walter Dean Myers. *Sunrise over Fallujah* (Scholastic): War-torn Iraq.
➤ Sanyika Shakur. *T.H.U.G. L.I.F.E.* (Grove Press): Los Angeles gang
culture.
➤ Janni Lee Simner. *Bones of Faerie* (Random House): Crumbling, post-
war American Midwest.
➤ Indra Sinha. *Animal's People* (Simon & Schuster): The slums of
Bhopal.

Style 159

have taken care to give a sense of a household—including the kitchen and bathroom facilities. Too much detail bogs down the narrative. The setting, its details, should become an integral part of the story. One shouldn't notice them."

Keeping setting from being too noticeable is often a matter of not giving too much detail at once. "No info dumps. You don't memorize every detail when you walk into a room. You see things gradually," says Mortimer. "Do the same with your setting and character descriptions. Oftentimes less really is more."

Express the details in a way that means something within the context of that particular story. "Here's my rule of thumb: If you're giving us a setting detail, you should have a reason. I don't care if the wind is blowing and the tree's leaves are shiny if it doesn't mean anything to the enhancement of the character and the plot," says Niehaus. "I care when the wind whispers like her father's murmurs, soft but somehow threatening, and how the leaves shine like her mother's locket used to before mom died and dad started getting scary."

Do not be fooled by the glitter sparkling from store displays. These settings do sell, but first they have to be deeply woven into the story, used to bring out compelling characters, tense plots, and just the right amount of detail. That is when they will pull in agents, editors, and your target audience, and leave them looking for another book with your name on it.

Beethoven versus the Crickets

Description in Fiction

By Sharelle Byars Moranville

Many writers find description the most difficult part of their craft. Kali Vanbaale, author of *The Space Between* (River City Publishing), recipient of the American Book Award for general fiction, says, "As much as I love writing details, I think it's the hardest skill in fiction writing to develop, and most often the last tool a writer adds to his or her toolbox."

Even separating description from the other writer's tools so it can be talked about is challenging. In the craft box, words are clearly *dialogue* or *not-dialogue, action* or *not-action*. But sorting words into description or not-description creates a third pile of *maybes*.

Mystery writer Mike Manno, author of *Murder Most Holy* and the upcoming *End of the Line* (both from Five Star Mysteries/ Gale), says, "Description is important to me, but for different reasons than for a writer of some other genre. Crime scene and evidence description is necessary, and so is description of all the red herrings used in the book."

While his novels are pegged as police procedurals, Manno views them as character-driven. "Of course, character can only be described by action, not words. You can't tell the reader about the character; you have to let him reveal himself to the reader. Thus I spend a lot of time creating dialogue that describes the character."

> "Character can only be described by action, not words. I spend a lot of time creating dialogue that describes the character."

He offers an example from *Murder Most Holy,* where policeman Jerome Stankowski is investigating the death of a young reporter's friend. There is ample evidence that the true target of the murder was the friend's father, Charles Winborn, who had bullied the young reporter, Buffy, off the staff of his newspaper. Stankowski conducts the interview knowing that the father died from a seizure shortly after seeing his daughter die. Buffy did not know that fact, and goes into a long list of grievances against the dad:

> There was a long pause. I could almost see the hate bottled up in her. I let her sit still for a minute. I cleared my throat, then asked her, "Did you know that Mr. Winborn died this morning?"
>
> I watched for her reaction very closely. Buffy Coyle was obviously a pretty little girl, and by little I mean just that, tiny. But today, whatever attractiveness she might have had was overshadowed by her venom.

"Good," she cried. "I'm glad." There was another pause; then she looked relieved. Her prettiness started to return. Her face, once drawn and tense, relaxed. She allowed herself to slump back into her chair. Now there was a twinkle in her eye when she returned my glance. Her small chest heaved as she inhaled. Extending her lower lip beyond her upper, she blew a wisp of hair from her eyes as she exhaled. Then she smiled.

"Wanna celebrate?"

This is a good example of taking description to its fullest meaning of revelation. Buffy's character is described by the mix of physical details, gesture, dialogue, and viewpoint.

The Viewpoint

Talking about the role of viewpoint in description, Rebecca Janni (author of the picture books *Every Cowgirl Needs a Horse* and the upcoming *Every Cowgirl Needs Dancing Boots*, from Dutton Books) tells a story of early morning bike riding with her eight-year-old son. As they pedalled through their quiet neighborhood, Janni heard beautifully played piano music drifting from a house.

"Andrew," she said, "listen! Is that Beethoven?"
"Beethoven?" he repeated.
"Don't you hear the piano?"
"No," he said. "All I hear is the sound of the crickets."

Janni says that her piano concert then faded to a symphony of crickets. "That is how an eight-year-old boy and an adult might pedal through the same scene and describe two entirely different experiences." Narrative viewpoint is key to what we describe and how we describe it.

 Style 163

"I find description most challenging in its potential to fall short," says Janni. "If I'm writing about a bike ride across the state of Iowa, I know with certainty that I can convey the basics —the bike, the time, the temperature. But can the reader see the fog lifting off the endless sea of riders? Hear the hum of spinning tires? Taste the salt of sweaty lips? Feel the heat rising off the sun-baked asphalt? Anything less has fallen short."

> "Can the reader see the fog lift off the endless sea of bike riders? Hear the hum of spinning tires? Taste the salt of sweaty lips?"

The best description pulls readers in and lets them share; makes them feel whatever the writer wants them to feel— whether it's the close-to-the-toad's-nose curiosity of a small boy or the grief of a mother whose son is a school shooter.

Words that simply describe the boy's curiosity or the mother's disbelief fall short of the ideal. But description that actually evokes that curiosity, wonder, or sadness in the reader and fuses the reader into the scene meets the mark.

The Visceral

While this may be a cerebral activity on the part of the writer, the result is—ideally—visceral to the reader. The reader must believe. Identify. Care. As Kimberly Stuart says, the best stories "draw out both belly laughter and a real life, empathetic heartache." Stuart is the author of *Balancing Act* and *Bottom Line,* from NavPress, and *Act Two, A Novel in Perfect Pitch* and *Stretch Marks,* from David C. Cook—all fast-paced and funny women's novels.

To achieve strong reader response, writers put themselves in the situation they are describing for their characters. In *The Space Between*, Vanbaale writes from the almost unbearable viewpoint of a mother whose teenage son takes a gun to school and shoots students, a teacher, and finally himself. About entering viscerally into an identity, she says, "Fortunately, I've never had to suffer the loss of a child, but I've been close to several families who have, so I largely drew on observations and just simply listening to them talk. That said, I'm also convinced I couldn't have written the story had I not been a mother myself. I don't think I could have imagined the loss of a child and gone to that dark place in my psyche without first knowing the overwhelming love and responsibility of a child. I also wrote this story right after the birth of my second child, so admittedly, a little postpartum depression didn't hurt."

With far lighter themes, teacher Eileen Boggess (author of *Mia the Meek, Mia the Melodramatic*, and *Mia the Magnificent*, from Bancroft Press) writes hilarious novels for teen girls. When it is time for description, she says, "I will act out a scene or movement in my living room to see how it looks and then I write about it. When I described Mia getting stuck on the bathroom floor in a suit of armor, for example, I acted out the scene. I tried to picture the bathroom floor of a girl's school bathroom. Luckily for me, but not luckily for my students, I had experience with people putting a face close to the floor of a school bathroom. During tornado drills, when the students in my class were directed to take *tornado position* in a safe place, they had to get on the floor of the bathroom and curl up in a ball, covering their head. I often thought that I would rather take my chances with a tornado than get on the floor and join them! A girls' school bathroom smell is just something that sticks with you." Writers know the value of sensory immersion.

Wendy Delsol, author of *Stork*, a young adult novel on Candlewick Press's fall 2010 list, says, "Descriptive passages will often require me to lift the fingers from the keyboard and really take a moment to inhabit the world I'm imagining. It also helps to close my eyes and imagine a scene almost as a mind's-eye movie. I walk through it two or three times to get the sequence of events and then I start to add the details."

Piling Up or Paring Down

Sometimes these details require actual sketches, reports Jan Blazanin. Discussing a revision to *Fairest of Them All* (MTV Books/Simon & Schuster), a novel about a teen beauty queen who goes bald, she says, "Because *Fairest of Them All* is for teens, I added more than what I'd consider my usual number and type of details for the characters' hairstyles, makeup, and clothing. I thought I'd done a pretty good job of it until I got an 11-page revision letter from my MTV editor, Jennifer Heddle. I quickly discovered that, by MTV standards, I had barely scratched the surface of description."

In one scene, Oribella tries on her gown for the Crowning Glory beauty pageant. Blazanin says, "Since I'd sewn the gown entirely from my imagination, I was quite pleased with the resulting description":

> I gasp at my reflection in the watery mirror. The opalescent fabric molds to my figure, making each of my curves shimmer. As I turn from side to side, the color changes from pale rose to mauve to the blue of an evening sky. The gown's straps are so tiny they're almost invisible.

But Heddle requested that Blazanin "describe the cut of the gown more. When my imagination hit a dead end, I took out a piece of paper and drew the gown as I imagined it. After several attempts I put together the following revised description of Ori's pageant gown."

> I gasp at my reflection in the wavy mirror. The full-length gown flows like a silken waterfall from my bust to just above my toes. Tiny tucks cinch in my waist so that it looks impossibly small. Below the waist, the tucks unfurl into a rippling skirt that's slim-fitting but loose enough to allow me to walk without ruining the lines of the gown. The opalescent fabric molds to my figure, making each of my curves shimmer. As I turn from side to side, the color changes from pale rose to mauve to the blue of an evening sky. The bodice is cut to show a hint of cleavage, and the silver chains sliding over my shoulders are so tiny they're almost invisible.

Sometimes the power of description lies in this kind of piling up of detail. But depending on audience and genre, sometimes the power is in brevity. Stuart says that a key element in her description is giving a "sensory sweep"—making sure that "the reader comes to smell, touch, see, hear, and taste the setting before too many words have passed. It's tough, isn't it? Vivid description that catapults a reader to the place the characters inhabit while still using an economy of words? Anton Chekhov said, 'Brevity is the sister of talent.' Keep description short, but pack a punch."

The familiar hardly ever packs a punch. Good description is the result of digging deep, finding the detail that is surprising, yet perfectly apt. In Tana French's psychological murder mystery *The*

Likeness (Penguin), Cassie Maddox is interviewing for a job in undercover operations. She describes the office desk of her soon-to-be boss, Frank Mackey:

> The desk was empty, not even a family photo; on the shelves, paperwork was mixed in with blues CDs, tabloids, a poker set and a woman's pink cardigan with the tags still on.

The surprising, vivid detail of the woman's pink cardigan with the tags still on pulls the reader into the scene with its freshness, and in only eight words traces a rich vein of Mackey's backstory.

Delsol aims for this kind of fresh description in her manuscripts. She says she moves in on "the things that my character would notice as out of the ordinary or unusual. I think it's the way we tend to take in the world: We skip over the familiars of a situation and zero in on what is new and/or out of place."

She tells of a writing instructor who "hated clichés of any kind. His physical reaction, and the angry red slash of pen, made quite an impression on me. I've since tried to look at things from all kinds of angles, and tried to use words and descriptions that are my own. I also try to find a humorous angle and inject a sense of fun into my writing. As an example, in the scene where Kat gives her new friend, Penny, a makeover, I wanted to find a way to describe the amount of hair spray used. I finally settled on 'and with enough hair spray to glue a cat to the wall.' I just loved the cartoonish image it brought to mind of a cat with its splayed limbs frozen against a stark wall."

Vanbaale says her favorite passage in *The Space Between* is from a chapter titled "Visitation," where the main character, Judith, visits her dead son's room. Vanbaale wrote this passage during a retreat with her writers' group as a timed exercise where the prompt was *a spinning top*. Vanbaale used the top as an extended metaphor to describe the chaos her son's act caused.

> Judith continued clutching the items to her chest, cradling them as she would a fragile newborn baby. She looked around the room again, at the mess and chaos, and saw what her son had created. Whether or not by intention, they had become like spinning tops, twisted between his fingers and dropped onto the hard floor, turning furiously out of control until their momentum dwindled, sputtered, and then stopped altogether, dizzy, disoriented, desperately changed. She felt certain that her son would feel not sadness at the uncontrollable motion he had created for his family, but pity.

As writers acknowledge, creating effective description is hard work. It requires stepping into the moment with visceral awareness. It requires conscious techniques of observation, deep digging for the perfect detail, and awareness of metaphor. It involves using tools like dialogue and action to reveal character. But as the central nervous system of a scene, it's what makes stories come alive.

Business Cards to Blogs

Creating a Marketing Platform

By Christina Hamlett

I t is hard to hear the phrase "don't toot your own horn" and not be reminded of the negative spin it has been given throughout the years by parents and teachers. While there is a practical side to warning children not to get too full of themselves by bragging, making a lot of noise about one's talents and accomplishments as an author is a cornerstone of survival, and success, in publishing today.

For introverts who have been conditioned to sing the praises of others more loudly than their own, the fear of launching a marketing platform for their books is usually driven by an expectation of failure or, worse, rejection. This hesitancy is further fueled by the misconception that the lion's share of public relations rests with the publisher, not the writer. The reality is that hawking books has become the least of most publishing houses' problems, especially in light of a worsening U.S. economy that has forced them to lay off staff, reduce their hours, and decrease the number of titles they can afford to produce.

Instead of asking "What kind of ideas can we expect from you in the future?" an acquisitions editor's first question to a prospective author is more likely to be "What kind of marketing can we expect you to do for us right now?" The answer you provide plays a pivotal role in whether you are going to be offered a contract.

Credentials and Access: Past, Present, & Future

The first step toward building your marketing platform is establishing yourself as an expert who has something unique to say. Whether the outlet for that expertise is fiction or nonfiction, it often derives from work experience, personal relationships, hobbies, or years of research on a topic you feel passionate about. Drawing attention to specific skill sets, connections, and knowledge in your cover letter or book proposal imbues it with a level of authenticity that intrigues editors.

Whomever you hung out with in the past, however, is immaterial to a publisher unless your present and future network of associates casts a wide enough net to actually sell books. If, for instance, you are still working in the profession that validated your claim to authorship, you have the stronger makings of a marketing platform than a memoirist whose social circle is all dearly departed or a hobbyist who eschews schmoozing. Someone for whom writing is a full-time career, or who is retired or supported by a partner or parent is presumably going to have more time to give talks, do book signings, go to conferences, write blogs, and be more visible than someone who works 40+ hours in a field totally unrelated to the subject of his book.

It is not just *what* you know; it is *who* you know that you can sell to, and how accessible they are to you on an immediate and ongoing basis. If you have written a nonfiction book, this means fostering relationships with businesses, trade associations, and organizations that have a passion for your topic (i.e., health care, biking, green living) and that would be willing to endorse it. For fiction, seek tie-ins with the physical setting of the story and its principal themes. These could include historical societies, school and scout groups, travel clubs, and athletic associations.

> It's not just *what* you know; it's *who* you know that you can sell to and how accessible they are to you on an immediate and ongoing basis.

Starting a (Cheap) Buzz

Social networking has burgeoned in recent years with entities like MySpace, Facebook, Twitter, Bebo, Gather, and LinkedIn. More focused on books and reading are Goodreads and BookGlutton. These sites are free to join and offer their members a wide array of photo, music, and file-sharing capabilities. They are not only forums for reconnecting with old friends and finding new ones, but are also effective tools for promoting one's work through chat rooms, videos, and links to websites.

For the author with a nonexistent budget for marketing, the social networking phenomenon is a low-stress way to join groups of like-minded individuals, share tips and advice, and slowly but surely establish yourself as someone who knows what she is talking about. It is a soft-sell approach to PR because it's easier to tell a friend (albeit a cyber pal) about your latest book than to give a speech to a room full of strangers.

Without question, social networking is a numbers game. The

more members you connect to, the bigger the ripple you can supposedly generate. The cautions about all this connectivity, however, are twofold. The first is that your objective as a writer is not to accrue votes in a popularity contest; it is to develop a supportive cluster of people who are sufficiently interested in your work to help spread the word. If you are going to use networking sites effectively to build your professional platform, limit the personal details you divulge—you don't need to talk about what you had for dinner or reveal why you're not going to your sister's wedding. The informality and ease of chatting in an electronic medium often spins a false level of comfort and can diminish your credibility as a serious author, especially if you're also posting goofy pictures of yourself quaffing margaritas.

Second, never feel compelled to accept everyone who wants to add you to their roster. Nor should you hesitate to defriend someone who proves annoying or duplicitous. My own experience involved a Kenyan woman who wanted to learn screenwriting so she could move out of her isolated village that had no electricity

Social Networking Sites

> **Bebo:** www.bebo.com
> **BookGlutton:** www.bookglutton.com
> **Facebook:** www.facebook.com
> **Gather:** www.gather.com
> **Goodreads:** www.goodreads.com
> **LinkedIn:** www.linkedin.com
> **MySpace:** www.myspace.com
> **Twitter:** http://twitter.com

Find a comparative review of the top ten sites at http://social-networking-websites-review.toptenreviews.com.

or phone service. (Odd, yes, that her computer connection worked just fine.) Eager to tap my services, she offered to wire me my consulting fee at once if I could just provide her with my banking information, social security number, and mother's maiden name.

The Blog, the Blog!

Understanding what is hot about your book topic and the demographic you want to reach makes you a prime candidate for a weekly, daily, or monthly blog. A blog offers the chance to incorporate excerpts from your book, chat about what inspired you to write it, give interesting backstory on the characters (some of which may not have made it into the final product), answer questions from your readers, and even give them a sneak peek at projects you have in the works.

The easiest place to start blogging is on a website devoted to your book. Include the URL on your business cards, promotional materials such as postcards and bookmarks, and as part of your e-signature on all correspondence. Some writers opt for an entirely separate blog in which they write on a variety of topics, invite free content and banner ads from other writers, and maximize Really Simple Syndication (RSS) capabilities to direct traffic to the book products that sites want to sell. The secret to generating high traffic is in making it as easy as possible for readers to subscribe to your blog:

➤ Offer freebie incentives to join (i.e., quick tips packages and e-books).
➤ Post comments in related forums.
➤ Become an enthusiastic guest blogger on other people's websites.

Just as with social networking venues, it is prudent to shop around before you jump in to blogging sites. Websites such as Blogger, WordPress, and LiveJournal have easy-to-use templates and tutorials. In addition, blog forums such as Thoughts.com allow you to create polls and reader surveys.

Another popular offshoot of blogging is the podcast, a do-it-yourself radio-style program that you can create and run from the comfort of your own home. This can take the form of a lecture or anecdotal chat where you dispense practical advice to fellow writers; a call-in scenario where listeners can ask questions on a specific topic; or Q&A sessions with published authors, agents, and industry experts. With resources such as Podblaze and Podomatic, a good microphone, a quiet room, and recording software such as Audacity and WavePad, your *show* can be up and running within a matter of hours.

Blogging Sites

➤ **Blogger:** www.blogger.com
➤ **LiveJournal:** www.livejournal.com
➤ **Thoughts.com:** www.thoughts.com/free-blog
➤ **WordPress:** http://wordpress.com

Plugging in to Your Peeps

Regional retailers love unique events that will bring customers through their doors. This, in turn, attracts the local media and enables both retailers and authors to benefit from the exposure. Weekly newspapers in particular are always on the prowl for human interest stories.

Suppose you have written a murder mystery that takes place

at a winery. Instead of sitting at a table in a bookstore and hoping someone will walk by and notice you, create an event that involves a reading or a talk at an area winery. Customers who buy an autographed copy of your book are then entitled to a modest discount on their wine purchase. Since they were already on the premises to buy a bottle or two, half your work is done before you even start talking.

Here are some more ideas:

➤ For cookbook authors, do a cooking demonstration at a gourmet shop that not only whips up excitement about the products and utensils they sell, but also reinforces your expert status. Pass out free recipe cards that feature the cover of your book on the back.

➤ Are you writing YA books? Offer to be a speaker for Career Day at neighborhood schools. In concert with the exciting advice you dispense about what it is like to be a writer, distribute pencils and pens with the titles of your books imprinted on them, hand out free bookmarks, and give students mini-teasers in the form of a trifold brochure or simple booklet that contains the first chapter and ends on a cliffhanger.

➤ Give your fictional YA characters their own blog and encourage teens and tweens to contribute to it, post reviews, and ask advice about writing, relationships, and life. This strategy will also keep you in the loop on the topics that interest them.

➤ Volunteer for literary events and festivals. Organize readings and discussion groups at the library. If it is not cost-prohibitive, attend national conferences or conventions and participate on panels. Leverage your expertise through consulting, mentoring, and training gigs. Teach

workshops at community centers or through distance-learning forums. Build your e-mail list from registrations and routinely forward articles of interest and monthly tips that supplement the classes your recipients have attended. The goal is to keep your name active for every outreach group with which you come in contact.

➤ Civic organizations are always looking for dynamic speakers for their luncheon meetings. Whenever you have the opportunity to give a talk to these groups, be sure to not only have copies of your books on hand but also a *one-pager* to distribute to attendees. The one-pager is a tidy summary of your background, your publications, your website(s), your professional affiliations and, most important, your availability as a speaker. Gregarious people typically belong to multiple clubs and organizations (including the Chamber of Commerce) and you can provide them with an easy way to make their next meeting a hit. The more you can become a known, and reliable, commodity, the more bookings you will get and, accordingly, the broader your platform will become.

Podcast Resources

➤ **Audacity:** http://audacity.sourceforge.net
➤ **Podblaze:** www.podblaze.com
➤ **Podomatic:** www.podomatic.com
➤ **WavePad:** www.nch.com.au/wavepad/masters.html

Generate Content

Every major market in the world is hungry for fresh content to fill their websites, newsletters, and direct mailers. They are not only willing to pay for premium articles and videos and use proprietary technology to optimize search engines, they also have no problem with writers using their own bylines.

Venues such as Demand Studios, About.com, Essortment, How to Do Things, and Real Simple enable you to build a portfolio fairly fast and, even better, encourage readers to get email alerts every time you publish something new. Even nonpaying markets such as *American Chronicle* attract more than 11 million annual visitors by using news aggregators such as Google, Lycos, and Topix, and will syndicate your articles to twenty affiliated online magazines throughout the U.S. and the world. That's a whole lot of marketing chatter that keeps working even while you sleep.

Web-writing Venues

- ➤ **About.com:** www.about.com
- ➤ **American Chronicle:** www.americanchronicle.com
- ➤ **Demand Studios:** www.demandstudios.com
- ➤ **Essortment:** www.essortment.com
- ➤ **How to Do Things:** www.howtodothings.com
- ➤ **Real Simple:** www.realsimple.com

Protecting Authors' Rights from Wrongs

By Mark Haverstock

"Occupation: Author. A noble tradition, but a precarious line of work . . . ,"

— *Roy Blount Jr., Authors Guild President*

Precarious? Yes.

Given all the new ways of *not* getting paid that new technology affords, the American Society of Journalists and Authors (ASJA), the Authors Guild, and other writers advocacy groups are busily scrutinizing contracts and business practices to help protect writers' rights, making it easier to earn a decent living. "Whether you're a writer of novels or a blogger, you have to be fairly compensated," says Salley Shannon, President of the ASJA.

The Amazon Jungle

Early on, Amazon was a kind of hero to small publishers and self-published authors. In a market where bookstore shelf space

181

was at a premium, Amazon offered virtual space on its website, showing and selling books to a worldwide audience. More recently, authors have not been happy in the Amazon jungle.

One of the most recent skirmishes has been over Amazon's popular Kindle 2, which rolled out in February 2009 with several new features, including text-to-speech audio. "They apparently hadn't talked to people in the publishing industry first before making their announcement: E-book rights don't come bundled with audio rights," says Paul Aiken, Executive Director of the Authors Guild. "Audio rights are separately placed by the author, the author's agent, or the book's publisher with audio book publishers."

Aiken notes that it is not contractually permissible to sell an e-book along with audio unless that right was specifically granted and specifically included with the e-book, which is almost never the case. Amazon's actions presented both a contractual and copyright problem for authors. "The practical effect," says Aiken, "is that we have to protect the audio book industry—a billion-dollar industry in the U.S." Interestingly, Amazon owns Audible, the largest online-based seller of downloadable audio books.

Blount's op-ed piece on this topic, "The Kindle Swindle?" (*New York Times,* February 24, 2009), touched off a firestorm of debate. The National Federation of the Blind accused the Guild of wanting to make it illegal to use the new technology, though exemptions for free audio availability to the blind have been in place for years. A lawyer at the Electronic Frontier Foundation issued a tongue-in-cheek warning that "parents everywhere should be on the lookout for legal papers haling them into court for reading to their kids."

Shortly afterward, Amazon agreed to let individual publishers request to turn off the text-to-speech capabilities. Aiken suggests that another sensible solution would be to make text-to-speech a purchase option. If you want to buy the audio along with the e-book, you pay a dollar or two extra and text-to-speech would then be enabled. There has been no response from Amazon on the purchase option yet.

It is no big deal to make such changes. Amazon has both the ability to adjust its pricing structure and reach into individual Kindles to make changes. This was proven in July 2009, when Amazon suddenly pulled and refunded purchases for two George Orwell titles, *Animal Farm* and, ironically, *1984*, from customers' Kindles because of copyright issues. After suffering a blast of bad PR for the action, Amazon founder Jeff Bezos quickly apologized for suddenly deleting the books.

BookSurge, or Else

A year earlier, Amazon had announced that it would require that all books it sells that are produced through on-demand means be printed by BookSurge, its in-house printer/publisher. Amazon explained this move as a customer service matter, saying it could deliver print-on-demand books more quickly and bundle shipments with other items purchased at the same time from the company. Amazon also put a green spin on the announcement, claiming that less transportation fuel is used when all items are shipped directly from its facilities.

Both the Authors Guild and ASJA believe something else is afoot, and are reviewing the antitrust and other legal implications of Amazon's move. Print-on-demand (POD) publisher BookLocker has already filed a class action suit.

Ingram Industries's Lightning Source has been the dominant printer for on-demand titles, and it seems to be quite efficient. It ships on-demand titles directly to the customer shortly after they are ordered through Amazon. It is a profitable business for

Ingram, which gets a percentage of the sales and a printing fee for every on-demand book it ships. Amazon appears to want Ingram's slice of the pie as well.

According to an e-mail sent to Authors Guild members, "once Amazon owns the supply chain, it has effective control of much of the 'long tail' of publishing—the enormous number of titles that sell in low volumes but which, in aggregate, make a lot of money for the aggregator [Amazon]." (www.authorsguild.org/advocacy/articles/amazonsqueezeslongtail.html) Since Amazon has become the major retailer of books, owning the supply chain would allow it to easily increase its profit margins on these books. This could be done by insisting on deeper discounts from publishers and authors, or it could simply charge more for printing the books.

"It's more about profit margin than it is about customer service or fossil fuels," says Aiken. "The potential big losers (other than Ingram) if Amazon imposes greater discounts on the industry are authors—since many are paid for on-demand sales based on the publisher's gross revenues—and publishers."

Shannon points out that the positive relationships that Amazon has built up over the years with authors and publishers will evaporate if the company continues its quest to be the only game in town. "With these grabby, strong-arm tactics, Amazon negates all that—and the years of goodwill it has built up with writers, who ultimately will bear the brunt of any price increases in the printing of independently published books," she says.

Google Settlement

That other Internet behemoth, Google, has been waging its own battles, some of them now against Amazon. In 2005, the Authors Guild and the Association of American Publishers (AAP) filed suit against Google, arguing that the Google Books

Facts at a Glance

➤ **Authors Guild:** www.authorsguild.org

The Authors Guild is an organization of and for published authors. It had its beginning in 1912 as the Authors' League of America, formed by 350 book and magazine authors, and dramatists. In 1921, the group split into the Dramatists Guild of America, for writers of radio and stage drama, and the Authors Guild, for novelists and nonfiction book and magazine authors.

The group now has about 8,000 members. Its current president is Roy Blount Jr.

➤ **American Society of Journalists and Authors:** www.asja.org

The American Society of Journalists and Authors (ASJA) was founded in 1948 as the Society of Magazine Writers, and is an organization of independent nonfiction writers in the United States.

ASJA is a member of the Council of National Journalism Organizations and of the Authors Coalition of America. All members are automatically enrolled into the Authors Registry.

Membership consists of more than 1,300 freelancers. The current president is Salley Shannon.

➤ **Association of American Publishers:** www.publishers.org

The Association of American Publishers (AAP) is the primary publishing trade organization. Its mission statement says its "mandate" is to cover "broad issues important to all publishers as well as issues of specific concern to particular segments of the industry." This includes intellectual property rights, technology and digital issues, censorship, and more. The goal is to expand American publishing markets at home and abroad, provide industry standards, and promote creativity by protecting rights.

Current membership numbers more than 300. The current President and CEO is Tom Allen.

Library Project—which was to scan thousands of books from libraries that included those at Harvard and Oxford—comprised "massive copyright infringement." Going back and forth in the courts, the Authors Guild and Google signed a settlement in September 2008. But the firestorms continued to rage, not least of all when Amazon filed a claim in September 2009 against the settlement, saying it would violate antitrust laws.

The Google Settlement is still not in place as *Writer's Guide* closes at the end of 2009. The *Wall Street Journal* called the situation deadlocked, although Google agreed to let go of some of its use of orphan works. The judge in the case preliminarily approved an amended agreement, and set a timeline for finalizing the case. Other publishers have been added as plaintiffs, as well, including Harlequin.

If this settlement is approved in amended form, Google will be allowed to digitize millions of out-of-print books, compile an archive of them, and make them available to readers and researchers. Rights holders of the books will share in 63 percent of gross revenues made by Google and its book database through ads or other fees, for sales and reprints. These funds will be paid through the Book Rights Registry, which will manage the accounts and pay the appropriate publishers or writers.

"What it would do is make out-of-print books available to people again, and that's good for consumers," says Aiken. "The settlement would make another 10 to 20 million out-of-print books available to the marketplace for free. For a rights holder, it's a no-brainer; you can decide whether or not to display your books, make use of the licenses the settlement enables or not, and you can change your mind at any time." For each publisher and author, account management will be handled through the Book Rights Registry.

The ASJA took a different decision, when its board voted in

The Book Rights Registry

The Book Rights Registry, which is being established in connection with the Google Settlement, will be a not-for-profit organization that represents the interests of rights holders with Google, as well as in potential licensing deals with other entities, subject to rights holders' authorization. The Registry will manage rights and payments for items included in Google Book Search, much like ASCAP does for the music industry.

Google has agreed to pay $34.5 million to establish the Registry, and to pay for the costs of the Class Notice Program and claims administration. After Google's payment, the Registry will be funded by taking an administrative fee as a percentage of revenues received from Google. Once the Registry is in operation, it will:

➤ represent the interests of the rights holders in connection with the settlement;
➤ establish and maintain a database of contact information for authors and publishers;
➤ attempt to locate rights holders;
➤ distribute payments received from Google for the rights holders' share of revenues;
➤ assist in the resolution of disputes between rights holders.

July 2009 to oppose the Google Settlement. It sought to partner with like-minded organizations to push for other options. According to Shannon, the ASJA is uncomfortable with handing over digital control to Google. "It sets a bad precedent for writers; it overturns copyright law," she says. "With the opt-out provision, everyone is in, like it or not, unless you opt out. We believe that anything as important as the registry of digital books should have a public oversight component and shouldn't be under the control of one corporation."

Tending to the Orphans

Another issue that provoked serious discussion and dissension, among the Guild, ASJA, and other interested writers' groups is the handling of *orphan works*. These out-of-print books are still held by copyright, but the rights holders cannot be found.

"People have been throwing out numbers saying that 60 or 70 percent of the books to be included in the Google database are orphaned works, which is crazy. That's the number of out-of-print works," says Aiken. "In reality, we are finding 80 to 85 percent of the rights holders for orphaned books."

The ASJA feels, however, that weakening copyright protection in any form is bad for writers. "Some people ask why should anyone be concerned about this because there isn't really a market right now," says Shannon. "But it strikes me that large corporations seldom act solely for altruism. I don't think that Google is scanning millions of orphan works for no reason whatever." She suggests that once these books become available to scholars and the general public, some of them will inevitably become "discovered" and could become hot properties.

Another issue is the diligence of the search. Authors or their estates could be left out because of weak attempts to find them. "We don't know how much effort will be put into finding orphan book authors," says Shannon. "I believe most writers that are living can be found."

Eight Hundred-Pound Gorillas

One of the biggest concerns of authors and publishers is how much money they will make. If Amazon and Google come to dominate their respective markets, they could conceivably dictate pricing for books or services because of their clout. That power could turn the publishing world on its head and redefine the way the writing business operates.

Right now, Amazon is selling Kindle e-books at a loss, and lowered the price yet again in late 2009. Take a look at the math, using a hardcover price of $30 retail as an example. According to Aiken, publishers hesitate to discount e-books much because they do not want to hurt hardcover sales, so they might price the e-book version at $25 retail. Amazon buys the e-book version at wholesale, for 50 percent off, for about $12.50. Then it sells the Kindle e-book at $9.99, going $2.51 into the red for each sale. "They're taking a loss on many of those sales, but they're trying to build a market and get customers locked into the [Kindle] device," he says.

Currently, it is still the publisher's contract with the writer that determines how much the writer will make. "This doesn't harm [authors] very much now because there aren't that many Kindles out there," says Shannon. "Potentially, it could be different—if a significant number of readers owned a Kindle and purchased most of their books that way. If the prices Amazon sets for Kindle e-books become lower than what a writer can get for the book in print, that harms you."

Everyone in the industry is wondering when that other shoe is going to drop, knowing that Amazon is becoming the 800-pound gorilla that can sit anywhere it wants. "Amazon is eventually going to say, 'We don't want to pay $12.50 for a book; we've got to make money and we've got the customer base,' and you have to respect that," says Aiken. "The big fear in the industry is that they'll want to buy the books at maybe $5 and mark them up to $9.99. Amazon is taking a loss now to build up their market, and will likely use that as leverage." He explains that the situation echoes the old book club model. Book clubs in their heyday were so large, with an audience that publishers wanted to reach, so the clubs could dictate terms.

Google is also an 800-pound gorilla, but the Authors Guild is

not overly concerned about its motives. "They're an 800-pound gorilla we have a tentative contract with," says Aiken. "Google is in the search engine business and always will be. They make a lot more money doing what they're doing now than they could distributing books. Since they are getting 37 percent of the revenue according to the settlement, there's no reason for them to be the bad guys."

Piracy

Another rights concern that has been surfacing is piracy, especially of electronic book or magazine versions that can be easily shared. "We can't be complacent," says Shannon. "Every writer knows that you can sweep the Internet once a month and likely find someone using your work without permission."

In a *New York Times* article, "Print Books Are Target of Pirates on the Web" (May 11, 2009), Motoko Rich reported that science fiction author Ursula K. Le Guin was perusing Scribd, a website where aspiring authors can share their original work, and found digital copies of books that seemed "familiar." In fact, they were her books, none of which had been authorized for electronic editions by Le Guin or her publisher. Rich wrote, "To Ms. Le Guin, it was a rude introduction to the quietly proliferating problem of digital piracy in the literary world. 'I thought, who do these people think they are?' she said. 'Why did they think they could violate my copyright and get away with it?'"

Rich cites other examples of illegal reproductions of copyrighted materials found on Scribd and Wattpad, as well as on file-sharing services RapidShare and MediaFire. Popular titles from J. K. Rowling, John Grisham, Stephen King, and Stephenie Meyer have popped up on these sites. Rich reports that David Young, Chief Executive of Hachette Book Group, says pirating is "exponentially up." Hachette's Little, Brown division publishes

Meyer's Twilight series, which is highly piratized.

One way to get around the hackers, suggests Aiken, is to have a functioning, fairly priced licensing system in place—one that works on several platforms. "We need an e-book sales system so there is an easy, legitimate way to get books. That was a problem the music industry ran into years ago with Napster."

Publishing in the Digital Age

What is in the digital future? How will authors and publishers face new technology, yet protect rights and the ability to make a decent living? "Two big fears are that piracy will become significant and take a big bite out of the industry, and the other is that a single aggregator will get control of the distribution of e-books—Amazon being the most likely candidate," says Aiken. "If that happens, it would be very unhealthy for the publishing industry."

He points to one scenario that is already happening between Amazon and the newspaper industry. Amazon keeps 70 percent of the profits from Kindle newspaper sales, and gets a sub-scriber list as well. "That's a sign of a weak industry, a strong aggregator, and what can result," explains Aiken. "Right now, it's a 50/50 split between the content provider and Amazon for e-books and it's going to tip one way or the other. If there is real competition in the distribution of e-books, then the distributor shouldn't get 50 percent, because they're just passing on data. A 70/30 split in favor of publishers and authors should be the standard if a truly competitive market develops for distributing e-books." He notes that the Guild will be watching closely, hoping to have some influence on the revenue share.

One of Shannon's primary concerns is payment to writers, particularly as more and more publications go online or appear on handheld devices. "This will change again the way writers are compensated," she says. "We can't always foresee what's

Pay-to-Play Papers

Publishing is undeniably an industry in transformation. Writers need protection of their rights and payment in the midst of shifting publication formats, new products (like the Kindle), and new services (like Google Book Search). But publishers too are facing new paradigms for how they do business and make money—especially newspapers and magazines.

Given the expectations of Internet users today, and the decline in newspaper print subscriptions and advertising, must the digital media continue to give away content for free? Can advertising support news reporting and analysis online? Must publishers consider subscription-only policies again, though many such systems have gone down in flames? Is the solution *micropayments*, or small fees for full access to stories? Will a combination of advertising, subscriptions, and micropayments keep more of the digital news media in operation?

Over the past year, the debate has been lively and very high-profile. *Time* had a cover story by Walter Isaacson, who wrote that "[t]he crisis in journalism has reached meltdown proportions" as ". . . news organizations are merrily giving away their news." He believes an iTunes-like, easy one-click purchase arrangement is the best option for making content payment work.

Michael Kinsley, founder of *Slate* and former editor of *The New Republic,* disagreed. *Slate* had begun as a subscription-only, premium online magazine. As Kinsley has written, "We were quite self-righteous about the alleged principle that 'content' should not be free." Today, he argues, news on paper thrown into the bushes by a kid on a bike or picked up at the corner newsstand is an anachronism, an artifact. He believes advertising will improve post-recession, and the strongest publications will still be around. Subscriptions or a micropayment system, he says, are not going to work.

But people like Steven Brill at Journalism Online, and Cynthia Typaldos at Kachingle think it will. At the end of 2009, Google, Microsoft, and Rupert Murdoch's News Corporation (which owns the

Pay-to-Play Papers

Wall Street Journal, one of the few newspapers with a successful online subscription policy) had entered the fray on the side of subscription/micropayment systems.

The Newspaper Association of America has now requested proposals for systems. Journalism Online reported in September that it had more than 1,000 publications signed up for its paid online model. At Kachingle, whose beta went live in November, users pay a ¢5 monthly fee that Kachingle distributes proportionately to the member sites ("content providers") the user visits most often.

Can the newspaper decline be staunched? John Ridding, Chief Executive of the U.K.'s *Financial Times,* has said the "free is good" premise must be abandoned, and cultural expectations changed.

Writers undoubtedly agree: Good writing and reporting is worth paying for.

Of Interest
➢ "Four Ways to Avoid 'Paid Content' Suicide," Josh Gordon, www.foliomag.com/2009/four-ways-avoid-paid-content-suicide
➢ "How to Save Your Newspaper," Walter Isaacson, www.time.com/time/printout/0,8816,1877191,00.html
➢ "Lots of Fee Ideas for Media Online," Richard Perez-Pena, www.nytimes.com/2009/09/11/business/media/11paper.html
➢ "Paid content the only way to safeguard journalism, says *Financial Times* chief," Katie Allen, www.guardian.co.uk/media/2009/oct/02/paid-content-ft-john-ridding
➢ "What Would Micropayments Do for Journalism? A Freakonomics Quorum," Stephen J. Dubner, http://freakonomics.blogs.nytimes.com/2009/02/18/blnk/
➢ "You Can't Sell News by the Slice," Michael Kinsley, www.nytimes.com/2009/02/10/opinion/10kinsley.html

➢ Journalism Online: www.journalismonline.com
➢ Kachingle: www.kachingle.com
➢ PaidContent: http://paidcontent.org

 Career 193

going to happen, but we must campaign to insist that writers be paid for their work and to oppose the idea that magazines or any other publication can rerun the work of any random blogger for no payment whatsoever. No matter who you are, if your writing is good enough that people want to read it, it's good enough that you should be compensated for it."

Shannon is also concerned about the content sites popping up on the Web that compensate writers at bargain-basement rates—or not at all. "I would advise writing professionals not to write for free. If someone says come and write for my website because it will give you great exposure, your response should be, 'Who will buy my groceries?'" she says. "If we continue to give our work away, it hampers the potential that writers will eventually be able to make a living on the Internet." Shannon advises writers never to work on a pay-per-click basis; you may write a great story, but could end up receiving only a few dollars for it. "We have to come up with some way that writers can be paid equitably for work that is published on the Web—I don't know what the final answer will be, but we do know what doesn't work."

For More Information

➢ **BookLocker suit:** http://antitrust.booklocker.com/
➢ **Google Settlement:** http://books.google.com/booksrightsholders/
➢ **Kindle 2:** www.nytimes.com/2009/02/25/opinion/25blount.html and www.engadget.com/2009/02/27/the-engadget-interview-paul-aiken-executive-director-of-the-au/

Grab 'Em, First Thing

The Art of Hooks & Selling Manuscripts

By Katherine Swarts

Often, the hardest part of writing is convincing people with the power to purchase your work that the results are worth reading. The only way to do that is quickly. Editors and readers alike are perennially rushed; if a query or proposal or manuscript or article or book doesn't *hook* attention with the first sentence, few people wait to see if things turn fascinating in paragraph four.

"There's often a reluctance to get to the point," says Moira Allen, Editor of Writing-World.com and author of *Starting Your Career as a Freelance Writer* (Allworth Press). "I remember one manuscript from my *Dog Fancy* editing days. It was a lovely story, but the writer prefaced it by explaining how she had gotten out of college, spent time looking for work, finally located a job on a farm, and 'That's when I met Shep, the most extraordinary sheepdog . . . ' I cut the first three or four paragraphs and led with something like 'I'll never forget the first day I met Shep . . . ' Take a look at your very first paragraph, even your first line: Does it set up the problem or question? If the first three or four paragraphs are about you, and the rest of the article is not about you, that's a real clue those paragraphs need to go!"

"I can't count the number of manuscripts I've seen that dump the whole backstory on readers before readers even have a chance to learn what the book is about," says freelance editor and history writer Sean McLachlan. "I advise writers to paint a quick picture of time and place, then forge ahead, filling in details on a need-to-know basis."

Some writers avoid the slow-start problem through a method recommended by professional writer and speechwriting teacher Donnell King: "Write the body of the speech first, and the introduction afterward. I can't introduce a speech until I clearly know that speech. After all, how could I introduce you if I had no idea who you were?" It's the same with article writing: "I simply start the article and sharpen the lead later. I regularly chop the first paragraph or two off to see if the article starts better that way. I keep various versions of articles in progress."

"I love rummaging through my writing in pursuit of the beginning," says freelance writer and speaker Jeri Darby, "a search best started after two or three days away from the work, so a writer can return with fresh perspective."

Hooks Readers Bite

Actual best beginnings come in many forms, but all good hooks arouse reader emotion. "I aim for openings that plug into the senses," says Darby. "Stimulating sights, sounds, and emotions pull readers in."

"For topics that promote change, I find that a surprising fact works well," says Wenona Napolitano, author of *The Everything Green Wedding Book* (Adams Media). "For instance, did you know that more than 20 tons of mining waste is generated to make one plain gold wedding band?"

True (or true-to-life) anecdotes are popular hooks because they make an impression that "this is relevant to real people like us." They also arouse a sense of action. "A starting anecdote raises the curtain in the middle of the action—what an editor I once knew called the *knee deep lead*," says King. "For instance, in 'Coping with High-Risk Pregnancy' (www.babyzone.com), I started with: "'We're going to refer you to a prenatal specialist, because it looks from the ultrasound that your baby has a two-vessel umbilical cord instead of the normal three-vessel cord." The nurse told

> "A starting anecdote raises the curtain in the middle of the action—what an editor I knew called the *knee deep lead*."

us this in late January; we were expecting a little girl to be born early in May.' I later painted in the journey that took us to that doctor's appointment, after the reader cared about it."

Andy Fink, Publisher and Editor in Chief of *Junior Shooters,* cites an opening involving real people: "'The young cowboy had a smile on his face as he looked at the older gunfighter.' The reader wonders why the smile, who these gunfighters are, and what is going to happen."

"I enjoy anecdotes because they engage readers and create immediate interest," says author and creative writing teacher Jennifer Brown Banks, who writes the Jennifer's Gems column for *Online Dating Magazine.* "Quotes would be a close second."

Consider what draws a specific market's readers, however. "Speaking as a writer," says Allen, "I prefer the anecdote. But

anecdotal hooks rarely work well in the articles I buy as editor for a writers' e-zine. There, a good hook poses the problem or question the article will address. For example, a hook on how to refresh oneself as a writer might open, 'Whether you've been writing for many years or just a few months, you're going to encounter days when you just don't seem able to find an original idea.' That hook isn't sexy—but it immediately tells the reader what to expect, and that this article may be worthwhile regardless of the reader's level of experience. It also sets up a problem most of us identify with. I call this type of hook a *promise* hook, because it promises to tell us how to resolve the problem. Obviously, a promise hook only works if, in fact, the article fulfills that promise."

"Hooks depend on subject and context," says McLachlan. For "a short, punchy magazine piece, surprising facts or statistics are good ways to grab a reader's attention. For history books, anecdotes that sum up the situation often work best. While reading a Confederate newspaper dating to late in the Civil War, I saw a charitable appeal to supply Confederate soldiers with tobacco. Imagine, all those Southern tobacco states and the rebel soldiers had nothing to smoke! It says volumes about how ragged the Confederate army had become and how poor their supply system was."

Before deciding what sort of hook to use, says Patricia Fry, an editorial consultant and President of the Small Publishers, Artists, and Writers Network (SPAWN), "I ask myself what this audience needs or wants to know. Isn't that what communication is all about—being tuned in to your audience?"

Query Letter Hooks

Before writers have the opportunity to tempt readers, they have to convince an editor or publisher to bring their work to

Opening Fiction with a Bang

Hooking readers immediately is particularly important with fiction. If a nonfiction title promises helpful advice, readers may endure a few dull paragraphs to reach the meat. But with fiction, they want pure entertainment and expect the writer to deliver quickly—or it's good-bye.

"The opening of your novel or short story is crucial," says science fiction and fantasy writer Will Greenway. "Line 1 [is] the hook—*the* most important line. This is the eye-catch, the mindshare, the part that invites the reader to continue . . . The line doesn't have to explode—it just needs to intrigue."

Greenway's website, www.ringrealms.com, has (on the Inspiration page) a two-part article on "Dynamic Beginnings" that includes more than half a dozen examples of powerful opening paragraphs. First sentences from three of those examples:

> ➢ "On Aarlen's eleventh birthday, Father gave her a sword and said by the time a year passed she would take a man's life with it."
> ➢ "Imagine a morning when the sun failed to rise."
> ➢ "I dangled over the cliff, only the will to live holding me suspended above the barnacle studded boulders."

Intrigued? Eager to hear more? Every fiction hook should trigger that same eagerness in readers.

readers. However good a manuscript, the first thing an editor reads is the query or cover letter. Many writers create excellent manuscripts and then sabotage themselves with dull or sloppy introductory letters.

"If your query or proposal is written poorly, I will not want to work with you, no matter how great your story," says Amy Thompson, Editor in Chief of Diversion Press. "I prefer that the author not give anecdotes, quotes, or facts, but rather offer an opening sentence that summarizes the manuscript and why I would want to read it. And I like the author to be very concise; my time is valuable."

"Clear, concise, and apt" queries sell, agrees Edward Wilson, Editor in Chief of Absey & Company. "No fluff, no 'My aunt, or Deepak Chopra loves my work.' They aren't publishing it. Grammar mistakes are deadly. I also stop reading if the first word of the manuscript is *it*."

Editors also like to know early on that an author understands who he is offering to write for—that publisher and their readers. "Make it obvious that the author has read our submission guidelines and is experienced in the field," says David Heath, Editor in Chief of Redleaf Press, which publishes early childhood resources. "The specific topic should be timely and fill a hole in our list."

Queries also should mention the first hook readers will see: the title. Not that finding the perfect title is a vital part of the writer's job—many editors substitute their own almost routinely —but a good suggestion does show that the writer can explain concisely what the text offers.

"Titles deserve ample thought and creative contemplation," says Darby. "I prefer snappy, clever types that unveil a takeaway."

"A title needs to grab attention and sum up what the reader's experience will be," says McLachlan.

"A title should give an idea of what lies in store," says Allen. "For newsstand magazines, keep in mind that editors think not only about titles but about how to convert your title into a *cover blurb*. But titles that are too clever and don't tell you what the article is about don't work. I recently ran an article whose author called it 'There's No Free Lunch.' What the heck is that about? It was actually an article on sources of free software. I kept the title, but added the free software element, and the article ran as 'There's No Free Lunch—But There IS Free Software!'"

> Many writers create excellent manuscripts and then sabotage themselves with dull or sloppy queries or cover letters.

"Clever and snappy titles really stand out," says Napolitano, "as long as they convey the message of what the work is actually about."

Conciseness counts. As with other writing, wordiness can ruin a title. Especially "when writing for the Web, it's wise to avoid very long titles or long, explanatory subtitles," says Allen. "I get a lot of titles like 'Hot and Heavy: Twenty Ways to Create Romantic Heroes Who Can Make You Feel the Heat.' But too long a title won't display properly in a Web browser—or on Google. And if you need a thirteen-word subtitle to explain a three-word title, maybe that original title needs some work!"

With nonfiction titles, basic-and-descriptive often wins over unique-and-unforgettable. "Many writers come up with really clever titles," says Fry, that "have little to do with the subject. In that case, I advise them to add a descriptive subtitle. Of course,

Sources

➤ **Absey & Company:** 23011 Northcrest Dr., Spring, TX 77389. www.absey.biz

➤ **Diversion Press:** www.diversionpress.com, diversionpress@ yahoo.com. Use e-mail to submit initial book proposals or to request the mailing address for anthology submissions.

➤ *Junior Shooters:* Junior Sports Magazines, 7154 W. State St., #377, Boise, ID 83714. www.juniorshooters.net

➤ *Online Dating Magazine:* Suite 202 - #188, 29030 SW Town Center Loop East, Wilsonville, OR 97070. www.onlinedatingmagazine.com

➤ **Redleaf Press:** 10 Yorkton Court, St. Paul, MN 55117. www.redleafpress.org

➤ **Small Publishers, Artists, and Writers Network (SPAWN):** PMB 123, 323 E. Matilija St., Suite 110, Ojai, CA 93023. www.spawn.org

➤ **Writing-world.com:** www.writing-world.com

Authors

➤ **Will Greenway:** www.ringrealms.com

➤ **Donnell King:** http://donnellking.com/

➤ **Sean McLachlan:** www.freewebs.com/seanmclachlan

➤ **Wenona Napolitano:** www.creativelygreen.blogspot.com, www.everythinggreenweddings.blogspot.com

it's great if the author can state the nature of the book or article in just a few words."

While most editors agree that titles are for grabbing attention and subtitles for explaining further, some prefer to put the most basic element first. Fink gives one example: "'Tips & Hints of the Week #5—Shooting Glasses.' If it started with 'Shooting Glasses' those not interested in glasses might not read further. Starting with 'Tips & Hints' attracts a broader reader base."

(See more on titles in "Titles that Sell," page 205.)

What Good Hooks Have in Common

Are different publishers attracted to different types of hooks to open a manuscript? "Absolutely!" says Heath. "The publisher's specific niche and audience are the most influential" factors in determining which kind of hook will work best. Authors are well-advised to study a dozen or more samples of what their target markets have already published.

Good hooks, however, share universal qualities. "It is important the reader have an inkling of what is happening," says Wilson. "Too much mystery, too much action, too much dialogue just gets in the way of the narrative."

"Your hook must show a reader why she should read the article," says Allen. "If readers don't know within the first paragraph why they should read on, chances are they won't. The point of a hook is not to show what a way you have with words. It's to convince readers to read the next paragraph, and the next." Once they make it to the end, "it's always good to come back to the hook. If you've used an anecdote, close with an anecdote that tells the reader where your *character* is at the end of your *story*," even for nonfiction, Allen continues. "If you've opened with a promise to answer a question, close with an indicator that the question is now resolved. I see lots of articles that

start with good hooks but have rotten, or nonexistent, endings —the article just stops when the information runs out."

Darby uses a memorable metaphor to reinforce the truth that good hooks are only the beginning of good writing: "Remember that some fish are caught with old hooks already in them; the first person did not reel them in. Hooks can be strong and sharp, but the writing that follows is what keeps readers swimming through your words to the end. When writing hooks, make sure that the rest of the piece is just as strong."

Titles that Sell

By Kelly McClymer

The *7 Habits of Highly Effective People*, Stephen R. Covey. *The Unbearable Lightness of Being*, Milan Kundera. *Kiss of the Spider Woman*, Manuel Puig. *The Time Traveler's Wife*, Audrey Niffenegger.

Don't Judge a Book By Its Cover

Despite the fact that readers care most about what is contained within a book, marketing departments at most publishing companies devote much effort toward designing eye-catching covers that entice readers to pluck a particular book from the shelf. Why so much focus on the packaging? As Sue Grimshaw, Borders Books Head Romance Buyer, says, "A great title, cover, and author quote all can impact the sales of a book, some more than others. I think readers enjoy seeing a catchy title not only because it is fun and clever, but it typically implies something about the story."

The Story Plant Publisher Lou Aronica, former Avon and

Berkley Publisher, agrees. "The best titles convey both how the writer is going to handle the material and whether the material is a particular reader's cup of tea. Looking at the current bestseller list, I think *The Guernsey Literary and Potato Peel Pie Society* is a great title for this reason. So is *Pride and Prejudice and Zombies."*

Since authors rarely control cover art, only two cover items are under their control—their own name and (to some degree) the title. While it is a running joke among writers that Nora Roberts and Stephen King could sell their grocery lists on the star power of their names, most other authors benefit from a great title on the way to building star powered author name recognition.

Sample Titles

➤ *The Lion, the Witch and the Wardrobe,* C. S. Lewis
➤ *All Creatures Great and Small,* James Herriot
➤ *Blink: The Power of Thinking Without Thinking,* Malcolm Gladwell

Finding a Great Title by Hook or by Crook

Like the titles listed in this article, a great title has the potential to help sell a book four times over—to agent, to editor, to bookseller, and to reader. So what makes a title great? Grimshaw, speaking as a reader, says, "One of my all-time favs is *The Secret Diaries of Miss Miranda Cheever.* Personally, I hate secrets and I'm one who has to find out everything about them if there are any." A great title engages the reader's imagination by being unique, evocative, intriguing, unusual, or funny.

Some authors are lucky enough to find a great title idea first. Vicki Lewis Thompson found her bestselling title *Nerd in Shining*

Armor while driving one day. "I passed a billboard that advertised *Geeks in Shining Armor*, and I rewrote it in my head as *Nerd in Shining Armor*. I was on the way to Sedona for a weekend away, and I ended up spending the whole weekend fleshing out the idea for the book. I couldn't help myself because the title told me exactly what the book would be about, and my only job was to write it down."

> A great title has the potential to sell a book four times over—to agent, to editor, to bookseller, to reader.

The same happened to me, when I attended a crowded editor's panel at a conference and misheard *The Salem Witch Trials* as *The Salem Witch Tryouts*. The character, the plot, and the natural humor suggested by the title had me scrambling for a notebook to outline the idea that led to a successful three-book series featuring a cheerleading teen witch.

Not everyone is so lucky as to have a title drop neatly into mind, but author Carrie Ryan did. "When I first started writing [one particular] book it was an experiment—I'd been thinking about the world [of this book] for a while but didn't have any plans to write about it," Ryan says. "On the way home from work one night, the first line popped into my head and when I got home I ended up writing the first chapter (totally out of the blue). When I saved it I had to come up with something to call the file and the only thing I knew about the story at that point was the setting, so I called it *The Forest of Hands and Teeth*." The title, pulled from the apocalyptic world's name for the

zombie-infested forest outside the fenced-in town, stuck.

If a great title hook doesn't suggest itself, there are three good ways to brainstorm one:

> ➤ Find a common phrase and give it a twist: *Dead Witch Walking*, Kim Harrison.
> ➤ Use a quote from the Bible: *On Wings of Eagles*, Ken Follett.
> ➤ Snip an evocative line of a famous poem: *Cover Her Face*, P. D. James.

Famous titles with a twist are proving to be fertile ground, too (*Prada and Prejudice*, Mandy Hubbard). The foundation for all great titles, no matter how they're found, is that the hook fits the audience.

Sample Titles

➤ *Jurassic Park*, Michael Crichton
➤ *The Horse Whisperer*, Nicholas Evans
➤ *A Time to Kill*, John Grisham
➤ *Where the Wild Things Are*, Maurice Sendak

Addressing Genres, Categories, Audiences

Grimshaw offers a reminder that readers' expectations play a part in finding a great title. "Criteria for titles can vary by sub-genre as well. Paranormal titles are typically one word and hero-centric, while historicals are more suggestive of the story line." A familiar phrase with a little attitude can make young adult readers and librarians sit up and take notice, as Teri

Brown found when she wrote *Read My Lips*, a young adult novel with a protagonist who is deaf. "We did market to the deaf community, but the big push was for hearing kids. It's not a deaf issues book." Brown adds, "I think the title does make people wonder about the thrust of the book. There are very few other books for teens out there with a deaf character."

In the quest to be unique and intriguing, avoid becoming outlandish. Nothing can sink a good book faster than a title that promises something other than what the book itself offers. Just imagine a children's book titled *The Killing Fields*. Or an adventure thriller called *Humpty Dumpty Takes a Dive*. Annie Kuhn, of the Briar Patch children's bookstore in Bangor, Maine, has found that some titles can unexpectedly put off a prospective audience. "I recall having a customer turn down my recommendation of Shannon Hale's *Princess Academy* because it sounded too *princessy*—even though I explained that it was really quite full of adventure and had a strong role model as a protagonist."

An uninspired title doesn't always mean uninspired sales, though, Kuhn points out. "In my own case, the title of *Three Cups of Tea* [by Greg Mortenson and David Oliver Relin] was a turnoff. Despite its amazing sales history, it sounded too goody-goody, nicey-nice for me to read what it was about. Only after getting a copy as a gift did I find out that it was this amazing adventure story!"

Unique, Intriguing, Unusual, or Funny

With the audience identified, choosing the right hook is key. Kuhn says that humor sells well at the Briar Patch. "Kevin Hawkes's *The Wicked Big Toddlah* always gets a chuckle from customers who spy it for the first time, and it's always at least picked up and looked over—often then sold, too."

For Ryan, the evocatively titled debut young adult novel *The*

Forest of Hands and Teeth helped her get an agent. "I included the title in the subject line of all my e-queries and I felt like I often got really quick responses (one agent known for a very long response time got back to me in two minutes). I even had a few responses pointing out that the title is what got them interested right away." The title continued to help deliver a good book deal, award nominations, and amazing reviews. In fact, Ryan adds, "I've also noticed that a lot of reviews mention they picked the book up or moved it to the top of the pile because of the title."

Sample Titles

➤ *The Girl with the Dragon Tattoo,* Stieg Larsson
➤ *The Hitchhiker's Guide to the Galaxy,* Douglas Adams
➤ *How to Win Friends and Influence People,* Dale Carnegie
➤ *Love in the Time of Cholera,* Gabriel Garcia Marquez

Series and Subtitles

Nonfiction writers can factor in the impact of a subtitle on their audience. Often this helps clarify an intriguing title (*Who Moved My Cheese? An Amazing Way to Deal with Change in Your Work and in Your Life,* Spencer Johnson and Kenneth Blanchard), or add intrigue to a general title (*Sway: The Irresistible Pull of Irrational Behavior,* Ori and Rom Brafman).

For fiction writers who plan an ongoing series, it is often wise to think about how titles will tie together. Sue Grafton is a famous example of a series author with long-range title planning. She began in April 1982 with *"A" is for Alibi,* and December 2009 saw the release of *"U" is for Undertow.* Other connections authors have used to tie series titles together are hobbies like cooking or knitting, or businesses such as bookshops and catering enterprises.

Sample Titles

- ➤ *Dying for Chocolate* (Goldy Culinary Mysteries), Diane Mott Davidson
- ➤ *He's Just Not That Into You: Your Daily Wake-Up Call*, Greg Behrendt and Liz Tuccillo
- ➤ *One for the Money* (Stephanie Plum Mysteries), Janet Evanovich
- ➤ *Whiskey Sour* (Jack Daniels Mysteries), J. A. Konrath

Take a Title Test Drive

Once the perfect title has been found, it should be taken for a test drive. Thompson was certain her *Nerd* title was an eye catcher, but her agent at the time didn't agree. Thompson's instincts were reaffirmed by her new agent and her enthusiastic publisher. "Irwin Applebaum at Bantam told me how much he loved the title." Thompson adds, "I'm also convinced the title and the cover were part of the reason Kelly Ripa chose the book for her book club—because the book was so easy to identify." After *Nerd in Shining Armor* was chosen for the book club on the morning talk show *Live with Regis and Kelly*, it became a bestseller. Thompson does not credit the TV exposure for all the word of mouth, however. "I got media attention even before Kelly chose it." As Thompson found out, "It turns out we have plenty of nerds in this country and they were thrilled to see themselves mentioned on the front of a book!"

Even a title that works very well can have a drawback or two. Ryan says, "I shouldn't be surprised, but many people have

a hard time remembering the title because it's a little different and long. I get a *lot* of people mistakenly calling it *The Forest of Hands and Feet* (so much so that I have a Google alert set for it, though it never bothers me)." Ryan gets around the minor drawback by handing out a business card with her book information.

Sample Titles

> ➤ *Dust of 100 Dogs*, A. S. King
> ➤ *Gone with the Wind*, Margaret Mitchell
> ➤ *The Prince of Tides*, Pat Conroy
> ➤ *The Sociopath Next Door*, Martha Stout

When Great Titles Go Bland

Sometimes, for marketing reasons, the publisher will choose a less than unique title (there are five novels and a Broadway play titled *Wicked*). Happily, though, as Grimshaw has seen in her tenure at Borders, "As long as it is a good story, readers will buy it, so I wouldn't be too concerned if you ended up with a title you weren't thrilled about."

Kuhn agrees. "Overall, I do not think that a title alone is a make-or-break issue in book sales. That said, I do think a title that is memorable or unique can get people to pick up a book or at least catch their attention enough that they then notice reviews or seek out the book after reading a review."

A Second Wind for Out-of-Print Books

By Kelly McClymer

I f a writer's dream is to see a published book shelved by the bookstores and cradled in a reader's hands, then a writer's nightmare must be when that book is no longer available in bookstores and has been deemed out of print by the publisher. Out of print is a form of limbo. The term indicates to booksellers and distributors that the publisher does not see profit in going back for even a small print run (1,000 copies). While a sudden onslaught of bookstore orders (or a movie deal) can change the publisher's mind, the odds are not in an out-of-print book's favor. Out of print is out of mind.

Alternative Directions

Over the last dozen years, authors have found creative ways around that pesky out-of-print designation. Nancy J. Cohen, the author of *Killer Knots* (Bad Hair Day Mystery), made the decision to use the decade-old Authors Guild Back in Print cooperative deal with iUniverse, whereby Guild members' books are available

213

in print-on-demand trade paperback editions. Cohen published her three out-of-print futuristic novels (written under the name Nancy Cane) and says, "It's nice to know my older out-of-print books are available should someone want to get them in a newer version." Because a trade paperback version can be more costly for readers, Cohen cautions, "The used bookstore route is a cheaper alternative for readers."

Neff Rotter wrote Regency and contemporary romance, and women's fiction under the names Laura Matthews and Elizabeth Neff for more than 20 years. She turned to e-publishing in the mid-1990s. Rotter says, "When I was unable to sell a book 'of the heart' in 1998, I self-published, creating Belgrave House as my publisher and setting up a website for it. In 1999, when two of my books, to which I had the rights, were 15 years old, I offered them as digital files on the website. Then in 2000 I offered an e-book of a book I had written with a doctor, which also didn't sell to [a] New York [publisher]. And that was how it all got started."

Today, Belgrave House acquires previously published—in print—fiction to offer as e-books. It specializes in women's fiction, mysteries, and contemporary and historical romance. Its sister site, Regency Reads, specializes in Regency and Georgian romance. As the website explains, "Our intention is to run a casual publishing partnership with authors (not agents) interested in making their backlists available as e-books. By this, we mean we prefer a 'gentleman's agreement' with our authors . . . ." Authors and Belgrave split revenue 50/50.

Fran Baker of Delphi Books similarly started up a publishing company that does a brisk print business in republishing out-of-print books. Baker read a three-part series in a newsletter put out by Novelists Inc. discussing the Authors Studio, which describes itself as "the first community of small presses owned and operated by multipublished commercial authors." Intrigued by the idea of a group of published novelists who had decided to start up small presses, Baker says, "I'd already had a very successful court reporting business before I began selling books so I wasn't afraid of starting another business. Those articles prompted me to start Delphi Books and publish *Once A Warrior*. The book got good reviews in *Publishers Weekly* and elsewhere, and sold all but a couple of hundred author's copies from its first 5,000-book printing. Now, eleven years later, Delphi Books are available worldwide via Ingram, Baker & Taylor, Brodart, etc." Delphi Books distributes mainly in Canada and Great Britain, but also in the Far and Middle East.

> Options for out-of-print books include print on demand, e-book formats, specialty publishers, and self-publishing.

The Future for Out-of-print Books

Over the last decade, the digital age has been both applauded and decried for its impact on publishing and authors.

Print on demand. On the positive side, print on demand (POD) and e-publishers have helped give new life to out-of-print books. Publishers like iUniverse, Fictionwise, Scribd, and Amazon (through its Kindle device) make it easy for authors to keep a book in print after rights have reverted to them. Deciding on the hows and whys of keeping a book in print through alternative means depends on the book's genre and target audience, as well as how well the book meshes with a publisher's format, distribution, and marketing.

Career 215

Rights Reversion

Saving the most important point for last: To rescue an out-of-print book by requesting a reversion of rights and then remarketing it, an author needs to ensure that the original contract includes a specific definition of when the book becomes out of print and when the rights revert. The Authors Guild website can illuminate with two important contractual clauses that will help a writer regain the rights to an out-of-print book: the *rights granted clause* and the *out-of-print clause.*

The key to if and when an author can claim out-of-print rights is in the original publishing contract. If an author sells *all rights* or the copyright on a book, the publisher then owns the book forever. Most publishers purchase limited rights, however: the right to publish in various countries (U.S. only, English-speaking countries, etc.) or various formats (hardback, trade paperback, mass market paperback, audio book, e-book, etc.). The rights bought (and the percentage of royalties paid to the author) should be explicitly stated in the contract. Writers should negotiate away any broad or vague language ("in any format now known or hereafter developed," for example, which the Authors Guild deems unacceptable contract language).

An author-friendly contract will grant the author control over any rights not specifically spelled out in the contract, and contain a

Almost all out-of-print reissues released through POD technology are hardcover or trade paperback format, which makes the book pricier than a mass-market paperback. Kassia Krozser, one of the founders of the Medialoper website and author of the Booksquare blog, says, "On the print side, unless the reverted title is a blockbuster waiting to happen, chances are the title will go through a print-on-demand, print-to-order, or other short-run printing process. This is more expensive for the

Rights Reversion

clause specifically stating when and how a book will be considered out of print. It used to be accepted that a book needed to be available for sale from the publisher or a retail distributor in order to be in print. Most publishers routinely included a period of time (usually between three and seven years) before reversion of rights could be requested.

The advent of electronic and print-on-demand options has created a gray area. Publishers have argued that a book available in e-format means it is still in print. Authors have argued otherwise, and an uneasy truce means that a good contractual clause on e-rights should set a certain amount of royalty income (or copies) that must be sold during a set time period (usually the six-month royalty reporting period) in order to maintain in-print status.

No matter what the contract stipulates, however, an author should get a letter from the publisher formally specifying that rights on a book have reverted to the author. This letter is not only a safeguard against any potential dispute with the publisher, it is a necessity when approaching new publishers.

Lastly, the newly reverted rights apply only to the manuscript you wrote. The cover art and any cover copy created by your original publisher are not your property.

publisher. The author needs to consider the *initial investment* and recoupment (has the book earned out?), and *subsequent investment* as part of negotiating a fair royalty [with the new publisher]. Will the book be rewritten, re-edited, given a new cover, and an additional marketing push?"

Large-print markets. Consider the specialty large-print market, too. Baker explored this market before she launched Delphi Books' large-print program. "I'm on a couple of librarians' lists and it seems there's less and less money for the more expensive large-print titles. I asked a lot of questions about what librarians would like to see in terms of quality and price." Recognizing that large-print readers include those with visual impairments, she adds, "Then, I contacted the National Association for Visually Handicapped (NAVH) to get their guidelines in hopes of also getting their seal of approval. Once I submitted a sample of Delphi's first large-print title to NAVH and received their seal, it was a go."

E-publishing. As for the e-publishing opportunities for out-of-print books, Krozser notes that e-publishing offers an author a chance at an audience not targeted by the original publisher. "Because the sales in digital publishing are *new* (customers who wouldn't or couldn't purchase the book in physical format, for various reasons); *additive* (customers who already own the book, but want a digital copy as well); and *replacement* (now buying digital instead of print), there are multiple opportunities for authors who hold reverted rights."

Rotter agrees. Her Belgrave House and Regency Reads websites together have more than 400 e-books and offer multi-published authors a publishing partnership where they retain the rights to their work and receive 50 percent of any income. "I think things are reaching critical mass in e-books," she says.

Multiple choice. Kathy Lynn Emerson, a prolific author of historical and cozy mysteries, chose to republish her out-of-print books in multiple formats. "Belgrave House has all my romance and mystery backlist, plus one of my nonfiction books and one YA that was sold but never published." Emerson also works with Delphi Large Print to re-release her Elizabethan Face Down mysteries. She enjoys receiving yet another, though small, advance for the books she has previously sold, but confesses, "The real intent is to keep the books available, and to make them

Websites

> **Authors Guild:** www.authorsguild.org
> **The Authors Studio:** www.theauthorsstudio.org
> **Belgrave House:** www.belgravehouse.com
> **Booksquare:** http://booksquare.com
> **Delphi Books:** www.delphibooks.us
> **Fictionwise:** www.fictionwise.com
> **iUniverse:** www.iuniverse.com
> **Medialoper:** http://medialoper.com
> **Regency Reads:** www.regencyreads.com
> **Scribd:** www.scribd.com

available to the library market in large print for older readers."

Baker is careful about which out-of-print books she accepts for Delphi. She keeps in mind the type of customers who frequent the website, and the library sales of her large-print editions. Baker looks for "books, preferably historicals, with good reviews that we can put on the back covers and in our flyers that we send to libraries. Because of the type size and margins required in large print, we try to limit acquisitions to a 60,000-word count. I'd like to put a good western in large print. Not too sexy a western because that's a little bit of a different audience, but some romance is fine. I wouldn't mind doing another Regency, either. Again, they would have to have good reviews that we can use in marketing."

Marketing, Distribution, and Payment

Out-of-print authors often have built-in readerships. They have published before, and perhaps since, the book in question. They have an audience from previous or current novels. Wherever

possible, they should highlight the republished books on web-sites and link to publisher websites for other books—especially those with author pages and/or newsletters. Baker says, "We ask the author to get the word out to their readers about their large-print title(s) [for us] and encourage those readers to ask for the books at their favorite bookstore or public library."

Before signing a contract with any publisher—whether the book is an original or reprint—an author should know the publisher's distribution methods, marketing outreach, and expectations for author promotion after the book is released.

While print publishers traditionally pay royalties twice a year, many e-publishers pay monthly or quarterly. Krozser cautions writers who are considering selling electronic rights to out-of-print books, "While digital distribution has some aspects in common with traditional distribution, the way the money flows makes paying on *net* practical, and, frankly, smart. Amazon is pushing base e-book prices lower, and setting consumer expectations." Many of its Kindle books sell for $9.99, at a loss to Amazon as it tries to build interest and consumer desire for the e-reader. "That cannot be undone, no matter how much publishers think they can *educate* the consumer to pay higher prices," says Krozser. E-publishing "is a different market, with different rules, and a different format. To make this work and continue to increase sales, a different way of calculating royalties is required."

Distribution is an issue for small publishers, for both print and e-books. Publishers that rely on POD should have books listed in the catalogues of the major book distributors, as well as on the major bookseller websites. While a publisher may help make sales to libraries, bookstores still hesitate to stock POD books; author marketing will be required. As for e-books, no format is favored by the consumer yet, although Amazon's

Kindle and the Sony E-Reader are emerging as front-runners in the e-book device marketplace.

The options for breathing life back into an out-of-print title continue to expand, but with complications that authors must inform themselves about. However you decide to give your book a second wind, Krozser offers advice on how you treat your intellectual property: "Remember, these rights are valuable. Don't sell too cheap!"

Agents Who Critique
Love Them or Leave Them

By Jacqueline Diamond

A highly recommended agent agreed to read my latest manuscript. Afterward, she telephoned with a list of what she believed needed fixing. Then she asked the key question: "Are you willing to revise?"

I had searched for months to find the right agent, and this one met my qualifications. Now I felt as if our future together hung on my reply. To some aspiring authors, the response might seem a no-brainer: Yes, yes, yes!

Not so fast.

For twenty years, I had been represented by a crusty older agent who believed in me and worked hard for sales. Critiquing, however, was not her strength. At least one manuscript that might have sailed to success given the right feedback had instead foundered on the rocks of her personal taste.

Hollow Voices, Real Voices

While theoretically a writer might return to the original vision

223

after a failed revision done at an agent's request, often the changes have been so profound and so draining that inspiration vanishes, and the book dies. After my agent's death, while I was on the hunt for a new one, friends told horror stories of their own.

"I had a negative experience with an agent who, along with her newly fledged assistants just out of college, kept asking for changes," says Kaye Wilson Klem, author of *East of Jamaica* (Coronet Books). "The upshot was a book that could not be sold, and one I abandoned after foolishly trying to implement what they wanted." She soon left that agency.

Rebecca Forster, author of the Witness series (Signet), has had a range of experiences, including one agent she credits with helping her revise and sell a series. "However, after the initial effort, she figured her job was done and never looked at another piece of work again," says Forster. At another time, she "had an agent who did read what I sent and directed me to cut out huge portions of the novel. I felt she had insight that I didn't and followed her advice. The book never sold. In this instance, I should have listened to my gut."

Although she still likes and respects her first agent, romance writer Kitty Bucholtz, who has sold short fiction, says disagreements over critiquing led to a breakup. "We came so close once —two publishers said they almost bought my first book," she says. Then she submitted another book she truly loved. "The agent didn't like it, made suggestions that required a page-one [complete] rewrite, and then didn't like the new novel either." It was never sent to publishers.

Initially, Bucholtz says, the agent liked her work, but over the course of several years, their tastes diverged. "The ideas she suggested were so different from where my energy and enthusiasm were that I ended up writing a hollow version of my real voice," she explains. "It's taken months to get her voice out of my head.

"My business school training to make a widget that people want to buy failed me here. I tried to write the books my agent wanted and I couldn't."

No Pushing

New York Times best-selling novelist Debbie Macomber, author of *Summer on Blossom Street* (Mira), cautions against allowing an agent to push you into writing to the latest trend.

"Yes, we need to think what's commercial, but far more important is we have to write from the heart and not what's on the best-seller list," Macomber says. "Almost always trends come and go, and by the time the book [is ready], the author has missed the peak. In addition, her heart won't be in the project and it tells in the writing and eventually in the sales. Following that kind of advice can hurt us more than help in the long run, and a good agent knows that."

Authors need to listen to their inner voices, not only about specific revisions but also about an agent's overall approach, says Karen Sandler, author of *The Family He Wanted* (Silhouette). After the retirement of her first agent, who critiqued lightly, she met an agent interested in representing her. "She took what I'd submitted to her and seemed to want to make it her own. She told me, 'You really ought to do this, this, and this,'" Sandler recalls. "Although my gut was screaming, I was on the brink of signing with her. One night I had a nightmare— I'd lost my home and I was grief-stricken. Talk about a metaphor smacking you in the face! I called her the next day to decline her representation."

Unpublished novelists may be particularly vulnerable because they doubt themselves. "I believe inexperienced-in-the-writing-business writers are more likely to be led astray," notes Bucholtz.

"They don't know what questions to ask or when to push back. If you and your agent don't both understand your vision, even the best agent can give you the kind of feedback that leads you astray. I believe that's what happened to me," she says. "Being new to representation, I wasn't sure how the agent-client relationship worked, and I labored under the misapprehension that I had to follow through on my agent's suggestions."

Sandler's story had a happy ending. "Sometime later, I sent a different book to Kim Lionetti at BookEnds. Her feedback was fantastic. She pointed out the problems, but let me solve them. I signed with her and after several weeks of work, we got the book ready to market. We're still waiting for a sale, but Kim's input made the book 200 percent better."

Lionetti says, "Most of the [first-time] projects I offer representation on are already publication-worthy, in my opinion. On subsequent projects, my clients' first drafts are often not publishable [because] they don't usually have the time to workshop and perfect like they did with that first book. I become their critique partner. So, I think my feedback has resulted in quite a few sales, but mostly just by speeding up the revision process."

Teamwork

Other agents also cite the need for teamwork.

"Every author has strengths and weaknesses, and I think that is to be expected. As a team we can minimize the weaknesses and show off the strengths," says Laura Bradford of the Bradford Literary Agency. "Maybe my author is a fabulous storyteller who writes lush, descriptive narrative with unique, relatable characters, but she writes a little more gritty than what the market will bear. Or that one section with the heroine and the accidental cat burglar that was supposed to be funny wasn't so much."

RITA winner Helen Brenna, author of *Treasure* and *First Come*

Agent Information

➤ **Laura Bradford, Bradford Literary Agency:** www.bradfordlit.com. Wants romance (historical, romantic suspense, paranormal, category, contemporary, erotic), urban fantasy, women's fiction, mystery, thrillers, and young adult. Nonfiction: Business, relationships, self-help, biography/memoir, parenting, narrative humor. Does not currently want poetry, screenplays, short stories, children's books, westerns, horror, new age, religion, crafts, cookbooks, gift books.
➤ **Kim Lionetti, BookEnds:** http://bookends-inc.com. Lionetti is particularly interested in women's fiction, mystery, true crime, pop science, pop culture, and all areas of romance.
➤ **Tina Wexler, International Creative Management:** www.icmtalent.com. Query by mail only. Looks at fiction, nonfiction, children's, adult.

Twins (Harlequin Superromance), says her agent, Tina Wexler at International Creative Management (ICM), has provided major help with revisions. The RITA is awarded by the Romance Writers of America (RWA) for excellence in romantic fiction.

"We don't always agree, but I believe her input has made every single one of my books better. I'm not sure my first Superromance, *Treasure*, would have won the 2008 RITA without her input," Brenna says. "The story involves a 400-year-old cursed cross, and she simply suggested that someone had to die in order for the curse to feel real. That led me to writing a prologue that really grabs the reader and propels her into the story in a way the first chapter never could."

Even an author at the top of the charts can benefit from input. While Macomber primarily relies on her editor of 24 years for advice, "My new agent did offer me feedback on *Twenty*

Wishes (Mira) that I found helpful. She wanted my heroine to be in her thirties because that made the story more attractive to Hollywood. I made the other heroine in her early forties, and another sixty."

For those of us lower on the food chain, market-savvy advice can be critical. "It's a crowded market, and neither authors nor agents should assume that an editor will overlook certain flaws in a manuscript just because the manuscript has a strong voice

> "Agents read constantly; we evaluate manuscripts constantly. Most agents are in the business because we love books, we love stories, we love language."

or a compelling plot line or engaging characters," said ICM's Wexler. "Editors are looking for the complete package: a strong voice, a compelling plotline, and engaging characters. Why give editors a reason to say no?"

Bradford concurs. "I think that sending out the best work possible is crucial. Publishing is so competitive that an author needs every advantage she can get. Her work needs to be pretty close to perfect and polished within an inch of its life to have a chance to compete. Two sets of eyes are simply better than one, and I would not want to risk my author missing out on an opportunity because of something silly that could easily have been fixed."

Experience gives agents a valuable perspective on a client's work. "Authors should keep in mind that agents read constantly; we evaluate manuscripts constantly," Wexler says. "We track what's selling and selling well and what isn't selling. In addition, most agents are in the business because we love books, we love stories, we love language. We may not be novelists (though some of us are), but we can tell when a character's behavior is inconsistent, when an ending doesn't work, when dialogue feels unnatural, when a scene needs to be added or cut. So, while I certainly believe that authors should beware of making changes that don't feel right, they should also refrain from ignoring feedback that doesn't instantly jibe with their way of thinking. Authors should let the critique sit for a while."

Bradford, too, says her insights are honed by familiarity with the publishing industry. "My opinion is often based on my experience, what I know about the success or failure of similar work, what I know about what houses want or what particular editors like or dislike," she says. "If an agent suggests a revision that is contrary to your vision of the work, or doesn't seem to be your style, or betrays your characters in some way, then you should discuss it. Don't ever be afraid to push back and champion your own work. But don't be a bonehead about it, either. Ask why a change is being suggested. If the reasoning is solid, consider making the change."

The Search for a Partner

The prospect of a sympathetic, market-wise partner sounds ideal, but as I discovered in my own search, such agents are hard to find. Despite my lengthy track record, several agents turned down my manuscript with only cryptic comments or none at all.

One disliked my heroine, a comment that sparked some revisions but didn't result in representation. Another said she preferred a more leisurely writing style, which was only helpful in the sense that it told me that agent wasn't right for my fast-paced approach.

During her agent search, Bucholtz also found some of the feedback helpful, at least in terms of shaping her pitch. "One agent sent me a wonderful personal reply thanking me for my 'lovely and intelligent' query, and telling me that she prefers more romance than what my query suggested. That was great because it made me take another look at my query and ask myself if I had represented my book properly."

Overall, however, her experiences have made Bucholtz wary of agent input. "I am not looking for an agent who critiques. I tried that the first time, and it didn't work out well for me. Having a successful agent wasn't enough; I need an agent who *gets* where I'm trying to go and will encourage me to take my own path," she says. "If I find the otherwise perfect agent for me, but they are big on critiquing, I will think hard about whether I want to go that route again. Still, I would not want an agent who wouldn't tell me that this kind of story is a hard sell, or that this new novel isn't as good as it needs to be yet. Without that, you're running a business blind."

For now, Bucholtz relies on input from a trusted friend. "One of my critique partners has known me for ten years, and she's brilliant. Our relationship has evolved into her knowing to be careful what she suggests because I trust that she knows where I'm trying to go and I'll likely take her advice. I hope to find an agent that I grow into that kind of trusting relationship with."

The multi-published Forster shares the same hope. "I am still searching for the perfect give and take," she says. "It may not exist, but I dream of the agent with whom I can have a dialogue about my work, who is encouraging and offers suggestions about the book I wrote, not the book she would like me to have written."

When there is a disagreement, is even the best agent necessarily more on target than the author? Agents note that they have had mixed responses from editors, who may share their view of a client's work—or may not.

"There have been times when I have given advice, the author declined to make certain changes, and then the project was rejected with the editor citing the same elements I wanted to change," says Bradford. "And there have been times when I have suggested a change and the author really wanted to stick

> "No writer should revise according to someone else's taste; authors should revise according to what the manuscript needs."

to her guns and it ended up working out beautifully. When it comes to critique and revision, there isn't so much right and wrong as there is opinion. I have an opinion, the author has one, and any number of editors do."

"Sometimes editors see the same problems, but other editors don't and then make an offer. This business is so subjective," comments Lionetti. "I think it's essential that both the agent and author are willing to work to bring the manuscript to its fullest potential. In order to do that, they need to bounce ideas off of one another. Authors need to be open to change and agents need to accept that they don't have the last say. The end product needs to be unquestionably the author's."

The process of reaching that potential can be a delicate one. ICM's Wexler cites a process that can work for both agent and author. "No writer should revise according to someone else's tastes; authors should revise according to what the manuscript needs," she says. "When I'm reading a manuscript with an eye

toward revisions, my first objective is to point out those areas where I'm tripped up by the story, the phrasing, the character's behavior. I may then offer a solution to the problem, but the goal isn't to get the author to revise the manuscript in the way I would; the goal is for the author to find a solution—be it the one I've suggested or not—that addresses the problem in a way that makes sense to the author and improves the manuscript."

"At the end of the day, it is the author's work, not the agent's version of the author's work," Bradford says. "The author should have the final say in the end-resulting manuscript. In fact, when I offer representation to an author for the first time, I make it a point to say that I do not expect that author to make any change I suggest just because I suggest it."

I can vouch for that, because it was Bradford with whom I was talking on the phone that day. I took careful notes of her comments about my manuscript, and every one felt on target. She obviously saw the book the same way I did.

"I'd be happy to revise," I told her, and was thrilled when she offered representation. Even though I belong to a critique group and keep up with the romance field through RWA chapter meetings and the national conference, I knew I needed expert feedback. I'd finally found the kind of agent I sought: collaborative and knowledgeable about the market.

Since signing with Laura, I've revised a number of manuscripts based on her well-chosen suggestions. Along the way, we have made several sales and hope to make more. She puts it this way. "There really isn't any room for ego in this. Sometimes I will be right, sometimes the author will be right. Hopefully, we will agree but sometimes we won't.

"It is about teamwork and partnership, and critiquing my author's work keeps me an active participant in her prospects for success."

The Case of the Paddlefish

Writers on Their Idea Files

By Veda Boyd Jones

I t has been fifteen years since my friend Joan Banks gave
me her paddlefish file. In it, she had stuck newspaper clippings about the fish in Oklahoma's Grand Lake that are
being illegally harvested for caviar. I had thought about writing
a novel set at the lake, and she mentioned the file. It was just
an idea file, really, and it is still just an idea file. Neither of us
have used it, but it's still in my bottom file drawer. That is
where I keep ideas. In individual files. There, and on odd slips
of paper stuck on my bulletin board. There, and in the cubby
hole shelves beside my computer. There, and in a slim notebook in my purse. There, and in my head.

Surely there are better systems.

Turns out, there are, and Joan even uses one. "Although I still
use napkins and odd bits of paper when an idea strikes me
away from home, once in my office, I transfer my ideas to a
computer program called Evernote." It lets her categorize ideas

by subject matter, which is useful to Joan, a freelancer who writes for both adult and children's markets. There are other note-saving programs available, free or for a small fee, which help pros aiming for a paperless office.

But most of the writers I surveyed have as haphazard a system as I do. All agree that ideas are everywhere and that ideas and research commingle. Here is an unscientific sampling of seasoned pros and their methods.

Lifecatchers, Etc.

➤ *Archaeological layers:* Brenda Seabrooke, author of 20 books for young readers, including *Cemetery Street* (Holiday House), is a lateral filer. "The creative process is a mystery to me, with the strangest things triggering forgotten people and events. I have archaeological layers of papers, books, notes on tiny scraps, tons of untidy notebooks, stacks of files around my desk." Once she grasps an idea, she keeps research in files, and adds to files when she stumbles over something she can use. "Usually the research hangs around in my head. I may need to refresh my memory by referring to the file, but usually it's still in my brain waiting to be used."

➤ *Divided notebooks:* Susan Martins Miller, author of 50 books (some for children, some for adults), doesn't "keep a huge idea file apart from concrete projects I'm working on." Once she signs up for a project, ideas pertaining to it are everywhere. "I'll make photocopies or jot notes, perhaps even sketches, and everything goes into a notebook behind labeled dividers that keep the project organized. Then wherever I am, if I have the notebook and my computer, I'm good to go."

➤ *Lifecatcher:* Vicki Grove, who has written ten middle-grade and YA novels for Putnam and hundreds of articles for adult and children's magazines, stores ideas in her *lifecatcher*, a four- by six-inch leather journal that holds yellow legal pads. She files hundreds of yellow pages in hanging files with headings such as *dialogue snatches, times when my feelings were hurt for no good reason, oddly shaped trees,* etc. "Every so often I thumb through those files, but as other writers have observed, by some strange process of word osmosis, simply writing down an idea and filing it in most cases seems to cement it into memory."

> "By some strange process of word osmosis, simply writing down an idea and filing it in most cases seems to cement it into memory."

➤ *Chevy-sized file cabinets:* Suzann Ledbetter Ellingsworth, who writes novels and nonfiction for adults, says her ideas spring "96.7 percent from reading—newspapers, newsmagazines, research books. Two monster four-drawer file cabinets take up as much floor space in my office as a mid-sized Chevy." She files under main headings: people, places, things. *People* is sub-divided into men, women, historic, and contemporary. *Things* includes turning points, trivia, inventions, and events. If an idea fits more than one category, Ellingsworth copies and files accordingly. "I have planted six trees in the yard (so far) as penance for all my tree slaying and paper filing."

➤ *Living document:* Michael Spradlin, author of *The Youngest Templar* (Putnam) and many other children's books, keeps a writer's notebook, a three-inch three-ring binder, for ideas that are "like air and water. They're around us all the time. My writer's notebook is a *living document,* so I'm always adding

ideas or additional sources to it, particularly as I'm working on something—articles from magazines, little Post-It notes with ideas scribbled on them, etc."

➤ *Multiple journals:* Mary Casanova, author of novels, series, and picture books for children, says, "I write about what intrigues me, haunts me, troubles me, and delights me. But the idea prompts often come from something I've read or something that I've experienced. My filing system for ideas is very loose. I jump around from journal to journal, with no particular order to my process. And occasionally, I file a journal entry or scrap of paper that holds possibilities for a good story into a file called Story Ideas. Every year or so, usually when I'm between projects, I peruse the file. When an idea still calls to me, then I know it's worth considering further. If I start to accumulate lots of information on one topic, then I have already started a new file for a story, given it a working title, and started gathering research more intentionally."

Good News

➤ *Story idea box:* Marti Attoun, a Contributing Editor for *American Profile*, has also written for dozens of national magazines, including *Ladies' Home Journal, Family Circle, Good Housekeeping,* and *Reader's Digest.* She claims her "niche is *good news,* and I find nearly all of my people to profile in newspapers, small and large. I buy newspapers, read them online, and sometimes while away an afternoon at the library reading newspapers. I also collect freebie newspapers and regional magazines found in convenience stores, truck stops, and flea markets. I subscribe to or buy magazines, collect them from friends and family, and haul them off by the musty boxful from garage sales."

Attoun continues, "My arsenal of low-tech tools includes index cards, cardboard boxes, and file cabinets. While reading, if I come across a possible idea, I jot it on a card. I tear out articles and throw them in a *story idea box*. When I begin researching and querying, I file each idea in a folder and move it to a file cabinet. On the outside of the folder, I write pertinent information: the interviewee's contact info, word length, magazine queried. Once I get an assignment, everything related to it, including the contract, research items, notes from interviews, goes into the folder." Attoun also incorporates higher tech. "On my computer, I keep a document labeled *story ideas* on the desktop so I can quickly add websites and articles that look promising."

➤ *Notebook of idea lists:* Cheryl Harness, who has written and/or illustrated over 40 books, mostly biographies for children, keeps a notebook full of idea lists. As an idea develops, she starts a file, "a plastic folder full of scraps, clippings, etc. The shelves of my library tables in my studio are piled with files and notebooks." In the file, she sticks information such as maps, costumes, any reference to the idea. Her flat surfaces may be cluttered, but her bookshelves, which line her studio, are organized by time period, i.e., *eighteenth century.* "As my interest is history, I'm ever on the lookout—on remainder tables, at used bookstores, in newspapers and magazines, and documentaries in the TV listings—for possible subjects and useful reference images that I'll be needing when the time comes to illustrate a book. Even if you're not illustrating yourself, the person who does will welcome this material. For instance, when I was doing the drawings for Julie Cummins's *Women Daredevils* (Dutton), Julie supplied me with a sheaf of photocopied images—most appreciated."

➤ *E-mail files:* Fern Reiss, Director of the International Association of Writers and author of the Publishing Game book series (Peanut Butter and Jelly Press), says her method is simple. "I put

each idea into a separate e-mail, referencing where the idea came from (another article I read, an online link, a conversation with a friend or colleague) and any ideas I have for follow-up resources. The e-mail automatically tracks the dates of the ideas. I name the subject line *Idea*, followed by a nutshell of the thought. Then I store it in an e-mail folder labeled *Ideas*. That way I can easily find it again when I need it, and sometimes I can cure writer's block just by scrolling through my e-mail idea

> "Sometimes I can cure writer's block just by scrolling through my e-mail idea folder to see the variety of things I've been thinking about over the year."

folder to see the variety of things I've been thinking about over the year. Periodically, if I notice that there are 27 different idea e-mails all related to the same topic, I realize that there might be an entire book rather than just an article there, and that gives me a basis for a new project."

➤ *Jottings to pages:* Gary Blackwood, author of more than 30 nonfiction books and novels for young readers, including the Shakespeare Stealer series (Dutton), says most of his ideas "originate with something I've read. I often stumble upon an idea for a novel or a picture book while I'm doing research for a nonfiction book. Mostly I manage to jot ideas down in a note-book dedicated to that purpose, but I also have a fat file folder crammed with sheets and scraps of paper containing scrawls that sometimes make sense and sometimes not so much. Some-times I make a note of where the idea came from, but usually I don't much worry about research sources unless I'm actively developing an idea, then I fill page after page with possible leads."

➤ *Color-coded pockets:* Ann Leach, freelancer, co-author with Michelle Beaulieu Pillen of *Goal Sisters: Live the Life You Want with a Little Help from Your Friends* (New World Library), and President of Life Preservers, a Grief Support Community (www.life-preservers.org), says, "I may see a news clip on TV or hear a friend's conversation and think, 'That would make a good article.' I have those expanding file pockets in a file drawer, and I label each with one subject. So I have one for *children and grief, businesses to profile, travel spots*, etc. Then as I see research or read something about any of these topics, I clip it or copy it, indicate the source, and put it in the appropriate folder. I color-code my subject files. Each topic has its own color, and I tag sources and news clips with Post-It notes of the same assigned color. I also use color on my Outlook folders of Internet research. I go through each file pocket once a year and weed out old research and outdated info."

➤ *External and internal:* Sneed B. Collard III, author of novels and nonfiction for children, gets plot ideas from day-to-day life. Collecting state quarters gave him an idea for his middle-grade thriller *Double Eagle* (Peachtree Publishers). But for character traits, he relies on ideas that come from his internal life, such as big disappointments or big successes. "Once I've written down an idea or put an article somewhere, I rarely go back to look at it. I find that if the idea is really compelling, it stays in my head." Once an idea becomes a project, he puts research in a hanging file for fiction. "For nonfiction projects, research files are too extensive for a hanging file, so I clear off a table and just spread things out until the project is finished. Then I pack the whole project in a box."

➤ *Bookmarks and notes:* Steve Reginald, freelancer in writing, editing, and consulting (and one of the best editors I have ever had), gets ideas from a variety of sources: "books, newspapers, websites, museums, just about anything can trigger an idea." He writes ideas on any piece of paper available. "I bookmark a lot of online resources while I'm researching. This way, I have easy access to information if I decide to pursue an idea."

At the company where Reginald worked in-house, brain-storming was common. "Generally, the editors would come up with ideas and present them to Sales and Marketing, who usually made or broke an idea. Sometimes Sales and Marketing would come up with ideas based on what they were seeing in the marketplace or what customers expressed a need for—a gap somewhere in the market." Once an idea comes out of the idea file, further research should involve market study.

My survey of writers reveals there really isn't just one system better than mine for organizing and maintaining idea files. The systems are as individual as the slant 14 writers would take on the same idea. And now that I have the file out, I wonder if the paddlefish idea still has possibilities.

Through a Child's Eyes

Childhood's Vivid Inspiration

By Leslie J. Wyatt

C hildhood—that fleeting, incredibly real time of our
lives—is beyond totally escaping, whether we enjoyed
it or just survived it. For writers, this is a good thing.
Childhood is a wellspring from which to draw inspiration.
Sights, smells, and sounds surface as fresh and new as the
moment we first experienced them. Happenings? Characters?
Settings? They are all stored away within us, and the variety is
as infinite and unique as humanity itself. Our early years inspire
not only by giving us specific locations, experiences, and people to describe and embellish, but also by influencing who we
are, how we approach the world, and the purposes and passions that drive us.

Profound Plots

Roland Smith, the author of more than 20 books including
the award-winning *Peak* (Harcourt), says, "Your entire life, including your childhood, influences your writing. How can it

not? You are writing from your own voice, experience, and imagination." He adds, "I remember my childhood well, and it has a profound bearing on my writing, and on my adult life, as is the case with most people. Our adult lives are partly formed by our childhoods."

Helen Kay Polaski agrees. She is the author of thousands of articles and editor of numerous books for adults, including *Christmas Through a Child's Eyes* (Adams Media). "My childhood is what formed me into the person I am today, and it is what forms my work," she says. "Because all feelings and all thoughts originated when we were children, something about my childhood always influences my writing in some manner."

For many writers, plot elements often spring from the wealth of material accumulated during childhood. Not that plots can usually be lifted intact from most of our real stories; day-to-day life contains mostly the mundane, no matter how intense it was for us growing up. But who said we had to use the bits and pieces verbatim? Mix, match, enhance, or borrow. There are no rules to break here.

Smith remarks, "I've used some actual events from my child-hood in a few of my novels, but they are greatly exaggerated to make them a lot more interesting than they actually were." He says that in the dozen or so novels he has written, the real events are just tiny seeds that grow into what may have seemed impossible things. "Think 'Jack and The Beanstalk,'" he says, where a small seed led to enormous adventure.

Kirby Larson, author of *Hattie Big Sky* (Delacorte), twists and turns genuine happenings "like warm taffy to shape them to fit my character's story."

Polaski finds that even when she dabbles in screenplay writing, she includes some aspect from childhood. "While I might come up with a story line or plot for a book or screenplay or short story that doesn't necessarily follow the same lines as a similar plot from my childhood, the beauty of it is that it can still skim the edges of my childhood, weave in and out of the story in much the same way as an adventure from my childhood."

One writer twists and turns real life incidents "like warm taffy to fit my character's story."

Beware, though. Sometimes using early experiences as a reference point can backfire. As historical fiction writer Lea Wait puts it, "Fiction is not real life; it is real life framed and tempered and distilled. I am wary of writing about incidents I experienced during my own childhood. I am afraid not enough time has gone by to have allowed perspective on the time or place." Some aspects of society have changed so much in the past twenty years that those incidents cannot realistically be placed in a contemporary setting.

Picture book and adult author Phyllis Walker agrees. "The hardest adjustment for me is to realize how much children have changed since I was a child. The exposure to words, ideas, lifestyles, travels, entertainment: It is quite a different world than I grew up in."

Characters, Settings, and Senses, Oh My!

Childhood also inspires our writing by providing a plethora of acquaintances from which to draw as we create believable characters. People we came to know in formative years often appear in our writing in one shape or another. Polaski says, "Even when I don't set out to do so, my characters tend to take

Ideas 243

on the inner workings of the minds of people I grew up with."
Wait mentions a similar phenomenon—characters and childhood memories form the beginning of incidents and characters,
"but they then morph into their own selves."

Here again, writers are an amazingly fluid bunch—though
they may draw from people they know, the characters seldom
mirror the original. A female character may inherit the charac-
teristics of a man you once knew. An animal may have the
same terrifying eyes as your kindergarten teacher, or the warm
personality of your beloved collie companion.

Of course, characters will not always spring exclusively from
childhood. Just as we ourselves are a blending of then and now,
our characters are a mix of old and new, composites of reality
and fiction melded into believability. Smith describes it in this
way: "As an adult, perhaps I see the characters both ways, as if
I'm peering through adult/child bifocals."

Writers often use elements from early days as settings. In
many ways, Wait says, she had a nineteenth-century childhood,
and finds that her love of history, and her familiarity with
eighteenth- and nineteenth-century New England is a part of all
of her writing, whether for children or adults. "I grew up with
both my parents and grandparents in a home built in 1774. I
was especially close to my grandmother, an antique doll and
toy dealer who introduced me to auctions, antique shows,
libraries, and nineteenth-century books for children. That time
and place are a deep part of me, and that makes choosing topics related to them natural." As a result, Wait has written four
stand-alone books for children set in Wiscasset, a small town
in Maine, as well as the Antique Print Mystery series (Scribner)
for adults, set in New England with the main character being—
what else?—an antique dealer.

In the words of John Betjeman, "Childhood is measured out

by sounds and smells and sights, before the dark hour of reason grows." Remember the first time you tasted cotton candy—how it smelled like toasted vanilla, how it melted on your tongue? How sticky your face and fingers soon became? When it comes to childhood memories, it only takes a moment to tap into a sensory extravaganza. Polaski gives an example. "When the sun

> "We can relive the exact feel of snow on our bare hands, the way an icicle felt in our mouth. I return to childhood for reassurance that what I'm writing is as vivid as life itself."

warms the top of my head, my mind whirls in a dozen different directions. All at the same time, I am reminded of eating pancakes on the front porch as the sun peeked over the horizon, picking flowers in the meadow at midday, catching tadpoles in the early afternoon, and walking along the shiny waters of the lake as the sun set again."

Polaski offers this tip for adding realism to writing: "As children, our memories were so vivid that when we step back into that role it helps us relive the exact feel of the snow on our bare hands, the way an icicle felt when we placed it into our mouth, the way the wind snatched our breath away. If and when I can, I return to my childhood for reassurance that what I'm writing is as vivid as life itself."

Larson says, "Do whatever you can to tamp down the adult perspective/viewpoint/understanding. Put on those kids' shoes and keep them on throughout the writing of your story."

 Ideas 245

Passion and Purpose

While we are not exclusively who we were as children, it is not hard to understand the multiple ways our growing-up years can inspire our writing. We may not be conscious of these influences as we write, but they are like a prevailing wind that causes all the trees to lean in one direction. Larson says, "When I write, I'm just trying to tell my character's story as honestly as possible. The other stuff—childhood perspectives and memories—is flitting around the edges, moth-like, but I'm not aware of it when I write."

The things we care deeply enough to write about are often built on youthful experiences. One might go so far as to say that in the struggles and joys of childhood are the seeds of thematic passions, because we once lived the experiences so intensely. Have you found certain subjects recurring in your writing? These may have their roots in the days when you were experiencing the mountains and valleys of life for the first time and trying to figure out what it was all about. Many of the convictions, priorities, and passions that we possess as adults begin in those early and intense times. This is one of the great gifts of childhood. As we tap into that resource—writing out of who we are and what is important to us—our writing takes on deeper intensity and realism.

What we did not have, as well as what we did, contributes to our take on life. "I think having moved around a lot predisposes me to empathize with the outsider," says Larson. "Also, I spent a lot of time figuring out how one makes friends and how one becomes a decent human being, both important themes in my writing."

Children's author June Rae Wood wrote *The Man Who Loved Clowns* (Perfection Learning) out of her experiences with a brother who has Down syndrome. If there was anger, neglect, or abandonment in your background, you are not alone. Bullying? Poverty? Prejudice? Sadly, many children are living through these very situations right now. For that matter, many adults are still processing the not-so-wonderful aspects of their own childhood. Here is an opportunity to right wrongs and to take those things that should never have happened to any child and make someone else's world better and brighter.

Walker finds that one way painful memories can be redeemed is by rewriting them—making the story turn out the way she wishes it had, rather than how it turned out in reality. By reworking those painful experiences, those awful surroundings, those mean real-life characters, or even the mean things we ourselves did, we find ways to rectify wrongs and give hope. Vicki Grove illustrates this in her book *Reaching Dustin* (Putnam), which includes a plot element based on something she had done to someone in fourth grade and wished she had not.

What a great privilege to be able to take what we have endured and redeem it, offering comfort and encouragement instead of pain, and furnishing tools with which our readers may transform their own lives for the better.

Benjamin Franklin once said, "Our whole life is but a greater and longer childhood." This is especially valid for writers as we visit and revisit those left-behind-yet-still-with-us years, recreating in infinite variations that which we have lived. What we care passionately about, along with plots, characters, events, settings, sensory details—these all intermingle, shimmering with richness, and whether we focus on them specifically or let them flow as an undercurrent, they lend realism and depth to our writings. Childhood as inspiration in writing? Definitively.

(To use some of your own childhood and family life as inspiration, try the writing prompts in "All in the Family," page 249.)

All in the Family

Writing Exercises & Prompts

By Christina Hamlett

Exotic locales and celebrity characters may be the dream subjects of swooning adolescents, and some would-be writers. But for writers of any age, the best ideas spring from something literally familiar and fertile: their very own families.

Whether you are writing fiction for young readers or adults, the influences of kith and kin tend to filter into plots and imbue characters with quirky, endearing, or downright scary personalities. The actions and reactions of writers' fictional alter egos similarly reflect life's conditioning: fright, fight, or flight instilled over the years by siblings, parents, mentors, instructors, and bosses.

The following exercises and prompts can be used to spin original plots and essays for use in stage, page, or cinema projects. They are also tools to help retrieve forgotten family memories, a critical component of autobiographical works.

Family Matters

➢ What is your personal definition of *family*?

➢ What are your family's three best qualities?

➢ What are their three worst traits?

➢ If a film were made about your family, who would you cast in all the roles (including yourself)?

➢ If you have siblings, did you ever wish you were an only child? If you are an only child, did you ever wish for siblings? If so, would you want them to be younger or older?

➢ What is your favorite family tradition? What is the weirdest?

➢ What is the best/worst place your family ever lived?

➢ What is your fondest vacation memory?

➢ What do you now know about your family that you wish you had known when you were younger?

➢ Which family ancestor would you most want to meet?

➢ In your family, who are the *talkers*? The *listeners*? The *doers*? The *waited upon*?

➢ Where was your favorite place to get away from family?

➢ What is the worst trouble you ever got into with your parents?

➢ Would you invite your parents to live with you in their old age? Would you want to move in with your own children?

Mum Knows Best

What would we do without mothers to feed us, clothe us, read stories, bandage *owies*, sew last-minute Halloween costumes, and let us lick the frosting bowl? On the flip side, mothers can be critical, snoopy, embarrassing, irrational, and totally out of touch (or so we think). Choose any historic figure from this list and compose a short story in which his or her mother offers unsolicited advice:

- Marc Antony
- Confucius
- Attila the Hun
- Marco Polo
- Eleanor of Aquitaine
- Joan of Arc
- Montezuma
- Christopher Columbus
- Copernicus
- William Shakespeare
- George Washington
- Ludwig van Beethoven
- Napoleon
- Elizabeth Barrett Browning
- Wyatt Earp
- Meriwether Lewis
- Florence Nightingale
- Calamity Jane
- Vincent van Gogh
- Theodore Roosevelt
- Mahatma Gandhi
- Agatha Christie
- Frida Kahlo

Medieval Mimes

Families engage often in unspoken dialogue that expresses their moods. The family in this exercise consists of a mom, a dad, a teenager, and a child. They are all mimes. Write a narrative or staged scene that uses no dialogue and revolves around the teenager coming home after curfew. Set the scene in:
- a medieval castle
- a log cabin

> a high-rise apartment in New York
> a space station

Real Life Meets Reel Life

If you could join any television sitcom household for a week, who would you choose and why? Here is a short list of possibilities to get started:

> *The Cosby Show*
> *Family Ties*
> *The Flintstones*
> *Fresh Prince of Bel-Air*
> *Gilmore Girls*
> *Hannah Montana*
> *Happy Days*
> *The Munsters*
> *The Nanny*
> *The Wonder Years*

For more ideas, visit www.sitcomsonline.com. Drama lovers? Construct a scenario wherein you go to one of your TV housemates for help solving a problem you are having at school or work. What ideas are sparked by the following television dramas?

> *Bonanza*
> *Dallas*
> *Little House on the Prairie*
> *My So-Called Life*
> *Smallville*
> *The Sopranos*
> *True Blood*
> *The Waltons*

Letters from Camp

Imagine you are ten and you have been sent off to summer camp. It is your first time away from home and you are not keen on the idea. Write a highly exaggerated letter to your parents to convince them to come rescue you at once. Write a second letter in the voice of the parent that addresses the camper's angst.

A Picture Worth a Thousand Families

Writers often draw inspiration for stories from works of art. Using the following examples, ascribe names and relationships to the individuals depicted and develop a family-oriented short story for each one.

> ➤ *American Gothic*, Grant Wood
> ➤ *Angelus*, Jean-Francois Millet
> ➤ *Breaking Home Ties*, Norman Rockwell
> ➤ *Compagnie Francaise des Chocolats et des Thès*, Theophile Alexandre Steinlen (poster)
> ➤ *The Fountain, Villa Torlonia,* John Singer Sargent
> ➤ *In the Omnibus*, Mary Cassatt
> ➤ *Migrant Mother,* Dorothea Lange (photograph)
> ➤ *Place de la Concorde,* Edgar Degas
> ➤ *On the Terrace,* Pierre-Auguste Renoir
> ➤ *Sunday on la Grande Jatte*, Georges Seurat
> ➤ *V-J Day Times Square 1945,* Alfred Eisenstaedt (photograph)
> ➤ Vietnam Women's Memorial, Glenna Goodacre (sculpture)

These works and many more can easily be found on the Internet by title or artist, as well as in art, travel, and reference books.

Trading Places

Reflect on friends from childhood, especially those with

Ideas 253

whom you spent lots of time at their homes.

> Which ones would you have traded places with? Why?
> In what ways would such a trade have influenced the choices you made as a teen and adult?
> How would your own family have handled your absence from their lives?
> What is the most memorable meal you ever had at your friend's house?
> To your best recollection, describe every aspect of that meal in terms of sights, smells, textures, tastes, and any background sounds that were going on.
> What did you learn about family relationships from observing these people?
> How did their family values differ from your own family?
> Did your respective families get along with each other? Why or why not?

Boyfriends Are from Venus, Dads Are from Mars

Your latest beau is not just a match made in heaven, he is literally out of this world: He hails from Venus, to be precise. You have put off introducing him to your family for as long as you can but they are starting to get suspicious. Both your parents, but especially your father, are very much opposed to interplanetary relationships, but you just know that if they only got to spend some quality moments with your boyfriend, their doubts would all evaporate. Pen a one-act play in which you bring your Venusian sweetie and your parents together for the first time. Write your first version as a comedy, then write a second one as a drama. You can also do this exercise as a short story.

Heir Apparent

Not every child wants to follow a parent cheerfully into the family business. The pressure is more pronounced in the case of an only child. For this writing exercise, put yourself in the role of a young adult who is given the choice of either commencing the training to be able to run the whole show someday, or being disinherited. Construct a three-part book outline that establishes the core conflict(s), escalates the tension, and leads to a resolution that may or may not be satisfactory to both sides. Be sure to identify why you find the family business so abhorrent, what you would rather be doing with your time instead, and the consequences beyond the issue of disinheritance.

The Quotable Family

Build your book theme around a proverb from one of these websites:

- ➤ Creative Proverbs: www.creativeproverbs.com
- ➤ Famous Quotes & Authors: www.famousquotesandauthors.com/topics/family_quotes.html
- ➤ Quote Garden: www.quotegarden.com/family.html
- ➤ ThinkExist: http://thinkexist.com/quotations/family

Life in the Past Lane

If you have grandparents or other older relatives, arm yourself with a notepad or a tape recorder and spend time asking them the following questions to learn what it was like to grow up in an earlier era. You might also want to check into the possibility of doing similar interviews at local retirement communities.

- ➤ What was it like growing up in [place]?
- ➤ What was it like growing up in [decade]?

Ideas 255

- What were your favorite subjects in school?
- What did your parents do for work? For fun?
- What did you want to grow up to be? Why?
- What kind of chores did you do as a child? As a teenager?
- What music did you listen to?
- What was your favorite book from childhood?
- What were your favorite toys?
- What were your hobbies?
- Which family member were you the closest to?
- Which relatives were the most/least fun to be around?
- What's the most amazing invention you've seen in your lifetime?
- When you became of voting age, who's the first person you voted for?
- Who was your first crush?
- What public figures did you most admire?
- What was your first paying job? How much were you paid?
- What was the most important holiday in your family?
- Who wrote to you the most often when you went away from home?
- What keepsakes do you still have from childhood?
- What was your favorite season as a child and how did you spend it?

Note: For additional questions, check out books such as Barbara Ann Kipfer's *4,000 Questions For Getting To Know Anyone and Everyone* and Margaret Tiberio's *The Book of Self-Acquaintance*. These books are not only invaluable for autobiographical projects but also contain queries to put to your fictional characters in order to give them depth and plausible motivations for the choices they make.

Missed Connections

During some dabbling in genealogy, you make the discovery that you are related to someone famous (or infamous). Identify the first three people to whom you would reveal this surprising news about your family tree and, in three separate scenes of dialogue, show how each one reacts.

Furs, Fins, and Feathers

The interactions of nonhuman families have long been fodder for cartoons, feature films, and television series such as *Meerkat Manor*. In this exercise, pick a group from Column A, a setting from Column B, and invent a family-themed premise for an anthropomorphic short book for children, and for an adult satire.

Column A	*Column B*
Beavers	A New Jersey housing project
Ducks	Ancient Greece
Penguins	Midwestern suburbia
Lemurs	The bright lights of Broadway
Chameleons	An inner city school
Dolphins	The American Revolution
Hippos	1920s Paris
Anteaters	A shopping mall
Koalas	An overgrown backyard
Hedgehogs	A toy store
Skunks	A fifth-century forest
Raccoons	A gourmet grocery store

It's All Relative

With which of your family relations would you least want to do the following?

Ideas 257

> go on vacation
> loan money to
> entrust with a secret
> work for (or with)
> invite to a party

Use one of these situations as the opening to your story.

Reality Show

Reality shows are all the rage, especially those in which individuals from diverse backgrounds are thrown together and forced to co-exist for a set amount of time. Instead of an island setting, the backdrop of the new reality show you are producing is a large house in which ten real-life celebrities of your choice will live together—as a forced family—for ten weeks and vote one another off each episode until only one remains. Write lists delineating:

> what the challenge will be each week
> whether members will compete individually or as teams
> how results will be measured

Next, write an account of what happens among the celebrities with each challenge.

"The family is like a forest," says a Ghanaian proverb. "If you are outside, it is dense; if you are inside, you see that each tree has its own position." The better you can understand what makes your own family tick through story-starters such as these, the more realistic foundation you can give your fictional characters as they embark on their own journeys into the woods and beyond.

Counting Candles
Writing Adult Characters
for Kids & Vice Versa

By Sue Bradford Edwards

C haracter-driven stories are sought out by more and more editors today. Compelling characters have perhaps never been so important to selling good fiction, even when action, plot, or even theme are a story's dominant trait. Readers want even the purest action/adventure/thriller fiction to have a memorable protagonist—to be someone with whom they can identify. For writers, the task of creating a top-notch protagonist becomes more difficult when the character differs in a significant way from the reader.

The greatest divide may be age. It is a regular pronouncement that children will not read books with adult main characters. Child characters in adult novels also face carefully limited roles. "I wish I read more adult literature that included realistic portrayals of children as fully realized people and not just a hindrance or a plot device," says novelist C. C. Finlay. Fortunately, some writers are willing to break these unwritten rules

259

to meet the demands of a particular story. At a time when character-driven stories are editor favorites, the ability to create characters with truly universal appeal—across ages and genders and interests—is a treasure.

Ladies, Gentlemen, & Children of All Ages

Every story has its own requirements. One setting will work where another will not. The voice for one story must be more formal than the voice for another. A serious book for adults may tell the story of a child. Sometimes a picture book demands a prominent adult character.

"When I did *Grandma U* (Peachtree Publishers), I just wrote the story I wanted to tell," about a soon-to-be grandmother who does not know how to be one. "I was new to writing for children, and only after the fact did I learn that most kids' books have children as the main characters," says author Jeanie Franz Ransom. "It made *Grandma U* a bit tough to sell, but I'm happy that it finally did find a home." She just needed to find a publisher who shared her vision.

Other picture book writers knowingly break with the convention of banning adults as the prominent character or subject. "Every story has a particular point of view that just seems right for that story," says author Kathryn Lasky. In her book *Georgia Rises: A Day in the Life of Georgia O'Keeffe* (Farrar, Straus and Giroux), "I imagine it is Georgia O'Keeffe's fierce independence that children might find appealing. Melanie Kroupa was my editor on this book and she seemed to sense instinctively what I was trying to do and helped me get there." Even when writing for a picture book audience—an audience fed a near-steady diet of preschool characters—some stories can only be told from the perspective of an adult.

Fiction for adults may, in turn, require the active participation of a child character. "I dive into the story and see where it takes me. Usually, the territory where I end up is fairly complicated. I am interested in how children have complex inner lives. They often have reactions that they might not be able to articulate at

> "I am interested in how children have complex inner lives. They often have reactions that they may not be able to articulate, but that I can put into words."

the time but that I, as a writer, can put into words," says novelist Elizabeth Graver. At the center of her novel *The Honey Thief* (Harvest Books) is 11-year-old Eva, whose kleptomania precipitates her mother's fears and decision to move from the city to the country, where the girl meets a middle-aged beekeeper. "*The Honey Thief* has three strands, and only one of them is from the point of view of a child," says Graver. Including this youthful character was necessary for the novel to function as Graver envisioned it. "I wanted that layering, that sense of three dimensions."

Child characters are an essential part of the fabric when a narrator is an adult looking back to examine life. "My idea for the novel *Billy Goat Hill* (Multnomah Books), which explores the nuances and complexity of the subject of forgiveness, was to craft a compelling story about two young brothers caught up in a twist of fate and how childhood events affect us far into the future," says author Mark Stanleigh Morris. "The story emanates from the point of view of a grown man recalling his childhood."

A story with integrity will speak its need and find its audience.

Ideas 261

Books that Get It Right

Child Characters for Adults:
- *Admissions*, Nancy Lieberman (Grand Central Publishing)
- *Asta in the Wings*, Jan Elizabeth Watson (Tin House Books)
- *The Bewildered*, Peter Rock (MacAdam/Cage)
- *Billy Goat Hill*, Mark Stanleigh Morris (Multnomah)
- *The Honey Thief*, Elizabeth Graver (Harvest Books)
- *Jim the Boy*, Tony Earley (Back Bay Books)
- *Prodigal Troll*, C. C. Finlay (Pyr Books)
- *Time Dancers*, Steve Cash (Del Rey)
- Traitor to the Crown trilogy, C. C. Finlay (Del Rey)

Adult Characters for Children:
- *A Couple of Boys Have the Best Week Ever*, Marla Frazee (Harcourt)
- *Dracula vs. Grampa at the Monster Truck Spectacular*, Kirk Scroggs (Little, Brown)
- *Georgia Rises*, Kathryn Lasky; illus., Ora Eitan (Farrar, Straus and Giroux)
- *Grandma U*, Jeanie Franz Ransom; illus., Lucy Corvino (Peachtree Publishers)
- Mr. Putter and Tabby series, Cynthia Rylant; illus., Arthur Howard (Sandpiper)
- *Mrs. Biddlebox*, Linda Smith; illus., Marla Frazee (Harcourt)
- *Officer Buckle and Gloria*, Peggy Rathmann (Putnam)
- *Santa the World's Number One Toy Expert*, Marla Frazee (Harcourt)
- *Skinnybones and the Wrinkle Queen*, Glen Huser (Groundwood Books)
- *What Do Parents Do (When You're Not Home)*, Jeanie Franz Ransom; illus., Cyd Moore (Carolrhoda)

J. D. Salinger wrote *Catcher in the Rye* for an adult readership, and while it still has that, the book soon became a rite of passage for teens. What you find out about your own intended audience might surprise you. "You may think you are writing a book for children and find out that it really is a book for young adults. Or maybe you thought it was for adults, but really it is for middle-schoolers," says children's author and illustrator Marla Frazee. "I think the story should determine the audience, rather than the other way around. Write the story. Then decide who it's for."

The Way It Is, the Way It Should Be

Empathy with the characters is the key—which is why character ages usually mirror that of the anticipated audience. Creating the necessary connection between reader and character can be more difficult when the reader and character seem to have little in common. In terms of age, this might seem most difficult when creating adult characters for children. How can a child identify with the history, complexities, and challenges of an adult?

"Adults—and their world—can trump the child very, very easily," says Frazee. "I have to work hard, as an author-illustrator of books for young children, to keep children and what matters to them as the primary focus of not only the writing, but of the illustrations. When an adult and a much smaller child inhabit the same image, it is difficult to have the physically smaller character be the focal point of the composition."

Examine your motivation for using an adult character in a book for children or teens. "An author should ask himself or herself what role the adults will play, and why having prominent adult characters is important to the story," says Ransom. "An author should never use an adult main character to solve

the problem or to teach a lesson. Neither is appealing to young readers."

To keep adults from taking over, it may be necessary consciously to push them to the side, and keep them in a supporting role. "*A Couple of Boys Have the Best Week Ever* (Harcourt) features two boys, James and Eamon, as the main characters, and two adults, Bill and Pam, as secondary characters," says

> "The questions of defining selfhood, of mortality, morality, community, independence, freedom, survival— these know no age."

Frazee of her book. "The text went through multiple revisions, each one focusing the story more on the boys and less on Bill and Pam. The text is written in counterpoint to what we see in the pictures, and I like to think of the words as being the adult perspective, the *way it should be*, while the pictures allow us to experience the story from a child perspective, the *way it is*."

Adult characters can be made more sympathetic by making them less like your average adult. "Even though my characters may be adults, they are young at heart. They're playful and have a sense of humor," says Ransom.

Frazee agrees. "I have written and/or illustrated other picture books where the main character is a grownup—*Santa the World's Number One Toy Expert* and *Mrs. Biddlebox* (both from Harcourt)—and in both cases, the adult character looks and behaves in a childlike manner. This allows the child reader to identify fully with the main character. In those books, the characters are small compared to their surroundings, and often highly emotional and volatile in their actions. They do not exhibit what we traditionally think of as grownup behavior."

Different Problems

Writing child characters for adults presents its own set of problems, but empathy is not as core an issue. "We were all children once. Many of us have children or are close to children in our lives. I also believe that there is not a stark line that separates childhood from adulthood," says Graver. "The human things that people struggle with—questions of defining selfhood, of mortality, morality, of community, independence, freedom, survival, etc.—these know no age."

Morris agrees. "Everyone was a child once upon a time, and I find that adult readers easily identify with well-developed child characters brought to life in well-crafted stories. I love to awaken and stimulate readers' childhood memories. Who doesn't occasionally long to be a kid again?"

Sometimes adults connect because of the role that adults play in the life of a child. "A child in danger from events beyond his understanding or power to change is compelling in its own right," says Finlay, speaking of his book *The Prodigal Troll* (Pyr Books), in which a human child is raised by trolls. "By the second half of the book, Maggot is trying to find his way in a world that is foreign to him, where he doesn't fit in, and doesn't understand all the nuances of the social interactions taking place around him. Many people identify with that, even when we're adults, but especially when we reflect on our experiences as young adults, striking out on our own for the first time."

Despite the presumed natural connection, writing realistic child characters for adults can be tricky. "One common pitfall is that it is very easy to exceed the reasonable actions and dialogue

Ideas 265

of children," says Morris. "Constructive feedback can help identify and correct this."

Writers who are careful not to make child characters sound too old often create another problem. "Pitfalls include being overly cute, overly coy, sounding false or cartoony, sounding like an adult trying to sound like a kid. Either the kid often sounds too kid-like or too precocious," says Graver.

Children and adults often react to the world differently, and that can be a challenge for writers to remember or portray. "The hardest thing about writing children, especially very young children, is conveying their natural brightness and curiosity without being cloying, their mercurial emotions without seeming arbitrary, their sometimes simultaneously graceful and clumsy physicality without relying on cliches," says Finlay.

The younger the character, the greater the potential divide from an adult reader. "It's important to remember that children —especially young, happy children—haven't built up all the usual adult barriers to their environment yet, and so they are constantly reacting to the immediacy of the situation," Finlay explains. "But the situation they notice isn't the same as what adults notice. They can be so focused on something specific that they miss a dramatic event, or they can be so sensitive to details that they see the thing that adults around them are overlooking."

Working through these complexities can also present writers with creative opportunities. In *The Honey Thief*, "I wanted to render both the true childishness of Eva's personality (she is only 11), and also the complexity of her position, her relationship to the past, her emotions," says Graver. "The tension between those things can be a bit tricky. I chose 11 for her age because it is a cusp age, between childhood and the beginning of adolescence, and as such, it is fascinating to me."

Creating characters is always challenging. You have to emphasize what the reader will identify with while keeping this trait within acceptable bounds. "When I wrote the Traitor to the Crown trilogy (Del Rey), a secret history about witches fighting a war behind the scenes of the American Revolution, children of various ages played important roles in every book," says Finlay. "The challenge was always to make them fully realized people."

Because no matter how young or how old, characters will come to life only when the story is alive and specific because of them. In a character-driven story, protagonists engage with readers because of what they have in common—a sense of fun, a unique way of looking at the world, the drive to prove themselves, or battles with demons. No reader, in the end, cares what the age of a character who strips the layers from the human condition: David Copperfield from child to man, Huck and Jim, D'Artagnan, Jo March, Holden Caulfield, Scout and Boo, Harry and Hermione, and even Edward and Bella.

Brainstorm Your Plot

By Kelly McClymer

E very piece of fiction needs a plot. Plot is the story line, the advance of events played out by characters in a short story, play, novel, or even narrative verse. In some stories, the protagonist's motivations drive the events, and in others, events propel the protagonist into actions and choices. But whether you start with a character (a dateless woman who decides she needs to be married within a year), or an event (the San Andreas fault is about to crack wide open), you have many pages of revelations, actions, reactions, obstacles, and conflicts to go until the woman has put together her new life, or a scientist discovers and averts impending disaster.

Sometimes it can seem that the best twists, turns, and tensions were used up almost as long ago as Shakespeare. Star-crossed lovers thwarted in their efforts to be together by a family feud? Done. A son in conflict with his mother and step-father to the point of murder? Done. So how can a writer push past familiar plot meanderings? One way is to use brainstorming tools to identify and unlock another level of creativity to make a story fresh and satisfying.

A Trinity: Idea, What If?, What Next?

No fiction writer ever stops asking *what if?* The question can be asked while doing dishes, working a day job, driving a car, or sitting at a desk scribbling away. Bestselling thriller author Tess Gerritsen describes using this process in her approach to beginning *Vanish* (Ballantine Books), which won the Nero Award for best mystery. "My original premise was *corpse wakes up in morgue.* The process then continued: *Q:* Who is this corpse? *A:* Maybe nobody knows. Maybe she comes in with no I.D. Maybe she doesn't say a word, only makes weird sounds, or speaks in a foreign language. Yeah, that's the ticket. Mysterious woman, nameless, opens up all sorts of possibilities. Maybe she's running from the law. Maybe she's a secret agent. Maybe she knows a secret that will kill her. Maybe someone tried to kill her, botched it, and that's how she ended up in the morgue."

What-if questions open up the possibilities for a little while, but then Gerritsen uses another stage of questioning to narrow down the plot possibilities: "*Q:* What happens next? *A.* Logically, the medical examiner would send her to the hospital, where she would recover and . . . Tell her story? (Too boring. Mystery solved too soon.) Gets attacked and survives—or dies? Attacked by whom, and why? Runs away and disappears? (Hmmm. Don't know where to go with this one.) Attacks a hospital security guard and takes hostages. Why would she do it? Is she scared? Homicidal? Hey, what if one of the hostages she takes is Detective Jane Rizzoli, my very pregnant series heroine?" Gerritsen knows when she has hit on a viable plot twist. "Now this is starting to sound interesting. It brings my series character into the story on a very personal level. I choose this option, even though I still don't know where the plot is going."

What-if questions also help when a writer runs out of ideas mid-plot, or even mid-scene. When Gerritsen needs to brainstorm what will happen next, she says, "I'll lie on the couch and stare at the ceiling. I'll get out a blank piece of paper and list as many possible plot pathways from that point. Sometimes a long drive in the car is also helpful. There's something about a highway that makes my mind start to work harder. I turn off the radio and just drive along in silence, mulling over possibilities."

Collaborative Push

An often overlooked tool for taking a plot to a new level is talking with others.

➤ *Brainstorm with friends.* Tina Ferraro, a young adult author whose books include *The ABC's of Kissing Boys* (Delacorte), begins with her title, but after about three chapters, she says, "I often turn to my online critique group (made up of about ten other female writers whose genres and target areas vary widely) for help with specifics on my *through-line*. Like 'uses for an unworn prom dress' or 'ways to hook a hottie' or 'everything we know about kissing.'" [The great acting teacher Constantin Stanislavski originated the concept of the through-line, which is the spine that connects a character's objectives and advances them through the plot.]

➤ *Far from the madding crowd.* Some writers take periodic days or weekends to brainstorm by means of a retreat designed specifically for generating ideas and moving stories ahead. Diane Amos, author of *Getting Personal* (The Wild Rose Press), has attended several retreats. She suggests that a few rules, and a moderator to make sure they are observed, can help keep the talk focused. "One rule we had at the MERWA (Maine Romance Writers of America) retreat brainstorming session was to set a

Programming Plots

Organization

While many writers use a basic word processing program like Microsoft Word, some have graduated to programs created specifically to help writers handle all the incidental information that goes into writing a book: character bios, background research, photographs, maps, timelines, and so on. Allison Brennan, bestselling author of suspense novels such as *Cutting Edge* (Ballantine), "recently started using Scrivener to write my first draft because I like the ability to write in scenes (something I've never really done before) and I love the ability to track keywords, link to research articles or facts, and have everything in one place."

Writer programs tend to give the user multiple ways to view the plot on screen—in outline form, as index cards, story templates—which can be an efficient (and green) way to adapt a formerly paper-intensive brainstorming method. Specific tools allow writers to organize a project by chapters and scenes, with easily accessible outlines, goals, and notes. The organizational features work for both those who outline fully before beginning to write, and for those who plot as they go.

Windows software: yWriter (www.spacejock.com); WriteWay Pro (www.writewaypro.com)

Macintosh software: Scrivener (www.literatureandlatte.com)

Both operating systems: Writer's Cafe (www.writerscafe.co.uk)

Brainstorming

Some software is specifically meant to boost brainstorming, not just for writers, but for students, teachers, artists, and others. These programs encourage mind-mapping, story-web creation, and on-screen image collage with existing templates, and also the freedom of user-created designs.

Windows: BrainStorm (www.brainstormsw.com/index.html)

Multiple systems: Inspiration (www.inspiration.com)

time limit" on each brainstorming task. Amos was so pleased by the results of the retreat that she created an ongoing brain-storming loop with the participants.

➤ *Interview an expert.* Talking to an expert in poisons may point a suspense author to a plant that seems innocent enough, until a few dried leaves are dropped into a cup of tea. An FBI agent may be able to steer an author to character actions and situations that fall within the rules of the Bureau (or away from those that do not). Never discount an expert's ability to open up new plot possibilities just by revealing facts and details that casual research won't always uncover.

➤ *Walk in the shoes of your character.* There is nothing like a trip to a location that will feature in the story. The only things needed are a notebook, a camera, and a vow to observe the smallest details that may be used to bring the story to life and offer a fresh turn to the plot.

See, Feel, Touch the Story

Hands-on methods let the five senses guide creativity as a writer considers which way the story wind is blowing.

➤ *Tarot cards and star charts.* Turning to ancient ways for answers can arouse creativity for some writers, whether you believe in them or not. Shuffle a Tarot deck and deal out a few cards to represent the conflict and characters of a given scene, chapter, or entire novel. When writing *Must Love Black* (Simon-Pulse), a gothic take on a not-so-goth teen, I researched Tarot. Stuck on the motivation for a key scene, I dealt out five cards and found my motivation in their interplay. There is no need to be a Tarot-reading expert, either. The act of shuffling, dealing, and the pictures on the faces of the cards are often enough to inspire a creative breakthrough. Some writers have also been known to cast star charts for their characters, using the information to help

A Page from the Masters

Many popular writers have written books describing the tools they use to come up with strong stories that are fresh and interesting. For brainstorming purposes, consider taking your favorite and heading straight to the section relevant to your brainstorming need—plot, character, or any other. Recommended titles:

➤ *Bird by Bird: Some Instructions on Writing and Life*, Anne Lamott (Anchor). A now classic inspirational writing book, with advice that can be used to unlock creativity.
➤ *From Where You Dream: The Process of Writing Fiction*, Robert Olen Butler (Grove Press). A series of creative writing lectures by a Pulitzer Prize winner. Stresses sense memories and emotional connections.
➤ *Writing the Breakout Novel*, Donald Maass (Writer's Digest). Uses case studies to inspire and illustrate how to write a novel that rises above the average.

uncover useful story conflicts.

➤ *Index cards and storyboarding.* Hollywood thinks in scenes, and so can writers. Writing important action on index cards—one card to a scene—and placing the cards in order on a wall or board is a great way to view the overall story without getting bogged down in sentences and paragraphs. Diana Peterfreund, author of the Secret Society Girl series (Delacorte) and the young adult fantasy novel *Rampant* (HarperTeen), uses a plotting board. She takes her first draft deeper by using a color for each plot thread. "A standard key for one of my plotting boards might show different colors for *main character arc, mystery plot, romance plot, subplot,* etc. A given scene might have several different colors because I touch on or develop multiple elements within the scene. I tend to organize the final board so that each row of scenes culminates in a climactic or turning point scene."

This helps give Peterfreund a bird's eye view of the story, and colorfully points out which areas of the manuscript need more development.

➤ *Collages.* Visual representations, key words or phrases, and even small objects—all related to characters or settings—can spur ideas. The collage process of thumbing through magazines or newspapers and gathering the pictures and words, or finding and contemplating objects that speak to the unfolding story, can free the unconscious mind. Charlotte Hubbard, author of the Angels of Mercy series (Leisure Books/Dorchester Publishing) and the new *Law of Attraction*, has found, "More than once, when I've let my mind go slightly out of gear as I select character photos (magazine pictures) for a story's collage, a face will insist on being in that story even though I don't know who it will be. And always, if I follow this gut instinct, I discover someone who becomes integral to the plot and the story's depth." The collage process has a second part: organizing the gathered images on a poster board or whiteboard. "Even the way the photos arrange themselves can suggest relationships between characters I didn't *know* about as I wrote up my proposal. I let the pictures flow into place around each other and am sometimes surprised about who knows someone else's secrets." Hubbard uses a bulletin board for her collage. "Their eyes and faces prod me if I reach a block or stall. Sometimes they suggest nuances or even subplots I wasn't expecting."

Remember, there is one simple point to any brainstorming method—the question, "What if?" So if you don't have access to any tools but a piece of paper or a long solitary stretch of road, begin with that question, and just keep asking it.

The Inside Story
Crafting Unique Material Through Interviews

By Jacqueline Adams

E very Saturday, loyal customers crowded Miller's Shoes in New Castle, Pennsylvania. Many drove from distant towns to shop in the little store. What was Ed Miller's secret? While other store owners took the self-service route, Ed used his decades of experience to painstakingly fit each customer in the perfect shoe. He gave his customers something they couldn't find elsewhere.

Writers can use the same idea to attract our customers: editors and readers. Writing based on secondary sources, such as published books and articles, offers readers information that is available elsewhere. But when we include information from original interviews, we give them something they cannot find anywhere else.

Susan Goldman Rubin, who has written more than 45 books for young readers, says, "An interview adds so much authenticity to your work, and originality, because you get an anecdote, a story, a slant, that would never have come about any other way. It sets your work apart from what's already been done."

Some writers feel overwhelmed by the idea of interviews, wondering where to find the right person to interview, how to approach a person and ask the right questions, or whether it is better to conduct an e-mail, telephone, or face-to-face interview. Four writers and two editors simplify the process by sharing their experiences and advice.

One Clue Leads to Another

Sometimes interesting people will present themselves to you—someone like Ed Miller, a good subject perhaps for an article in a local paper or regional magazine. But when you begin with a general topic and need firsthand information, the first challenge is finding a potential interviewee. In some cases, writers can enlist the help of someone they know. Sara Louise Kras, author of 23 children's nonfiction books, explains, "When trying to find the correct person to interview for a polar bear story, I began with a known, friendly contact who was the owner of a helicopter company in Churchill [Canada, where Kras took a polar bear tour]. He then pointed me in the right direction. He gave me names and in some cases e-mail addresses of experts who lived in the area."

When Rubin wanted to interview survivors of Terezin for *Fireflies in the Dark* (Holiday House), she found an ally in the Director of Library and Archival Services at the Simon Wiesenthal Center's Museum of Tolerance in Los Angeles. The director wrote letters of introduction on her behalf, and one survivor responded. "Through her, we met a host of adults who had been kids in Terezin, men and women who were so eager for me to tell their story," Rubin says. "One clue leads to another."

More often, writers start without a known contact. When

Laura Hillenbrand researched *Seabiscuit: An American Legend* (Ballantine Books), she conducted a broad search to find people who had witnessed the story's events. She started by placing ads in racing publications. "And I did a lot of cold calling to people in the racing industry," she says. "I must have made a hundred phone calls just to this organization or that organization, a training organization, or the press box at this racetrack. I would say, 'Who do you know who was around in the 1930s?' People would say, 'Oh, you've got to talk to this track veterinarian. He's like 90, and he'll tell you things.'" For her current work-in-progress, a book about a World War II bombardier, Hillenbrand again ran ads. "Every time I interviewed one person, I'd say, 'Who do you know who also knew these guys?' That's been really helpful, to skip from one person to another."

Jeanna Bryner, a Senior Writer for LiveScience.com, often calls the press office of organizations related to her subject. "If I'm writing about family values or perhaps a piece on the science behind why men cheat, I would contact the press person at the American Sociological Association. Recently, I wrote an article about the guidelines for breastfeeding mothers and drinking alcohol. I contacted the American Academy of Pediatrics and they gave me a few contacts."

Bryner also uses Internet search engines to find names of scientists in the field she is researching. The same tactic works for locating everyday people. *Dog Fancy* Editor Susan Chaney suggests, "In addition to just looking for *people who love dogs,* for example, look for online articles about the subject you're writing about. You'll find people in those articles who could be sources for you. You can use Yellowpages.com, Facebook, etc., to find them—sometimes. Don't, however, contact the article's author and ask for their sources' contact info. If they're smart, they'll tell you to do your own reporting."

Winning Approach

Chaney suggests a simple way to approach a potential interviewee. "Call or send an e-mail saying, 'Hi, I'm ___, and I'm working on an article about ___ for ___ magazine. I understand that you've had an experience with ___, and I'm hoping that I can interview you about it. Would that be possible? When would be a good time for an interview?'"

Kras gives potential interview subjects "a detailed description of who I am and what I am doing. Then I ask if it's okay to ask a few questions about the topic. I do this so they know that I am contacting them for a real purpose and have a direction in mind." Even when she is writing on speculation, she does not hesitate to seek interviews. "If I don't have a contract, I make it known. I tell them I will be attempting to sell the manuscript once it is completed."

Hillenbrand also found that lack of a contract was no barrier. "People generally like to be interviewed. With *Seabiscuit*, I had been researching for two years before I had a book contract. Initially, I was just hoping to sell the story as an article. I just said I was researching for an article, and everyone was happy to speak to me."

Providing samples of past work, along with a respectful attitude, can help remove obstacles. Rubin's *Steven Spielberg: Crazy for Movies* (Abrams) depended on interviews with Spielberg's family. Her contact at the Simon Wiesenthal Center offered to introduce her to Spielberg's mother, Leah. Rubin brought two of her published books to Leah's restaurant. She relates: "Leah took the books and—it was very crisp—said, 'No, no, no, I can't agree to any interview. It's only Steve who gives permission.' So I said, 'Okay, I'm just delighted to have met you. And I want you to have these books as a little gift.'" Leah left to speak with other customers, but soon returned and said, "I like the books. I like you.

Let's do it." She told Rubin how to get her son's permission.

Another part of a respectful approach is requesting an appointment instead of expecting the person to do the interview on the spot. But occasionally someone will respond, "How about right now?" Wise writers prepare as much as possible before making contact.

Prepared, but Flexible

Good preparation involves researching the person and the topic. Learning the basics about your selected subject shows respect for the interviewee and lets you, as the interviewer, make the most of the allotted time. "I do all of my basic research first so I'm not asking them questions which can easily be answered via other means such as the Internet or already published books or magazine articles," says Kras.

This research, along with thinking about what readers will want to know, will help you formulate a list of questions. Elizabeth Carpentiere, Editor of the children's magazine about cultures, *Faces*, has advice about interviewing children that can extend to adults as well. She suggests wording that will yield the most information. "Avoid asking questions that can be answered with a simple yes or no—more often than not, that is how the person will answer and you will not have much to work with. Rather than ask a child, 'Do you like school?' ask, 'What do you like best about school?' or a similar question that will involve a more detailed answer. And don't forget to ask 'Why?' if the interviewee doesn't elaborate. 'Why is art your favorite subject?'"

Interviewing is a core technique of journalism, and the traditional journalistic questions offer a good way to structure your interview. "Start some questions with *when, why,* and *how,*" Chaney suggests. "For example, 'When did you know that you would become a Yorkie breeder? Do you remember the exact

To Record or Not to Record

Some writers rely solely on note-taking, while others record their interviews and listen to or transcribe them later. If you record, always ask the interviewee's permission. Most people are fine with the idea, and some even prefer it because they feel it protects them from being misquoted. Whichever method you use, take measures to ensure accuracy.

Author Laura Hillenbrand isn't a fan of depending on notes alone. She explains, "You're just falling over yourself trying to keep up with someone speaking. And when you're doing that, you're not focusing so much on understanding what they're saying; you're just trying to copy it down. And so you're going to miss the question that pops into your head later." She records interviews in order to be free to listen and formulate follow-up questions. Her other concern is accuracy. When her book *Seabiscuit* hit the best-seller list, she had to switch sides of the desk and become an interviewee. "I have been misquoted so many times," she says. "Some of them have been these award-winning journalists who've been very, very sloppy, and it's because they're just copying it down and they're not really thinking. It has shown me how easy it is to get it wrong if you're not taping it."

Having interviews on tape helps Jeanna Bryner, a science writer who must explain technical information. "If I am working on a feature, I often transcribe so that I can get better or longer quotes

moment?' or 'Why did you want to explore that line of research? Did anything in your personal life push you in that direction?' and 'How did you come up with that idea?' 'How did you make that decision?'"

Hillenbrand cautions against forming preconceived ideas and then looking for quotes to match. "I like to go into an interview not assuming I understand what their thinking is and being very open-minded about their point of view, approaching it as, 'I am your student; you teach me what you know.'" Banishing

To Record or Not to Record

and also so I can go back and listen to the source explain any complex ideas," she says. "Since transcribing takes time, I don't transcribe for quick-turnaround stories that I need to get out in 30 minutes to an hour."

Susan Goldman Rubin switches between methods, depending on the circumstances. When she can't record, she later double-checks the quotes with the interviewee to make sure she got the correct wording. "Even when I do record an interview, I take notes at the same time," she says. "For example, when I interviewed Steven Spielberg's sisters Nancy and Sue I recorded the conversation, but they talked so fast and so much that I jotted down brief notes to remind me who said what. It was hilarious. All I had to do was ask, 'What was it like growing up with Steve as your big brother?' and I never got another word in."

If you're not recording, *Dog Fancy* Editor Susan Chaney stresses taking the time to get it right. "If you get behind, feel free to say, 'Sorry. I got a little behind. Let me catch up here.'" She points out that it's fine to ask someone to go back to the beginning of a good quote that you didn't catch completely. Also, use a notation to show which lines you wrote down word for word and which you para-phrased. She says, "The one I've used for years is quote marks for perfect quotes, quote marks hatched through for imperfect quotes."

preconceived ideas also means having the courage to ask so-called stupid questions. She says, "So many things are counter-intuitive, and so many times you can assume you understand something, and it turns out you're not right about it. And so I like to just say, 'Look, this is a dumb question, but . . . .' And often I'll be surprised by the answer."

To keep from missing interesting details, Hillenbrand likes to begin with general questions. "For instance, if I were talking to someone who saw the Seabiscuit-War Admiral match race, I'd

say, 'Tell me about that day,' because that leaves it so wide open that someone can begin with what his general impressions were, and things that you might not specifically ask about. He might say, 'This amazing thing happened in the parking lot when I was on my way in.' You would never have thought to ask, 'Did something happen to you in the parking lot when you were on your way in?'"

> "You might get a response you didn't expect that will lead your interview down a different direction. Don't be a slave to your scripted questions."

Although preparation is important, writers must remain flexible. "You might get a response you didn't expect that will lead your interview down a different direction. Don't be a slave to your scripted questions," says Carpentiere.

Listening carefully, rather than thinking about the next question on your list, allows you to ask follow-up questions. Bryner says, "When I really listen to my sources, I naturally come up with questions to ask and the interview flows better." She wraps things up with a final open question. "At the end of the interview, I like to ask my sources if there is anything they'd like to add, or if I missed something important about their research or study."

Common Challenges

Skillful questioning can help draw out someone who is not talkative. But what about the other extreme—people who go off on lengthy tangents? When the interviewee can grant you only a limited amount of time that does not allow for meandering, you must tactfully get back on track in order to get needed information. Chaney suggests, "Wait for him to take a breath (not finish the story), then rush right in: 'Can we go back to ___? I'm really curious about how . . .'"

If people have time to talk and a side story is reasonably related to the subject, Hillenbrand likes to let them go. One reason is respect. "But also, so often when people have gone off on tangents, eventually they hit on something that's a gem." She recalls an elderly man who went off on a long tangent while being interviewed for *Seabiscuit*. "None of it was useful to me, but I thought, 'Well, he's enjoying talking about it, so I'll let him talk.' Then in passing he said, 'That was the year that the pile of manure at Tijuana racetrack was hit by a flood and crashed into the track and wrecked it.' I thought, 'Wait a minute. Back up.'" She called back other sources who hadn't mentioned this event and found that they, too, had witnessed it.

Sometimes the challenge is not the interviewee, but the writer. Writers may hesitate to conduct interviews out of fear that they are not good conversationalists. But if so, that quality can be a plus. "Say as little as you can about yourself," Rubin advises. "In other words, it's not a regular social conversation but an interview. Keep your own opinions and experiences out of it. Focus completely on the person you are interviewing."

The more you talk, the less you will hear from your interviewee. Interjecting to let the person know you're still listening can ruin a good quote. "Many writers/reporters think and speak quickly, and tend to finish people's sentences for them. Don't," Chaney says.

Going Electronic?

Writers sometimes wonder whether they should skip the

Ideas 285

Back for a Fact Check?

Some editors require writers to send a completed manuscript back to interviewees for a fact check, while others forbid this. When you have a choice, what should you do? Opinions vary greatly, but hearing from experienced interviewers can help you weigh the factors involved.

"I always love to send the complete manuscript (or partial manuscript if the interview only relates to a small part of it) back to the interviewees if they are willing to take the time to read it. This gives them a chance to check my and their wording," says children's author Sara Louise Kras. She feels that sending her manuscript for *The Galapagos Islands* (Marshall Cavendish) back to her contact at the Charles Darwin Research Station was a great help. "It never hurts to go over the material again to ensure it is 100 percent correct."

"I don't typically send a completed manuscript to the interviewee for a fact check," science writer Jeanna Bryner says. "Sometimes if it's a complex topic and I am familiar with the researcher, I will send sections to the interviewee and ask him or her to let me know if there are any inaccuracies."

When author Laura Hillenbrand wrote articles on veterinary medicine for *Equus*, she was grateful that the editors allowed her to send the articles back to her interviewees. "I'm not a veterinarian, and I was coming in as a complete neophyte every time I wrote a story," she says. She felt that sending the article back for review protected her and her interviewees in case she had misunderstood technical information. "When I went into the interview saying I wanted to do that, people felt more comfortable talking to me, knowing I wasn't going to just print something that was totally off the mark and they wouldn't know about it until it came out." In one case, an interviewee who read her draft alerted her that a second interviewee had taken credit for other people's research. Hillenbrand verified the claim and made corrections.

Susan Chaney, Editor of *Dog Fancy*, thinks that asking for a review is fine in the case of highly technical material that the writer

Back for a Fact Check?

may not completely grasp. Otherwise, she cautions against the practice. "As a writer, you don't want to get into a discussion with a source about what he wants the article to be about. He may not like the tone, the voice, the conclusions, your choices of other sources, etc. That's not the source's prerogative. Interviewees only own their quotes, not what you do with them, and not the rest of the article." If the writer wants to send back quotes only, rather than the entire article, she finds that acceptable. "However, if the interviewee said something colorful or bizarre, are you willing to change it or remove it? If not, best not send quotes back for review."

Susan Goldman Rubin had that experience when she sent quotes for *Andy Warhol: Pop Art Painter* back to her interviewees. "Len Kessler decided at the last minute that he didn't want me to quote something he had said about visiting Andy's house when they were both students," she says. "It would have been a wonderful insight into Andy's growing up but I had to respect Len's wishes and omit it." Even though Rubin was disappointed, she still feels that clearing quotes with interviewees is important.

What if you send your manuscript to someone who goes beyond fact-checking and requests inappropriate changes? "I let them know that this is against editorial policy and try to explain in polite terms," Bryner says.

This happened only once to Hillenbrand when an interviewee disliked the article's style. "I just said to her, 'I will make changes only to your quotations and the facts in this story, but not my style.' And that was fine."

Kras says, "I thank them very much for their comments and nothing else. I'm the author and it's my book. I don't think any comment is necessary. No need to upset the interviewee."

Whether or not you run the manuscript past your interviewee, don't neglect to fact check it yourself. An interviewee may or may not catch something you've missed, but the final responsibility for accuracy rests with the writer.

telephone or face-to-face interview in favor of e-mail responses. The type of interview often depends on such factors as distance, deadline, or the interviewee's preference. But when they have a choice, most writers and editors opt for a face-to-face interview. Reasons cited include: The contact is more personal, you can observe body language and facial expressions, it is easier to ask follow-up questions, and the person is often more at ease and gives more colorful answers.

Telephone interviews came in second for preference. Our panel points out that these interviews are convenient, time-saving, and make it easier to record the conversation (with the interviewee's permission, of course). Interviewers can still ask follow-up questions and sometimes get an interview on the spot.

Rubin sums up the general feeling toward e-mail interviews: "Better than nothing."

Chaney warns, "You will never get the kind of quotes from an e-mail interview that you'll get in person or even on the telephone. Quotes are what give life and color to an article. You need to hear the person's words, tone, inflection, etc. You likely will not catch the person's passion or emotion in an e-mail."

E-mail sometimes has advantages, however. A person with a challenging schedule may hesitate to grant another type of interview. Carpentiere says, "E-mail interviews can be great for people with a busy schedule. They can complete the interview anytime, day or night."

Bryner, who interviews scientists from many countries, finds e-mail helpful when a language barrier is involved. "I like e-mail interviews also when there is a big time difference or when I am getting responses from a bunch of scientists/sources for a story—when trying to get a sense of where the field stands on certain issues. E-mail interviews also can be efficient in that

I can send the questions and move on to another project."

When researching *Andy Warhol: Pop Art Painter* (Abrams), Rubin contacted Warhol's nephew, who preferred e-mail. "I asked very specific questions that only he could answer." Using this approach and taking time to follow up with more e-mails, she discovered previously unpublished anecdotes.

In other words, she applied Ed Miller's secret: Give your customers something they cannot get anywhere else. If you do the same by conducting interviews, you may also find your work in demand.

The Art of Field Research

By Katherine Swarts

Fiction or nonfiction, reference book or graphic novel, few manuscripts can be completed without research. Research fills holes, verifies facts, and brings the credibility of outside expertise.

Field research—away from the computer desk, out of the library—additionally provides writers with personal experience. Writers who have lived their topics are more effective writers. For those who have not *been there* already, introduce yourself to the idea of field research and get out in the field for firsthand observation.

Why Field Research?

"Seeing for yourself sets a writer apart," says Vicki Cobb, author of more than 85 nonfiction books. "Firsthand experience adds a depth of knowledge not possible by just reading." Cobb is expert at noting detail: "In Peru researching *This Place is High* (Walker Books), I noticed that llamas had brightly colored tassels

291

in their ears; each rancher branded his llamas with his own color."

Lisa Wade McCormick, investigative reporter and children's author, concurs: "Isn't it more interesting to read how butter is made when a writer [who has observed the process] can paint with words how it smells, tastes, and even sounds when it's churning?"

> "Isn't it more interesting to read how butter is made when a writer can paint with words how it smells, tastes, and even sounds when it's churning?"

Field research is no less important with fiction. "I can't tell you how many novels I've read where the details just do not ring true," says Amy Efaw, author of *Battle Dress* (HarperTeen) and *After* (Viking). "For my novel *After*, one of the settings is inside a juvenile detention center. If I hadn't visited an actual detention center, I would never have known that its classroom didn't look like a jail, but instead resembled a kindergarten classroom with crayoned coloring book pages of Disney princesses on the walls."

"It's extremely difficult to create realistic settings without traveling to a location," says techno-thriller author Ralph L. Cates, whose works include *Black October* (Mystic Publishers) and its in-progress follow-up novel, *The Phoenix Agenda*. "Even with extensive video, sound, and written works available for research, fiction [tends to be] bland and unbelievable" if the author made no on-site observations.

Children's science author Loree Griffin Burns notes "an added bonus" of field research: It is "a great way to win respect and cooperation. Once people recognize that I am fascinated, they are more than happy to share their passions. I've beachcombed with oceanographers in California, sampled bees in a commercial apiary in Pennsylvania, and collected butterfly tags in the mountains of Mexico." Burns's books include *Tracking Trash* and the new *The Hive Detectives,* both from Houghton Mifflin's Scientists in the Field series.

"Another advantage is the time you spend with whomever you're interviewing," adds Mary Kay Carson, another Scientists in the Field author. "There's a lot of downtime, driving from here to there or waiting for bats to fly into nets. It's much less stuffy and formal than a sit-down interview, and often leads to more kid-friendly and spontaneous information."

Serendipity may be a gift of field research interviews. "Sometimes I stumble across some fascinating piece of information," says McCormick. "Or someone may give me a tip on a person who has even more knowledge."

"Be open to dropping prepared questions if the interview takes a surprise turn," says novelist Tish Cohen. "Be prepared to drop what you think you know. In my research for *Inside Out Girl* (Harper Perennial), I was shocked to learn how being bullied permeates the day-to-day worlds of youngsters with nonverbal learning disorders. That discovery altered the plot of the novel."

Of course, surprises have their disadvantages. "Sometimes facts become very inconvenient," notes Efaw. "Research may reveal that the story's foundation is unsound and require that drastic changes be made. Some authors would rather plead ignorance than change their stories to fit the facts. That is a gross disservice to the audience."

Discovering the need for major rewrites can put a dent in an author's passion for a project. On the other hand, many writers find that field research stimulates that passion. Says science and geography author Tanya Lloyd Kyi: "Field research in the early stages can boost your enthusiasm. Speaking to a dedicated scientist is much more inspiring than paging through reference books."

Science and math writer Vijaya Bodach concurs: "Even with lab work, seeing the work done can give you more insight. With citizen science-type projects, a visit to the site is a must. You learn so much by being part of the team."

The Hard Side

Field research also gives writers the opportunity to value—and help readers appreciate—the struggles of professional field-work. "It's never a guaranteed experience," says Carson. "I've spent days driving around with cave scientists and not seen many bats. Weather is always a variable. Then there's the meshing of schedules—often a deadline doesn't allow time."

Security concerns are also possible, if rare. "There are times when working in the field is dangerous," notes McCormick, especially in investigative work. "I've had interview subjects threaten to take my notes or videotapes. A reporter I worked with was even attacked."

Long-distance travel may bring problems. While research in distant fields is certainly easier than it was before air travel and quick long-distance communication, it is probably not as easy as it was a generation ago. Economic problems have reduced writers' travel budgets; terrorism concerns have reduced site availabilities. "When I wrote *Saving the Baghdad Zoo* (Greenwillow), visiting war-torn Baghdad wasn't an option," says Kelly Milner Halls, author of more than a dozen children's books and more than 750 nonfiction articles. "I had to depend on my co-writer, William Sumner, who had been in Iraq as the adventure unfolded. If I can't go to the mountain, I depend on someone who has gone."

If travel money is limited, says Bodach, "the next best thing is to interview someone who has conducted professional research." Nonetheless, writers for whom direct field research is not an option have to accept that there really is no ideal substitute.

Even having been to a location before may not be enough. "Tecate, Mexico, a small border town southeast of San Diego, figures prominently in *The Phoenix Agenda*," says Cates. "Since I haven't visited Tecate in years, I plan to revisit to make sure the lay of the land is current and realistic. I will eat in small restaurants, talk to taco vendors and the border patrol, perhaps tour the beer factory."

One partial solution to travel difficulties is Cobb's suggestion to "contact tourism offices in that part of the world. They can be very helpful in organizing your fieldwork. A major benefit of a contract or assignment is that you can get a lot free, particularly when it comes to travel." Careful planning and budgeting have helped many writers accomplish field research that looked impossible at first glance.

Perhaps an even better solution is to consider the field-researchable topics already close at hand, which has the advantage of a writer already being familiar with area-specific details. "There are wondrous things to discover close to home," says Halls. "I hope writers will expand their local reach, even as they hope for fiscal relief."

Setting Parameters

But even when a field is convenient, and even when everything goes smoothly, research is not always simple. "Field

research can be a complex thing to master," says author Maude Stephany, who has published research-heavy articles in children's and parenting magazines. "It takes time, trial, and error to really get it right. The biggest disadvantage, aside from how much time it takes, is you keep finding new things you feel you must explore. That can keep you from writing."

Kyi agrees: "You can spend your time gazing through microscopes, hiking through parks, and chatting with experts instead of actually writing."

Advance planning can help curtail temptations to wander. "When I pitch a project," says Burns, "I have a good idea of the story and how I can tell it most effectively."

It is best to plan "in relation to the project you're doing," says Stephany. "You probably don't want to spend a whole day on field research if you're getting paid only $50. Make this topic you've spent so much time and energy researching serve as more than a one-trick pony." Research pays off long-term when writers save their notes for future projects.

When brand-new to a topic, "do as much background research as you can" before starting the field part, says Efaw. "Gain a firm grasp of what questions really need answering. You may also stumble across the name of an expert to target for answers. Shoot for the moon! The expert may be the top forensic psychiatrist in the field, but you may end up being pleasantly surprised by the cooperation you receive—that happened to me while I was researching *After*."

Most authors do find locating field research opportunities fairly easy; indeed, first steps for many projects begin with casual encounters. "During a recent trip to a live butterfly exhibit," says Burns, "I came upon a mating pair of Transandean cattleheart butterflies—surprising because breeding is not typically allowed in these exhibits. I was curious enough to ask the docent, who introduced me to the curator. After a long conversation and an impromptu behind-the-scenes tour, I am now working on a book about butterfly farming."

"When I visit a new place," says Stephany, "I take in as much as possible. Almost any experience can be applied to research for present or future works."

When writers are actively seeking opportunities, suggests Carson, "conservation groups, parks, or local universities" are good places to look. There are "experts and likely field research opportunities at any major museum," says McCormick. "Writers sometimes have to think outside the box, but opportunities are there for those who keep digging and asking questions."

It isn't just experts that field researchers can learn from, either; the ordinary-people perspective is invaluable to much writing. McCormick continues: "If you're writing a story about a famous Civil War battle, do locals ever talk about seeing ghosts around that battlefield? Ask them."

It is not surprising that lay people and researchers alike are willing to share information. Like everyone else, they are passionate about their key interests and eager to see that passion spread. "Scientists like to talk to me," says Cobb, "because I am genuinely interested in their work."

"An author can't be afraid to cold call!" Efaw reminds writers. "Even if you don't get the right person the first time, you'll find that people are generally glad to point you in the right direction. It's important to be persistent and risk feeling like a fool. You have to operate outside your comfort zone; almost always, you'll be glad that you did."

On the Scene

Sensible writers, however, plan ahead to minimize discomfort during actual field experiences. "On my first dinosaur dig,"

Field Research, Human Subjects

"When I conceived the concept for *Authors Kids Love* (Enslow)," says series author Michelle Parker-Rock, "I decided to base each book on a live interview and offer my readers a unique personal connection. I arranged to meet face-to-face with each subject in his or her home or place of work. The meetings lasted anywhere from five hours to three days; each was a different experience.

"At my own expense, I flew to California, Missouri, New York, Washington DC, Massachusetts, and Ontario. I stayed in my subjects' homes or in nearby hotels. For the interviews, I used a Panasonic desktop cassette transcriber/recorder. An open-ended questioning framework allowed the subjects to speak freely and openly, and me to be spontaneous and responsive.

"The authors gave me snapshots of themselves and their families at various ages and in various places, and they also allowed me to photograph them in their own surroundings. Later, I transcribed the recordings, organized the anecdotes and quotes, and sorted through the photos. Follow-up questions and manuscript reviews were conducted via snail mail, e-mail, and phone."

Authors featured in the series include Alma Flor Ada, Joseph Bruchac, Bruce Coville, Christopher Paul Curtis, Sid Fleischman, Jack Gantos, Bruce Hale, Patricia and Fredrick McKissack, and Linda Sue Park.

says Halls, "I only brought one pair of socks. I didn't realize we'd have to hike through a knee-deep stream. I never forget now to ask if I'll need backup supplies."

Writers need their own professional supplies as well. "Always carry business cards," says Burns. "Invest in a nice recorder, preferably digital, and keep spare batteries with you. But keep in mind that background noise, such as airplanes flying overhead, will wreck your recording."

"Tape recorders are important," says Halls, "but they can, and often do, fail. So take lots and lots of notes on good old-fashioned paper."

"I always carry a pencil," says McCormick. "As a young reporter, I was covering a holiday tree-lighting ceremony in Colorado, and the ink in my ballpoint pen froze. The photographer I was working with handed me his pencil and said: 'I've never had the lead in a pencil freeze.'"

McCormick notes that preparation also includes a mental aspect: "I review my notes before I go, to be sure I know the questions I want to cover. I also make sure I have all the contact information for my sources."

Once in the field, good notes don't stop with just the facts. Halls advises, "Besides your expert's comments and physical procedures, note the weather, regional smells, the look of the landscape, and how the sensory feedback makes you feel. Don't assume you'll remember accurately."

"It's crucial to transcribe as soon as you get home," recommends Burns. "Many little details can be added while the experience is fresh. Then contact your hosts to thank them and ask any follow-up questions. When your article or book comes out, send a copy to every researcher who helped you. Remember: You are a professional. Act accordingly."

Being a professional in science-related fields sometimes means looking eccentric. "Be prepared to look like a lunatic," says Stephany. "I get my share of crazy looks when talking into my recorder."

Good writers do not let this bother them; readers appreciate their genius. What readers appreciate most is a book or story that feels real, personal, alive. Field research, as Cobb puts it, "brings writing to life!"

ideas &
research

An Idea Miscellany

Compiled by Marni McNiff

Spark your imagination, and your writing, with one or more of the many facts that follow. Some are based on anniversaries that take place in 2010; some are recent news; some are fascinating; some are strange. Taken together, they represent a great breadth of possible ideas. Select an idea that appeals to you and brainstorm, research, and create.

The ideas here are divided into the following categories:

➤ 2010 Anniversaries
➤ Animals
➤ Arts and Literature
➤ Cultures and Traditions
➤ Family Life
➤ Food
➤ Fun Facts
➤ Geography
➤ Health

➤ History
➤ Holidays
➤ Music
➤ Popular Culture
➤ Religion
➤ Science and Technology
➤ Sports

2010 Anniversaries

➤ 400 years ago, on January 7, 1610, Galileo Galilei discovered four of Jupiter's moons using a homemade telescope.

➤ 350 years ago, Italian Baroque composer Alessandro Scarlatti was born. Among his famous operas are *Pirro e Demetrio, Gli Equivoci Nel Sembiante,* and *Il Pompeo.*

➤ 350 years ago, composers Giovanni Battista Pergolesi and Thomas Augustine Arne were born.

➤ 300 years ago, Samuel Pepys began his diary of London life during the 1660s. He described living through the Great Plague and the Great Fire.

➤ 200 years ago, Mexico's War of Independence (the struggle to gain independence from Spain) began. The Mexican Revolution (against the sitting government and the beginning of a civil war) began 100 years ago, in 1910.

➤ 200 years ago, composer Frédéric Chopin was born. His famous classical works include *Revolutionary Étude* and *Minute Waltz.* His compositions were primarily written for the piano as a solo instrument.

➤ 200 years ago, composer Samuel Barber was born. Barber was an American composer of orchestral, opera, choral, and piano music.

➤ 175 years ago, the first assassination attempt on a U.S.

president occurred. Unemployed house painter Richard Lawrence attempted to shoot President Andrew Jackson as he left a Congressional funeral. Lawrence's gun misfired. Jackson is said to have clubbed Lawrence with his walking cane until bystanders jumped in and restrained him.

➤ 150 years ago, Bohemian-born John Neumann, the first American bishop to be canonized, died. He moved from Bohemia (the modern Czech Republic) to be ordained in the U.S. and became one of the founders of the Catholic education system in America.

➤ 150 years ago, Ukrainian short story writer Anton Chekhov was born. His famous short stories include "Neighbors," "Ward Number Six," and "The Murder."

➤ 150 years ago, the first president of the Republic of Ireland, Douglas Hyde, was born. He served as president from 1938 to 1945 and was also the founder of the Gaelic League, one of Ireland's cultural organizations.

➤ 125 years ago, the American Telephone and Telegraph Company (AT&T) was founded.

➤ 125 years ago, an appendix was successfully removed for the first time by an Iowan doctor named William West Grant. Since then, improvements on the operation have included the appendix being removed both vaginally and orally.

➤ 125 years ago, Wilson A. Bentley was the first person to photograph a single snowflake.

➤ 125 years ago, Coney Island's roller coaster, Switchback Railway, was patented by LaMarcus Adna Thompson.

➤ 100 years ago, the Metropolitan Opera House in New York was the scene of the first live, public radio transmission of a performance anywhere. Performers included Enrico Caruso.

➤ 90 years ago, Isaac Asimov, an American author known for

his works of science fiction, was born. His 1941 short story, "Nightfall," was voted the best science fiction short story ever written by the Science Fiction Writers of America in 1968.

➢ 100 years ago, the youth organization Boy Scouts of America was founded by Chicago publisher William Boyce.

➢ 100 years ago, the Union of South Africa was created. It had two capitals, Cape Town and Pretoria.

➢ 100 years ago, revolution broke out in Portugal on October 5, ending Portugal's monarchy. King Manuel II was deposed and the Portuguese First Republic was established. King Manuel II went into exile until his death in 1932.

➢ 100 years ago, Japan annexed Korea with the Japan-Korea Annexation Treaty, which was signed on August 22, 1910. It became effective on August 29, which started the period of Japanese rule in Korea. Today, August 29 is viewed by Koreans as a national day of shame.

➢ 100 years ago, Angel Island became an immigration center for Asians coming to the United States through San Francisco.

➢ 100 years ago, Thomas Edison presented the kinetophone, adding sound to film.

➢ 100 years ago, Halley's Comet was first seen via photographs. The comet itself has been observed since 240 BC, but was not recognized as a periodic comet until the eighteenth century. It can be seen every 75 to 76 years and is named for Edmond Halley, the first astronomer to track its orbit.

➢ 90 years ago, the first black baseball league, the Negro National League, started.

➢ 90 years ago, Italian artist Amedeo Modigliani died at the age of 35.

➢ 80 years ago, Walt Disney's Mickey Mouse first appeared, in the *New York Mirror*.

➤ 80 years ago, Clarence Birdseye's first frozen foods went on sale in Massachusetts. Birdseye invented and commercialized a method of quick freezing foods in easy-to-use packages.

➤ 75 years ago, Bruno Hauptmann was convicted of kidnapping and killing Charles Lindbergh's baby son on February 13, 1935. Hauptmann received the death sentence for his crime and was executed by electrocution on April 3, 1936.

➤ 75 years ago, Amelia Earhart was the first woman to fly solo across the Pacific.

➤ 75 years ago, Woody Allen, Julie Andrews, Diahann Carroll, Christo, the Dalai Lama, Pete Hamill, Rafer Johnson, Sandy Koufax, Jerry Lee Lewis, Seiji Ozawa, Jacques Pépin, Gary Player, Elvis Presley, and Calvin Trillin were born.

➤ 75 years ago, the spectrophotometer, a device that measures light intensity and wavelength, was patented by MIT's Arthur C. Hardy.

➤ 75 years ago, Jockey shorts were first produced.

➤ 75 years ago, beer cans first appeared, from the Kreuger Brewing Company.

➤ 70 years ago, Russia bombed Finland in WWII.

➤ 70 years ago, Britain gave the People's Republic of China official recognition.

➤ 60 years ago, in Boston, MA, the Great Brinks Robbery took place. On January 17, 1950, 11 armed robbers stole $1,218,211.29 in cash and more than $1.5 million in checks and money orders from the Brinks Building. At the time, it was America's largest robbery ever. The 11 thieves were eventually arrested.

➤ 60 years ago, Eric Arthur Blair, who wrote under the name George Orwell, died.

➤ 60 years ago, the Federal Bureau of Investigation (FBI) published its first Ten Most Wanted Fugitives list.

Ideas 305

➤ 60 years ago, Jerusalem was named the capital of Israel by the nation's parliament, the Knesset.

➤ 60 years ago, India gained its independence from Britain, installing its first president, Rajendra Prasad, and establishing its constitution.

➤ 60 years ago, anti-apartheid riots erupted in Johannesburg.

➤ 60 years ago, the U.S. Atomic Energy Commission was instructed by President Harry S. Truman to continue developing the hydrogen bomb. On January 31, 1950, Truman said, "It is part of my responsibility as Commander in Chief to see to it that our country is able to defend itself against any possible aggressor. Accordingly, I have directed the Atomic Energy Commission to continue its work on all forms of weapons, including the so-called hydrogen or super-bomb."

➤ 50 years ago, Cameroon declared itself independent of Britain and France. The same year, Chad gained independence from France.

➤ 50 years ago, the Aswan Dam construction began in Egypt.

➤ 50 years ago, Michael Hutchence, of INXS, was born.

➤ 50 years ago, a Payola scandal surrounding disc jockey bribes occurred.

➤ 50 years ago, the ocean research boat called a bathyscaphe, the *Trieste*, dove to the deepest point of the ocean reached up until that time. It descended into the Mariana Trench, to about 36,800 feet.

➤ 40 years ago, the Boeing 747 Jumbo Jet made its first regularly scheduled flight ever, from New York to London.

➤ 35 years ago, Elizabeth Ann Seton was canonized, making her the first American-born saint.

➤ 30 years ago, Robert Mugabe was elected Zimbabwe's first

black prime minister.

➤ 30 years ago, President Jimmy Carter made the decision to boycott the 1980 Moscow Olympics to protest the Soviet invasion of Afghanistan.

➤ 20 years ago, Russia's first McDonald's fast food restaurant opened in Moscow.

➤ 15 years ago, Japan was devastated by the Kobe earthquake, in which more than 6,000 people died.

➤ 10 years ago, Charles Schulz's last original *Peanuts* comic strip was published.

➤ 10 years ago, a group of five British women became the first all-female expedition to reach both the North and South Pole.

Animals

➤ Since 2008, the giraffe population has been increasing again in the wilds of Niger.

➤ Flamingos get their pink feathers from the carotene they consume. The birds live 20 to 30 years.

➤ A hippopotamus can open its mouth wide enough to fit a 4-foot person. Hippos are the third largest land animal but despite their enormous size can outrun a human.

➤ A shark can detect one part blood in 100 million parts of water. The largest species of shark is the whale shark, which can grow to 50 feet.

➤ Emus cannot walk backwards. They are the second largest member of the flightless bird family called ratites. At 5 to 7 feet tall, they can run 40 mph with single strides over 9 feet.

➤ The peregrine falcon has been recorded at speeds greater than 200 mph; the cheetah at 70 mph; the pronghorn antelope at about 60 mph; and the lion at 50 mph.

➤ Polar bears are undetectable by infrared cameras, which

has given rise to myths and to a scientific debate about ultraviolet light, fiber optics, and polar bear hair, which is clear.

➤ A cockroach can live up to nine days without its head.

➤ Catfish are the only animal with an odd number of whiskers.

➤ Camels have three eyelids that protect their eyes from blowing sand.

➤ Blue and fin whales make the loudest animal sounds.

➤ The basking shark and whale shark are the two largest species of sharks in the world. They are also the least dangerous.

➤ Some sharks lay egg cases, while others give birth to live babies. Sharks have a very sharp sense of smell. Some can trail prey from a mile away, following the smell of microscopic proteins.

➤ Through hairs on their pincers, scorpions detect vibrations in the air and ground that help the creatures locate prey.

➤ A poison arrow frog contains enough poison to kill 2,200 people. Indigenous to rain forests, they are only about a half-inch in length and have bright, distinctive colors.

➤ Elephants are the only animal that cannot jump. In one day, an elephant can drink up to 80 gallons of water. Their trunks can hold about 18 quarts at a time.

➤ Starfish have eight eyes, one at the end of each arm.

➤ Moles dig so quickly they can finish 15 feet an hour, and look like they are swimming through the soil.

➤ Koala fingerprints are very similar to human fingerprints. Their fingers and toes have patterned ridges.

➤ The average lifespan of a hermit crab is 75 years.

➤ The praying mantis can turn its head and look at its own back, which no other insect can do. Its forelegs are like arms, with sharp hooks, and it can catch prey faster than a fly. The praying mantis is used around the world for pest control.

➤ The loris is an Asian primate, tailless or with a short tail, that is nocturnal and tree-dwelling. The slow loris has glands on its elbows that produce a poison, which the mother mixes with saliva. She licks it onto her children as protection from predators.

➤ The platypus and echidna (or spiny anteater) are the only animals classified as monotremes, mammals that lay eggs and suckle their young. Both animals are indigenous to Australia, New Guinea, and Tasmania.

➤ Armadillos sleep an average of 18.5 hours each day. Like opossums and sloths, they sleep away 80 percent of their lives.

➤ The porcupine is a nocturnal rodent. It cannot shoot its quills, but the quills do rise and come out easily enough to embed in predators. The porcupine is buoyant and swims well.

Arts and Literature

➤ In 1961, Matisse's *Le Bateau* hung upside down for two months in New York's Museum of Modern Art. None of the museum's 116,000 visitors noticed.

➤ The world's first history book, *The Great Universal History*, was published by Rashid-Eddin of Persia in 1311.

➤ *The Tale of Genji* is considered the first novel. It was written in 1007 by a Japanese noblewoman, Murasaki Shikibu.

➤ The oldest daily newspaper in the world is the *Wiener Zeitung* of Austria. It has been published every day since 1703.

➤ *Murder on the Orient Express* was the first novel to be sold through a vending machine at the Paris Metro Station.

➤ The 1939 novel *Gadsby*, by Ernest Vincent Wright, is a lipogram, a writing task in which one letter is never used. In all of *Gadsby*'s 50,110 words, there is not a single *e*. Wright died at 66, within days of the book's publication.

➢ *The Nutcracker* ballet opened in Russia in 1892. At the time, it was a flop. Composer Pyotr Ilyich Tchaikovsky, who died of cholera a year later, never saw its ultimate success.

➢ The Bolshoi Ballet began as a dance school for the Moscow Orphanage in 1773.

➢ Edgar Allan Poe's famous short story, "The Mystery of Marie Roget," was based on the real-life murder of a New York tobacconist shop girl named Mary Rogers, who was found floating in the Hudson River. Poe changed the city to Paris and the river to the Seine. He believed his story solved the actual murder case, which remained unresolved by New York police.

➢ Vincent Van Gogh only sold one painting during his lifetime. His most popular work, *The Starry Night,* was done while he was in an asylum in Saint-Rémy-de-Provence, France. Contrary to popular belief, Van Gogh did not cut off his ear, but rather a small portion of his ear lobe.

➢ *Tom Sawyer,* by Mark Twain, was the first novel to be written on a typewriter.

➢ Geoffrey Chaucer was the first poet to be buried in London's Westminster Abbey, beginning what is known as Poets' Corner. Today, 29 poets or authors are buried there, among them Ben Jonson, John Dryden, Robert Browning, Charles Dickens, Thomas Hardy, Samuel Johnson, Rudyard Kipling, and Alfred Tennyson. Also interred there are actors David Garrick and Laurence Olivier, and composer George Frideric Handel.

➢ A first edition of Geoffrey Chaucer's *Canterbury Tales* that was printed in the fifteenth century was put up for auction by Christie's in 1998. The book sold for £4.6 million ($73,581,815).

Cultures and Traditions

➢ In Thailand, it is improper to touch someone, even a small child, on the head. This stems from the belief that a person's soul resides in the head. It is also considered rude in Thailand for a person to point with their feet.

➤ In Paraguay, dueling is legal as long as both participants are registered blood donors.

➤ A Thai honeymoon lasts for three months and it is up to the bride and her family to cover the expenses.

➤ In ancient Greece, tossing an apple to a girl was a traditional way of proposing marriage.

➤ A Swedish superstition claims that a girl who collects seven or nine different flowers on a midsummer evening and places them under her pillow will dream of her future spouse.

➤ A Vietnamese legend states that all Vietnamese people are descended from Lac, a dragon lord, and Au Co, an immortal princess.

➤ It is considered unlucky in Turkey for a person to step on a piece of bread.

➤ It is a Czech tradition for a single woman to toss her shoes over her shoulder on Christmas Eve. If the shoe lands with the heel facing the door, she will be single for another year. If the toe points toward the door, she will be married. Families would also traditionally float walnut shell boats carrying lit candles at Christmas. If a boat made it across a bowl of water, the owner would have a long, prosperous life. A sinking boat meant bad luck.

➤ The word *honeymoon* may have originated in the ancient custom of giving a newly married couple the gift of mead for a month, to encourage happiness and fertility. Mead is a honey wine.

➤ *Hogueras*, or bonfires, are part of the celebration of the winter solstice in Spain. People jump over small bonfires to ward off illness.

➤ The tradition of using a baby to signify the New Year began in Greece around 600 BC. To honor the god of wine, Dionysus, a baby would be paraded around in a basket representing the god as the spirit of fertility.

➤ It is a Norwegian tradition for people to hide their brooms on Christmas Eve. It was thought that witches and evil spirits would come out on Christmas Eve looking for brooms to ride.

➤ In Atlantic Canada, a birthday child is ambushed and their nose is greased with butter for good luck. The belief behind the tradition is that a greased nose makes the child too slippery for bad luck to catch them. This tradition may be Scottish in origin.

➤ In past centuries, wedding bells were often heard in spring and summer—thus the popularity of June weddings—when it was warm enough to bathe.

➤ Mary Queen of Scots wore a white dress at her marriage to the King of France, Francois II. The color was atypical at the time, and in fact may have been associated with mourning. The marriage was a disaster and ended in his madness and divorce.

Three centuries later, Queen Victoria of England married in white, and the choice became virtually official. The white gown was meant to echo ancient traditions of Christianity: the white christening gown, the white dress of communion, and holy orders.

➤ In Victorian England, the wedding reception might include a ribbon pull. Various silver charms were tied to ribbons and tucked between layers of the wedding cake. Before the cake was cut, the bridesmaids each pulled a ribbon to discover a charm meant to be a sign about their future.

➤ Traditionally, Irish brides often wore a blue wedding dress, signifying trustworthiness and purity. It was also an Irish tradition for the bride and groom to walk down the street to the church together. Onlookers threw not only rice at the couple for good luck, but also larger items, like pots and pans.

➤ An old Scottish wedding custom was "creeling the bridegroom." The groom carried a large creel (fishing basket) filled with stones through the town until his bride came and kissed him.

➤ The ancient Incas believed that a couple was officially married only after they took off their sandals and handed them to each other.

Family Life

➤ The United States has the world's highest marriage rate, as well as the world's highest divorce rate.

➤ A study by an architecture firm found that students who took standardized tests in rooms with more natural light scored as much as 25 percent higher.

➤ National Family Literacy Day takes place on November 1. About 8,000 groups sponsor activities on this day.

➤ The number one Father's Day gift is a necktie, followed by tools and sporting goods.

➤ A 2008 survey found approximately 140,000 stay-at-home fathers, caring for 234,000 children under 15 years old.

➤ According to the Institute for Women's Policy Research, the best places for women to live and work—based on earnings, job numbers, and managerial or professional positions—are the District of Columbia, Maryland, and Massachusetts. The worst are Arkansas and Louisiana.

➤ Women buy 93 percent of all greeting cards. More than a billion Valentine's Day cards are sold each year in North America.

➤ The most common cause of poisoning in children at home is dish detergent.

➤ A dishwasher uses about 10 ¹/₂ gallons of water to clean a load. Hand washing the same dishes takes about 20.

➤ The typical American home has between 3 and 10 gallons of hazardous material at any given time.

➤ Toothpaste was first packaged in plastic, rather than in metal, during World War II.

➤ James Ayscough invented sunglasses. BluBlocker sunglasses were developed with lenses that were used in the NASA space program for American astronauts.

➤ While working for the Timberlake Wire and Novelty Company in Jackson, Michigan, Albert Parkhouse was apparently frustrated to find no coat hooks available. He took a piece of wire, bent it into a form to support his coat, and hung it up elsewhere. Thus was the wire clothes hanger born, in 1902.

➤ Pollution inside the average American home is ten times greater than outside.

➤ Jigsaw puzzles hit their height of popularity in the U.S. during the Great Depression, when they were sometimes given away as advertising premiums. New York's Einson-Freeman Company gave the first premium, with toothbrushes, in 1931. Puzzles were inexpensive family entertainment during difficult times.

➤ A woman named Patsy Sherman invented Scotchgard while working as a research chemist at 3M. She noticed that a spill from an experimental compound on her new white tennis shoes was resistant to water and solvents. She and a colleague, Sam Smith, made the intellectual leap and developed the compound into a polymer that repelled liquid. Scotchgard was introduced to the public in 1956 for use on fabrics and carpets.

➤ Another accidental invention was Teflon, by Roy Plunkett, a scientist at DuPont. In 1938, while Plunkett was working on the coolant Freon, a gas canister malfunctioned. He opened it to find a solid, white, and slippery powder. He eventually reproduced the substance, patented in 1941. Teflon was first used on machine parts, and in the early 1960s found its large market in nonstick cookware.

➤ The first wrench, that staple of home repairs, was invented in England in 1835 by Solymon Merrick—though the British call it a *spanner*. The *monkey* wrench was devised by Charles Moncky about 50 years later. Jack Johnson, the first African American heavyweight boxing champion, patented improvements to the household wrench in 1922.

➤ Noah and Joseph McVicker invented Play-Doh in 1956, based on an off-white wallpaper cleaner they had developed for the family soap company. They later added colors, and formed a new company to sell the nontoxic compound for play.

Food

➤ Thomas Jefferson smuggled a strain of rice from Italy, where it was illegal to take rice seeds out of the country. Jefferson also was responsible for introducing brussels sprouts, broccoli, cauliflower, and eggplant to America.

➤ The most chocolate sold in any single location in the world is at Brussels National Airport. Belgium annually produces 220,000 tons—which amounts to 22 kilograms of chocolate consumed by each Belgian each year, or 61 grams a day.

➤ Cheese can be made from the milk of 24 different kinds of mammals.

➤ There are more than 450 types of cheese in the world and more than 250 of them originated in France.

➤ Grapes are the world's largest fruit crop, at an annual 66 million tons harvested. Oranges are second, at 63 million tons.

➤ Ancient Egyptians used thyme in the mummification

process. Thyme was also placed in coffins to ensure passage into the next world.

➤ Tootsie Rolls were the first wrapped candy in America.

➤ Kopi Luwak, the most expensive coffee in the world, comes from the feces of a civet. The cat-sized mammal feeds on ripe coffee berries and excretes the partially digested beans.

➤ Coconut water can be used intravenously in emergency situations to rehydrate a patient, because it is sterile, has an ideal pH level, and is chemically similar to blood plasma.

➤ The first soup for which evidence has been found dates back to 6000 BC and was made with hippopotamus bones.

➤ The kiwi fruit first came from South China and was called the Chinese gooseberry. Although not native to New Zealand, it was cultivated there and became an important export. With marketing in mind, New Zealanders in the 1950s renamed the fruit the kiwi after the flightless bird that is the country's symbol.

➤ Americans consume 75 to 100 acres of pizza each day, which is roughly 350 slices a second, and 40 slices a year per person. Anchovies are the least popular topping, and pepperoni the most, included in 36 percent of all pizza orders.

➤ Peaches, the third most popular fruit grown in America, are part of the rose family.

➤ In the early 1960s, McDonald's introduced the Hula Burger in an effort to give Catholics, who abstained from eating meat on Fridays, another choice on the menu. The burger was actually grilled pineapple and cheese on a bun. The Hula Burger failed, as did the McPizza, Arch Deluxe, and the McLean Deluxe, which contained a seaweed extract.

➤ According to the National Coffee Association, 35 percent of coffee drinkers take it black.

➤ Fortune cookies were invented in the U.S. Some say they

were first made in 1918 by David Jung, but that claim is disputed by others.

➤ Americans purchase more than 20 million pounds of candy corn each Halloween season.

➤ Honey is the only known food that does not spoil.

Fun Facts

➤ *Uncopyrightable* is the only English word with 15 letters that does not repeat a letter.

➤ *Queue* is the only English word that is pronounced the same way with and without the last four letters.

➤ *Set* has more meanings than any other English word.

➤ The only English words that cannot be rhymed are *orange, month, silver,* and *purple*.

➤ It was long believed that no piece of paper could be folded in half more than 8 times, but in 2001-2002 a high school junior named Britney Gallivan developed a mathematical formula for extra credit in math, and folded a 4,000-foot piece of toilet paper in half 12 times.

➤ The typical pencil can draw a line 35 miles long, or write about 50,000 English words.

➤ Wang is the most common surname in China, shared by more than 93 million people. Other countries' most common surnames are: France, Martin; Germany, Müller (which means *miller*); Greece, Papadopoulos (*priest's son*); Ireland, Murphy; Israel, Cohen (*priest*); Italy, Rossi (*ruddy*); Japan, Sato; Mexico, Hernandez; Spain, Garcia; Sweden, Johansson; U.K. and U.S., Smith.

➤ A ten gallon hat holds about six pints.

➤ The only letter that is not on the periodic table is *J*.

Geography

➤ Ninety percent of the world's ice covers Antarctica. Nonetheless, the continent is the driest place on the planet, with an average precipitation of about two inches a year and an absolute humidity lower than that of the Gobi Desert.

➤ Canada is home to more lakes than any other country.

➤ Istanbul, Turkey, is the only city in the world located on two continents.

➤ The Republic of Nauru is an eight-square-mile island whose economy was once based on phosphates derived from guano, now depleted. It has no official capital. Nauru is a member of the British Commonwealth.

➤ Siberia contains more than 25 percent of the world's forests. Covering about 75 percent of modern Russia, the region has more natural resources than anywhere else. Oil and gas from Siberia make up about 40 percent of Russia's revenues.

➤ Russia covers one-seventh of the globe. It neighbors more countries than any other nation and is bordered by 22 seas.

➤ Liechtenstein and Uzbekistan are the only two countries in the world that are doubly landlocked—that is, surrounded by other landlocked countries. To get to any coastline, two borders must be crossed.

➤ Bolivia has been landlocked since 1879's War of the Pacific, when it lost its coastal region, Litoral, to Chile. Bolivia still has access to the Atlantic via the Paraguay River.

➤ Alaska makes up more than half of the U.S. coastline.

➤ Japan is an archipelago nation comprised of more than 3,000 islands. The four major islands are Hokkaido, Honshu, Shikoku, and Kyushu.

➤ Niagara Falls is the second largest waterfall on Earth, after Zimbabwe's Victoria Falls. About 150,000 gallons of water pass over Niagara each second. Sixty-three-year-old Annie Edson Taylor was the first person to go over the falls in a barrel and survive.

➤ Angel Falls in Venezuela is the tallest waterfall on the planet, at 3,212 feet.

➤ The Dead Sea in Israel is the lowest point on Earth at 1,315 feet below sea level.

➤ The Dune du Pilat in France is the tallest sand dune in Europe, measuring 384 feet high, 1,640 feet wide, and almost two miles long.

➤ The Kalahari Desert covers two-thirds of Botswana. Its Okavango Delta measures 2,000 square miles part of the year, and up to 4,600 square miles during the annual floods. It is the largest inland delta in the world.

➤ Bahrain comprises 33 islands in the Arabian Gulf, between the east coast of Saudi Arabia and the Qatar Peninsula. It has one of the fastest-growing economies in the Arab world.

➤ The largest cave in the world is the Sarawak Chamber in Malaysia. It measures 2,300 feet deep, 980 feet wide, and 230 feet high.

➤ The only state in the U.S. that has never had an earthquake is North Dakota.

➤ The largest shopping mall in Europe is the Nordstan, located in Gothenburg, Sweden.

➤ The great pyramids of Egypt have shifted 3 miles south due to the shift in the Earth's surface over the last 4,500 years.

Health

➤ The number of bones in the human body is 350 at birth, and 206 in adulthood. Bone plates fuse as we age: the femur somewhere between ages 18 and 20; the tibia, 15 to 18; the

humerus, 16 to 20; and the radius, 18 to 20.

➤ Each person sheds a pound and a half of skin every year, or about 105 pounds by age 70. On every square inch of our skin are about 32 million bacteria.

➤ Every three or four days, our stomachs produce a new lining to deal with the acids that digest our foods.

➤ The human tongue has a unique print.

➤ Humans recognize about 50,000 scents through about 5 million olfactory receptors. Dog noses are up to 1,000 times more sensitive, with 220 million receptors. The average adult is able to process approximately 10,000 different smells; each odor has the potential to recall a certain memory.

➤ The body pumps 2,000 gallons of blood 60,000 miles every day. The average adult's heart beats about 70 times a minute. The heart rate of infants is slightly higher at 120 beats a minute.

➤ Babies are born without knee caps. The knee caps are fully formed between the ages of two and four.

➤ Twenty-five percent of the bones in a human body are located in the feet.

➤ A fetus develops its fingerprints at 18 weeks.

➤ In an average lifetime, a person inhales approximately 44 pounds of dust.

➤ People can sneeze as hard and fast as 100 miles an hour.

➤ In the 1600s, thermometers were filled with brandy rather than mercury.

➤ The average red blood cell has a lifespan of 120 days. In just 3 drops of blood are more than 1 billion red blood cells.

➤ The average office desk has over 400 times more bacteria than a toilet.

➤ Humans produce about 10,000 gallons of saliva in a lifetime.

➤ Phosphenes are the stars and colors you see when you rub your eyes. They can be caused by mechanical, electrical, or magnetic stimulation of the retina.

➤ Israel has more in-vitro fertilizations per capita than any other nation in the world.

History

➤ Contrary to popular belief, Cleopatra's lineage was Macedonian, not Egyptian. Her first two marriages, which were arranged, were to her younger brothers, Ptolemy XIII and Ptolemy XIV. She may have married Julius Caesar, though he did not acknowledge the marriage. Cleopatra was later married to Mark Antony, although the union was not deemed legal in Rome.

➤ Alexander the Great, Julius Caesar, and Fyodor Dostoevsky all suffered from epilepsy.

➤ The Imperial Throne of Japan has been occupied by the same family for 1,300 years. The Yamato Dynasty has had 125 monarchs since Emperor Jimmu took the throne in 660 BC. The current emperor, Akihito, took the throne in 1989.

➤ According to some, all the Russian tsars were of Swedish Viking descent. The medieval Russian Rurik dynasty was believed to descend from the Scandinavian prince Rurik.

➤ Russian Tsar Peter the Great instituted a tax on men with beards.

➤ The world's longest war was the ill-named Hundred Years War between Britain and France, which actually lasted 116 years, from 1337 to 1453.

➤ King Edward the Confessor was the first English monarch to be declared a saint. He was the patron saint of England until 1348, when he was replaced by St. George.

➤ King Henry VI of England was the youngest European

monarch ever, ascending the throne at the age of nine months on August 31, 1422. Henry VI also became the king of France upon the death of his grandfather, Charles VI, on October 21.

➢ Benjamin Franklin was the only one of the United States' founding fathers to sign five of its most important documents: the Albany Plan of Union; the Declaration of Independence; the Treaty of Alliance, Amity, and Commerce, with France; the Treaty of Paris, with Great Britain; and the Constitution.

➢ The first U.S. state to abolish slavery was Vermont, in 1777. The last state to recognize the Emancipation Proclamation was Texas in June 1965.

➢ Great Britain was the first country to issue adhesive postage stamps, beginning with the Penny Black, in 1840.

➢ The first postcards were made and sent in the Austro-Hungarian empire in 1869 and 1870. The hobby of collecting postcards is *deltiology*.

➢ Edinburgh, Scotland, was the first city in the world to organize a municipal fire brigade, in 1824. Before that time, insurance companies in London formed brigades, but would only fight fires at buildings on which they held policies.

➢ Scotland's motto is *Nemo me impune lacessit*: No one provokes me with impunity.

➢ The U.S. motto, In God We Trust, was adopted in 1956.

➢ The first zoo in the U.S. was in Philadelphia, Pennsylvania. Benjamin Franklin developed the idea for the zoo, but it wasn't until 1859 that it was chartered by the state. The Civil War delayed the actual opening, which took place in July 1874.

➢ The first submarine to sink an enemy ship was the *H. L. Hunley* during the American Civil War. It was able to attach an explosive to the *U.S.S. Housatonic,* and detonate it, sending the *Housatonic* to the bottom of the ocean. The victory was short-lived as the *H. L. Hunley* also sank, killing the Confederate crew of eight.

➤ February 1865 is the only month on record not to have a full moon.

➤ The shortest war in history was between England and Zanzibar in 1896. It lasted only 38 minutes before Zanzibar surrendered.

➤ The first subway system in America was built in 1897 in Boston, Massachusetts.

➤ Hawaii is the only state that used to be a kingdom.

➤ Iceland is the world's oldest democracy.

➤ New Zealand was the first country to give women the vote, and South Australia, then a colony, was the second.

➤ During World War I, the language of the Choctaw Indians was used to encode messages.

➤ In 1922, Pan American airlines made its first around-the-world commercial flight.

➤ Harry S. Truman was the last person without a college degree to become president of the United States.

➤ San Francisco's cable cars are the only mobile National Monument.

➤ There have been more than 200 political coups and counter-coups in Bolivia.

➤ Sirimavo Bandaranaike was the first woman to become prime minister of a country. She served three terms governing Sri Lanka, from 1960 to 1965, 1970 to 1977, and 1994 to 2000. She was the widow of another prime minister, Solomon Bandaranaike.

Holidays

➤ At Easter, Bulgarians traditionally use onions, nettle,

apples, and walnuts to dye their eggs. The eggs are often treated with elaborate wax designs. The family's oldest woman dyes the first egg and uses it to bless the children.

➤ *Sobótka,* or St. John's Night, was celebrated in Poland and other eastern and central European countries in conjunction with the summer solstice, on June 24. The pagan festival became the Christian St. John's Night somewhere around the tenth century. The holiday incorporated rites of fire, water, and fertility.

➤ Candlemas is one of the four *crossquarters* of the year, occurring on February 2, between the first day of winter and the first day of spring. For Christians, it was the day on which the infant Jesus was presented in the temple and the day of the Virgin Mary's purification. It has been tied to Groundhog Day, possibly through a legend that hibernating animals would come from their sleep to acknowledge the purification.

➤ *Sagra dei Garagoi* is an Italian celebration dedicated to the garagoi, or sea snails, which are cooked in tomato sauce with lots of pepper.

➤ In Wales at the stroke of midnight on New Year's Eve, a back door is opened and then closed to signify the release of the old year and all of its bad luck.

➤ June 12 marks Russia's newest holiday, Independence Day, which commemorates the adoption of the Declaration of Sovereignty of the Russian Federation in 1991.

➤ Christmas in Russia is celebrated on January 7, in accordance with the Julian calendar still used by the Orthodox Churches. All of Europe used the Julian calendar until 1582, when Pope Gregory XIII corrected its errors related to leap days. The Gregorian calendar became standard in most Roman Catholic countries. Eastern Orthodox countries retained the Julian calendar, and while those nations eventually changed to the Gregorian (as late as 1927), the Orthodox churches did not.

➤ Berchtold's Day commemorates the founding of Switzerland's capital. According to legend, in the twelfth century Duke Berchtold V declared he would name the city after the first animal he killed. It was a bear and he named the capital Bern, a variation of the German plural for *bear* (Bär(e)n).

➤ Icelandic children are visited by 13 Santas with names ranging from Meat Hook to Sausage Snatcher to Pot Scraper. Each leaves presents for the children who have been good.

➤ Since 1944 the town of Buñol, Valencia, Spain, has celebrated *La Tomatina* on the last Wednesday in August. The week-long festival, where people gather and throw tomatoes, is called the world's largest food fight. The origins are unclear.

➤ Australia Day, January 26, commemorates the day when ships filled with convicts arrived in Sydney harbor. Britain used Australia as a penal colony, deporting convicts who committed minor crimes. The reasons for British colonization of Australia are intensely debated, but include a scheme to relieve the prisons in Britain; to get rid of *undesirables*, whether truly criminals or those seen as inferior, such as the Irish; to make up in part for the loss of the American colonies; and to develop a strategic sea position in the Eastern hemisphere.

➤ *Swieconka* is a Polish tradition in which the Easter meal is blessed in the church. A typical Easter table is filled with ham, kielbasa, cakes, and eggs, brought to the church on Holy Saturday and then set aside for Easter morning.

➤ *Diwali* is the five-day Hindu celebration of the new year. The most important time is the night before the new moon when small oil lamps, called *dipas*, are burned in honor of Lakshmi, the goddess of good fortune, wealth, and happiness.

➤ Saint Andrew's Day is celebrated in Scotland on November

30 to commemorate its patron saint. One of the twelve apostles and the younger brother of Simon Peter, Andrew is credited with spreading the gospel to Romania, Greece, and Russia. Legend has it that the Emperor Constantine had Andrew's bones moved to Constantinople, and that either a Greek or traveling Irish monk had a dream telling him to move the bones for safety. They ended up in Scotland.

➤ The Vietnamese holiday of Tet has been celebrated for more than 4,000 years. It occurs between January 21 and February 19 and lasts for three days. During Tet, Vietnamese people visit family and friends and reflect on their blessings. Children receive gifts of money in small red envelopes, called *li xi*.

Music

➤ The average piano has 230 strings; each string has 165 pounds of tension. Pianos come in many sizes, from the largest, the Concert Grand, to the smallest, the Spinet.

➤ The CD (compact disc) was widely released to the public for the first time in 1983. Going back in time, Columbia Records' Peter Carl Goldmark helped develop the vinyl LP, 33 1/3 rpm, in the 1920s. The first discs, or records, were developed by Emile Berliner. His United States Gramophone Company was selling 78 rpm records in the early 1890s. Thomas Edison had invented the phonograph in 1877, using tinfoil cylinders at first, and then wax.

➤ The largest drum ever made was 12 feet in diameter and weighed 600 pounds. It was used in the Boston World Peace Jubilee of 1872, which celebrated the end of the Franco-Prussian War. The festival lasted 18 days.

➤ Benedictine monk Guido Aretinus is regarded as the inventor of modern musical notation. His form of staff notation replaced neumatic notation. He authored *Micrologus,* the second most widely distributed treatise on music in the Middle Ages.

➤ Mozart's *Requiem*, unfinished at the time of his death, was completed by his student Franz Süssmayr.

➤ The most prolific classical composer was Georg Philipp Telemann, a contemporary of Johann Sebastian Bach, who was also prolific. It is estimated that Telemann wrote about 3,000 works, though only about 800 are still in existence. We have about 1,127 of Bach's compositions.

➤ Johannes Brahms did not compose his first symphony until age 43. He composed four symphonies between 1876 and 1885.

➤ The longest piano piece ever written is "Vexations," by Erik Satie. It runs 18 hours and 40 minutes and consists of a 180-note composition repeated 840 times.

➤ "When Irish Eyes Are Smiling" was written by German-born George Graff, who never even visited Ireland.

➤ Harry Belafonte's 1956 *Calypso* was the first album to sell one million copies.

➤ Diana Ross performed on at least one hit single every year between 1964 and 1996.

➤ The American Film Institute lists the theme to *Star Wars*, by John Williams, as the most memorable film score of all time.

➤ In 1955, Neil Sedaka was one of the founding members of the Linc-Tones, at Abraham Lincoln High School in Brooklyn, New York. Two years later, Sedaka left, but the group changed its name to the Tokens, and had a major hit in 1961 with "The Lion Sleeps Tonight."

➤ In 1987, Aretha Franklin was the first woman to be inducted into the Rock and Roll Hall of Fame.

➤ Jimi Hendrix, Kurt Cobain, Janis Joplin, and Jim Morrison all died at the age of 27.

➤ Michael Jackson's video for "Billie Jean" was the first video by a black artist played on MTV.

➤ The only father and son both inducted into the Country Music Hall of Fame are Fred and Wesley Rose.

➤ Roy Rogers is the only person inducted twice into the Country Music Hall of Fame; the first time was as a member of the Sons of the Pioneers and the second was as a solo artist.

➤ "Video Killed the Radio Star," by the Buggles, was the first video to be played on MTV, on August 1, 1981, and also the millionth video to appear on the channel, on February 27, 2000.

➤ Paul McCartney's company owns the rights to Buddy Holly's songs.

➤ Hip-hop music and culture originated in the Bronx, New York, in the 1970s. Urban, black, Latino, and Caribbean influences came together for the music and style.

➤ The origins of hip-hop are strongly associated with graffiti, especially the graffiti art of Lee Quinones and Michael Tracy (TRACY 168). A 1980 article by Richard Goldstein in *New York Magazine* was the first high-profile piece to link graffiti and rap music and view them as a cultural phenomenon.

➤ *Rap*, as in rap music, comes from the 1960s slang for having a conversation. The music, a part of hip-hop, derived in part from Jamaican disc jockeys in New York who would talk over the music they were playing.

Popular Culture

➤ Warner Communications has owned the rights to "Happy Birthday" since 1998.

➤ Pamela Anderson's first claim to fame is that she was Canada's *Centennial Baby*: the first baby born on the centennial anniversary of Canadian independence.

➤ Speak & Spell, made by Texas Instruments, was the first talking educational device that sold commercially, in 1978. It used digital speech synthesis by which computerized circuits replicate a human voice that *speaks* words to children, who learn spelling and vocabulary.

➤ Only a third of the episodes of *Gilligan's Island* were devoted to the castaways getting off the island.

➤ The theme music for *Star Trek* has lyrics. The music was written by Alexander Courage, without words. *Star Trek* creator Gene Roddenberry later wrote lyrics (never used, or seemingly meant to be), claimed co-creator status, and took half the royalties.

➤ Grossing $69.6 million opening weekend, the movie *Twilight* had the biggest opening ever for a female director. Catherine Hardwick directed the famous film, but opted out of directing its sequel, *New Moon*. Chris Weitz directed *New Moon*, which made $140.7 million opening weekend.

➤ Each day, more money is printed by Parker Brothers for its Monopoly games than is printed by the U.S. Treasury.

➤ Walt Disney's Tinkerbell character was created using Marilyn Monroe's body for a model.

➤ Chocolate syrup was used for the infamous shower scene in Alfred Hitchcock's movie, *Psycho*.

➤ Patents are not permitted on U.S. gambling machines.

➤ Chewing gum may not be sold in Singapore for reasons of environmental cleanliness.

➤ The pitcher's name in the famous "Who's on First" routine of Abbott and Costello is Tomorrow.

➤ The Road Runner was caught only once by Wile E. Coyote.

➤ Estimates of how many advertisements (in many forms) a typical American is exposed to every day range as high as 3,000.

➤ In 2001, a movement began in Australia, New Zealand, and Britain to classify Jedi, based on the *Star Wars* films, as an official religion. Largely joke, partly political statement, the movement

was widespread enough for the 2001 census in England and Wales to count 390,127 Jedi.

Religion

➤ *Mudderschprooch* is the language spoken by the Amish. It is a German dialect.

➤ Christianity is the world's largest religion when all of the denominations, Catholic, Protestant, and Orthodox, are combined, with more than 2.1 billion members. Islam is the next largest, with 1.5 billion people. But Muslims outnumbered Catholics in 2008, according to the Vatican, and became the single largest religious denomination.

➤ *Islam* means *peace through submission to God*. A Muslim is literally one who submits to God's will. Its five pillars are confessions of faith; daily prayer; charity; pilgrimage to Mecca; and fasting during Ramadan. The Qur'an (Koran) reveals God's 99 names, according to Muslim belief, which help human understanding. They include the All-Merciful, the All-Knower, the Protector, the Provider, the Helper, the Near, the One, and Source of Peace.

➤ Buddhism, founded by Siddhartha Gautama in northern India in the sixth century BC, is the world's fourth largest religion. It has two sects: Theravada and Mahayana. Its eightfold path consists of right beliefs, right aspirations, right speech, right conduct, right livelihood, right effort, right mindfulness, and right meditational attainment.

➤ 80 percent of India follows Hinduism.

➤ The largest religious building ever built is Angkor Wat in Cambodia. It was built between AD 1113 and 1150 and spans 402 acres. Originally consecrated to the Hindu God Vishnu, it was converted to a Buddhist temple in the thirteenth century.

➤ Scientology holds religious status in the United States and

Australia only. Germany has taken steps to ban Scientology.

➤ The first temple of the Church of Jesus Christ of Latter-day Saints (LDS, or Mormonism) built outside the U.S. was in Cardston, Alberta. The second was in 1952 in Bern, Switzerland, which was also the first non-English-speaking temple. Most temples have a statue of the angel Moroni, who visited the religion's founder, Joseph Smith. Moroni had been a prophet and a warrior.

➤ The highest proportion of female ministers in the world is in Belgium.

➤ The Czech Republic has one of the least religious populations in Europe, with only 19 percent of respondents polled in 2005 saying they believe in God.

➤ The traditional names of the two robbers crucified next to Jesus Christ were named Dismas and Gestas.

➤ Saint Médard is the patron saint against bad weather.

➤ Saint Isidore of Seville is the patron saint of the Internet. The early seventh-century scholar was renowned for his classification of a wide range of knowledge, including histories and an encyclopedia called the *Etymologiae*.

➤ The Christian evangelical sect, Jehovah's Witnesses, was founded in 1879 by Charles Taze Russell. Russell was an Adventist who believed that the Second Coming was to occur in 1914. He also taught that there is no hellfire or trinity. The religion stresses moral, clean living, and the Bible, and does not use the cross, or celebrate holidays such as Christmas or birthdays.

➤ The Russian Orthodox Church is the official religion of Russia. Although Russia is famous for its elaborate and ornate churches including St. Basil's Cathedral, the role of religion decreased significantly during the years of the Soviet Union.

➤ Cao Dai or Caodaism is a Vietnamese religious movement that began in 1926. It combines nationalism with elements of

Confucianism, Taoism, and Buddhism. Is holy figures include adherents' ancestors, as well as Pericles, Julius Caesar, Joan of Arc, Victor Hugo, Jesus Christ, Muhammed, and Sun Yat-Sen, all admired by founder Ngo Van Chieu. Karma and rebirth are the primary elements of belief about the afterlife.

➤ Ásatrú is a modern form of an ancient Germanic religion, and is taken from Old Norse words to mean *faith in the gods*. Sveinbjörn Beinteinsson succeeded in having the religion officially recognized in Iceland, Denmark, and Norway in the 1970s. The tenets are based on myths found in the Eddas, two epic poems from the twelfth and thirteenth centuries.

Science and Technology

➤ The newly discovered Anglo-Saxon hoard in Staffordshire, England, contained more than 1,500 items in gold and silver. Revealed to the public in September 2009, the hoard dates to about AD 700 and was probably booty hidden during a period of ongoing warfare.

➤ In September 2009, archaeologists discovered the remains of a couple from ancient Troy. The man and woman died around 1,200 BC. Experts are using radiocarbon dating to determine if, in fact, the two died during the Trojan War.

➤ In October 2009, Lucy was displaced from her long-held position as the oldest recovered fossil of a human ancestor. Lucy lived about 3.2 million years ago. The newly found skeleton is a female named Ardi (for *Ardipithecus ramidus*). Ardi was discovered in Ethiopia, and lived about a million years earlier than Lucy. The discovery indicates strongly the theory that our evolutionary ancestors are not related to chimpanzees, but much older apes.

➤ An osteologist studies bones, and an osteoarchaeologist excavates and analyzes historical skeletal human remains. Scientists can determine the sex, age, diet, general health, and more about an individual, based on bone fragments.

➢ Mehrgarh is a Neolithic site in Baluchistan, Pakistan, occupied from 7000 to 2500 BC. It is one of the earliest sites with evidence of farming and herding in South Asia. It was discovered in 1974 by French archaeologists led by Jean-Francois Jarrige.

➢ Fabricated diamonds made in the laboratory are now almost identical to natural diamonds. Scientists began trying to synthesize the gem in the 1950s.

➢ The oldest decorated object in existence is from 77,000 years ago: a reddish brown, polished stone, with parallel lines encasing crosshatches and a single line. It was found on the east coast of Africa by Norwegian archaeologist Christopher Henshilwood.

➢ Scientists in Cambridge, England, are developing a process to desensitize children with peanut allergies. It uses peanut flour.

➢ Five complete fossils of octopuses, 95 million years old, were discovered in Lebanon. Since the octopus does not have a hard skeleton, the discovery is extremely rare.

➢ The Swedish botanist Carolus Linnaeus devised a biological method of classification in 1758 that is still used today. It organizes all organisms based on their structure. He created the definitions of genera, species, and binomial nomenclature, the system for naming organisms.

➢ DNA was discovered in 1869 by Swiss physician Friedrich Miescher.

➢ The discovery of the double-helix structure of DNA was made in 1953 by James Watson and Francis Crick. This discovery was an enormous breakthrough for various fields of science, and provided more proof for the theory of evolution.

➢ Human eyes remain the same size from birth, but the nose and ears never stop growing. Between the ages of 30 and 70 a

nose might grow half an inch, and ears a quarter of an inch.

➤ Venus is the only planet that rotates clockwise. It is also the hottest, with an estimated surface temperature of 864° F.

➤ Cold water weighs more than an equal amount of hot water, because the cold water is denser.

➤ A dry snow avalanche moves at a speed of 60 to 80 mph, but has been known to travel at up to 225 mph. Wet snow avalanches travel at about 20 mph.

➤ Loud noises do not cause avalanches, except in rare circumstances. Those that take lives have usually been caused by the weight of a person. Most avalanches are large slabs of snow that shatter. Less common loose snow falling down a mountain is called a *sluff*.

➤ Autumn leaves change color with the change of air temperature. Lower temperatures cause the chlorophyll inside the leaves to break down, revealing the pigments inside other than green, thus producing shades of yellow, orange, and red.

➤ The largest recorded meteorite was found in Hoba, Namibia, and weighed in at 60 tons. One or two meteors reach the surface of the Earth each day.

➤ Recycling one aluminum can saves enough energy to power a television for three hours. An aluminum can that is thrown away will still be a can 500 years from now.

➤ By recycling one ton of paper you save: 17 trees; 6,953 gallons of water; 463 gallons of oil; 587 pounds of air pollution; 3.06 cubic yards of landfill; and 4,077 kilowatt hours of energy.

➤ Oxygen is the most abundant element in the Earth's crust, water, and atmosphere. Twenty percent of the Earth's oxygen is produced by rain forests.

➤ Tungsten's melting point is 6170° F, the highest for a metal.

➤ The brightest star in the sky is Sirius. It is located about 51 trillion miles from Earth.

➤ In October 2009, the Spitzer Space Telescope revealed that Saturn has a larger ring around it, one never seen before. The material in the ring starts about 3.7 million miles from the planet and extends out another 7.4 million miles. Before this discovery, Saturn was known to have seven major rings.

➤ The Nova laser at Lawrence Livermore National Laboratory in California is the world's most powerful laser. It generates a pulse of energy equal to 100,000,000,000,000 watts of power for .000000001 second to a target as small as a grain of sand.

Sports

➤ Since the modern-day Olympics began in 1896, only Australia and Greece have participated every time. The youngest athlete ever to compete was ten-year-old Dimitrios Loundra in 1896. He won a bronze medal on the men's parallel bars. At age 72, Oscar Swahn was the oldest athlete to compete, although he did not win a medal. In earlier Olympic Games, he had won three gold medals, a silver, and two bronze medals.

➤ An ice hockey puck is often frozen before games to decrease bouncing and friction on the ice.

➤ Soccer is the world's most popular sport. It is played in more than 140 countries.

➤ Until 1859, an umpire in a baseball game sat in a padded chair behind home plate.

➤ In 1943, so many players were serving in World War II that the Pittsburgh Steelers and Philadelphia Eagles temporarily merged. Though officially called the Eagles (with no city name), the team was nicknamed the Steagles by fans.

➤ The National Hockey League's Stanley Cup was originally 7 1/2 inches high. The silver bowl listed the names of the winning

players, coaches, and managers. Today, the Stanley Cup measures 35.25 inches and weighs 34.5 pounds. The original bowl sits on top.

➢ Germany's Horst Preisler completed 949 marathons between 1974 and 2000.

➢ The fastest baseball pitch ever recorded was 100.9 miles an hour, by Nolan Ryan in 1974.

➢ Women's boxing will make its Olympic debut at the 2012 London Olympic Games. Female boxers will compete in three weight classes.

➢ Golf and rugby will be played at the 2016 Olympics.

➢ Table tennis, commonly referred to as Ping Pong, was banned in the Soviet Union from 1930 through 1950 because it was allegedly harmful to the eyes.

➢ Parker Brothers trademarked the name Ping Pong for the noise the ball makes when it hits the paddle and the table. The game has also been called Flim-Flan, Gossima, and Whiff Whaff.

➢ Janet Guthrie was the first woman to compete in the Indianapolis 500, in 1977, and was also Top Rookie at the Daytona 500.

➢ In 1983, the *Australia II* won the America's Cup yacht race, ending America's 132-year domination of the event.

➢ Baseballs are never used straight out of the box. They are mudded down by the umpires. Traditionally, the mud used is from New Jersey and is called Lena Blackburne Baseball Rubbing Mud. It takes off the shine but doesn't soften or blacken the ball, or smell. A baseball typically lasts eight days in professional play.

➢ About 23 percent of golfers are women.

➢ In October 2009, Nullarbor Links in Australia became the world's longest golf course. The 72-par 18 holes stretch 848 miles across the outback and can take a week to play.

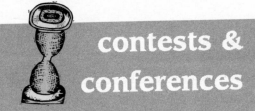

Attending a Writers' Conference? Pack These Tips

By Judy Bradbury

Writers are loners. No matter how social they may be in personality, the writing is ultimately done alone, in the mind and at the desk. In such a field, attending a professional conference and being in the company of others who *get* the ups and downs of the business is rewarding and affirming. It is an experience that refreshes, inspires, and renews the spirit. We writers spend so much time working on our own that the opportunity to sit in a room with like-minded professionals and absorb up-to-the-minute information, useful advice, and timely tips is like a shot of B-12 for an anemic.

Attending a conference also can be an intimidating experience. Depending on the size, length, or structure of the event, and the scope of our individual personalities, a conference can feel overwhelming. But we can overcome trepidations through preparation for the experience.

Enumerate Aims

Let's assume you have plunked down money to attend a conference, the agenda has arrived, and your travel arrangements are complete. It is time to prepare for the experience. Begin by making a checklist of what you hope to accomplish as a result of attending this particular conference. Be specific. Do you want to meet writers from your area in the hopes of forming or joining a critique group? Do you desire to hear a particular keynote speaker or attend a specific session or focused workshop?

Review the agenda carefully as soon as it becomes available. Read the biographies and visit the websites of featured speakers. If the presenters are authors, scout out their work. Read their blogs. Peruse current releases and award-winning titles published or represented by editors and agents on the faculty. Browse the Web pages of publishers and agents for details on submission guidelines, how the publisher or agent operates, their success stories, and what they are currently interested in reviewing. Your knowledge of featured speakers at the conference, and the books they have created, edited, or represented, is directly proportionate to what you will gain from the conference sessions. It is common for authors to use examples from their own novels to make a point, for instance, and the concept is far more likely to sink in if you understand the reference.

As you compile your list of objectives for attending the conference, allow for flexibility in your planned outcomes. Once you arrive on site, you may find that intriguing sessions have been added. Last-minute substitutions for speakers may be scheduled, or unforeseen opportunities may present themselves. I attended a national conference a few years ago at which I intended to sit in on a session about the current state of the market. When a Publisher and Editor in Chief suggested to me that I join them for breakfast, I weighed my options. (The eggs were delicious.)

Network

"With the current global financial slowdown affecting publishing as deeply as other parts of the economy, writers' conferences emerge as even more essential tools for the professional writer," observes children's and mystery author Cheryl Zach, who oversees more than 60 Regional Advisors for the Society of Children's Book Writers and Illustrators (SCBWI). "Publishing houses have been forced to let even longtime editors go and to cut staff at multiple levels, making it commonplace for remaining editors to wear multiple hats. These hard-working—and hard-pressed—editors still, however, must look for good books to publish and have less time than ever to find them. Writers' conferences are therefore better places than ever for authors, editors, and agents to connect."

Once you leave your hotel room and head for the elevator, smile. Chat with people—at the coffee urn, at lunch, at the conference bookstore, and in the inevitable restroom lines. "Don't be shy," says Claudia Harrington, Southern California Regional Advisor for SCBWI. "Remember that participants represent a broad spectrum of levels, and many are on yours, whether you're a first-timer or a veteran. As Lin Oliver, Executive Director of SCBWI, says, we are a tribe. That doesn't mean face paint! It means there's a spirit of camaraderie, of peers wanting to help each other be the best they can be. Introduce yourself to those around you. You'll most likely make some lifelong friends."

Briefly introduce yourself and your work, and then listen and learn from people you meet. If you are not good at retaining names or details, jot down particulars on conferees with whom you interact as soon as possible. Later, transfer notes onto the conference roster of attendees. When you run into that person again over the course of the conference (and you will be amazed at how many times you will), be sure to say hello by name. If the two of you really click, consider exchanging business cards. At one of my first professional writers' conferences I met a woman while waiting in line for Eve Bunting to sign our books. As we inched up to the autograph table, we became fast friends. Now, some 17 years later, although we live on opposite coasts, we keep in close contact throughout the year and look forward to meeting annually at that same conference.

Attend scheduled and impromptu events. Although many writers are introverted by nature, it is a good plan to be open to possibilities at conferences. Join in the fun. Is there a contest? A costume party? A yoga session? You never know who will be doing the downward-facing dog on the mat beside you! "Mingle with editors, agents, fellow writers, and illustrators," advises Harrington, "keeping in mind that they are people, not golden tickets."

Be Open and Listen Up

"Go with an open mind and absorb everything. Take it all in," Harrington suggests. "Conference schedules can be overwhelming at times, so write things down. You can go over your notes later. You'll be energized for weeks after the conference!"

If you attend a session that makes a positive impression on you, think about what made it so special. If you spot the presenter grabbing a cup of coffee or browsing the bookstore, approach her, introduce yourself, and thank her for the helpful information she imparted. Explain specifically—and succinctly—what you learned from her talk. Speakers appreciate sincere feedback, and they expect to be approached; it is understood that they are there for the benefit of attendees.

Do not, however, corner a speaker or interrupt a conversation she may be having with a colleague or another conferee. Use common sense and remember your manners. Be sensitive to a speaker's right to privacy. "Do not hand off manuscripts at any time," warns Harrington. "Editors and agents don't come with extra suitcases." Refrain from asking questions personal to your manuscript unless your conversation clearly moves in that direction. Use discretion and create positive impressions. "Make meetings memorable in the best possible sense," says Harrington. "If you make a connection and the editor or agent would like to see your work, great! Send it after the conference— following careful revision based on what you learned at the conference."

"The most important piece of advice I can offer is *listen*," says Amy Emm, SCBWI Regional Advisor for Western and Central New York. "This applies to lectures and critiques. Listen to craft talks given by authors who have been in your seat so you can find out how they did it and get inspired. Listen to editors' needs, and be honest with yourself when evaluating if your work would be a good match for their house. Once you get home, don't waste your time (or the editor's) by sending, for example, a middle-grade fiction manuscript when an editor specifically requested young adult fiction."

Critical Opportunities

Whether daylong events or full-week junkets, conferences often offer a coveted and valuable optional feature: a one-on-one critique with a professional. Typically, these sessions are arranged weeks in advance of the conference and come at an additional cost. "Sign up for a critique," encourages Emm. "Getting professional advice is critical to improving the quality of your work. Don't be disappointed if you are assigned to a published author instead of an editor. The point of a critique is to improve your work, not sell it right then and there."

Follow the guidelines, cautions Emm. "If you are supposed to send 20 pages, double-spaced, font size 12, do not send illustrations, a single-spaced document, or use font size 10. Following

directions is the first step to a professional presentation. It is insulting to editors to receive work beyond what they have been asked to evaluate, and it's also very telling: How can they expect you to work professionally in an editorial relationship if you can't follow a few simple directions?"

Kim Turrisi, Director of Special Projects for SCBWI, and the person who screens every manuscript submitted for critique at the organization's midwinter and summer conferences, adds, "Know the industry and know what you're doing. Work on your craft. Join a local or online critique group. Submit a manuscript for critique at a conference once you're ready." Noting that editors are hungry for "fresh voices and compelling stories," Turrisi says, "the first line of a YA or middle-grade novel is crucial for catching interest. Editors know in the first five pages whether a story has merit." The same holds true for adult writing, and for any genre or category of writing.

Emm offers advice for the face-to-face critique. "Do not defend your work. Do not explain it. Do take notes. Listen with an open heart and mind. Try not to get emotional. This is hard to do, but you'll get more out of the critique that way. Do not immediately think, 'Well, she just doesn't get it.' Banish such judgments until you've had time to evaluate the critique objectively."

Critiques can be a valuable step in the writing process. Turrisi has a collection of tales that prove the point. Kristin Venuti's journey to publication (see sidebar on page 344) is one. Another success story involves Jill Alexander's debut novel *Sweetheart of Prosper County*. "When Jill originally submitted her manuscript at an SCBWI conference, her fresh voice stood out. After a critique, she revised her story and it grew into a wonderful YA novel that blew me away," says Turrisi. "Alexander eventually landed a book and audio deal with Editor in Chief Liz Szabla at Feiwel & Friends, and the novel was selected as one of six books to watch at the BEA in June."

Time for loosely organized get-togethers is usually built into the conference schedule. Writers can drop in and participate in peer critiques. Consider taking advantage of these valuable (and free) feedback experiences. "If there are informal critique sessions, go. If you have a manuscript that is ready for a critique, do it," encourages Harrington. "Critiquers—whether they are publishing professionals or fellow writers—are there to help you get better. They want you to succeed."

Think Locally

Not every conference is national or large in scope. "Don't overlook regional conferences, which often are smaller than national events and offer more chances for personal interaction," advises Zach. "Often at these events, during a break or at lunch, there may be time to chat with a junior editor who is eager to add to his or her stable of writers. The SCBWI puts on a wide variety of conferences, from editor, writer, and illustrator days to writers' retreats, illustrators' showcases, and many other activities around the U.S. and throughout the world."

Whether it is a big gathering or a smaller, more intimate event, meet the organizers or advisors, "and other writers from your area. Find out what's going on locally so you can attend events. Volunteer. The more you do, the better you get at it, and the more fun you have. It's an un-vicious circle," Harrington suggests. "Be intent on the journey. Attend a conference to meet like-minded people, better your craft, and learn. Don't worry about the golden egg of being published. That will come. Raise your own bar. There are people there to help you do just that."

Pack up your smile, your polished manuscript, your checklist, and your sense of adventure. Happy travels!

Three's a Charm

"I feel like the poster child for SCBWI [the Society of Children's Book Writers and Illustrators]," says author Kristin Clark Venuti. "I can't stress enough the value in getting a manuscript critiqued at a conference." The first time Venuti submitted her work for evaluation at an SCBWI conference, she sent in the required 15 pages of a story for which she had written only 40 pages. "I wanted to see if I was headed in the right direction," she recalls. The editor encouraged her to finish the manuscript and send it to her. By the time Venuti's middle-grade manuscript was complete, the editor had moved to a different publishing house and her needs had changed. "So, I submitted my revised story at the conference the following year," says Venuti. This time, "it wasn't a meeting of the minds." Although she believes the agent who critiqued her manuscript pages didn't "get it," she credits him with asking "some very good questions," which she addressed in further revision.

Fast-forward to the next annual conference, where Venuti submitted pages from her beloved story again. The third time proved to be the charm. Agent "Tracey Adams read it, liked it, and offered to represent me. She sold the novel to Elizabeth Law at Egmont," and, Venuti is pleased to report, *Leaving the Bellweathers* was released in September 2009. "I credit the SCBWI for such a remarkable opportunity, and [manuscript critique coordinator] Kim Turrisi for her insight and super-helpful attitude."

Along her book's way to publication, Venuti says, "It always remained my story, my project, but the direction I received at those critiques made my story stronger. I worked hard and fabulous things happened. I know my experience is not 100 percent typical, but your chances are greatly enhanced if you take advantage of professional critiques offered at conferences. It's a great way for your work to get seen."

Conferences for Adult & Children's Writers

**American Society of Journalists and Authors
   Annual Writers Conference**
1501 Broadway, #302, New York, NY 10036
www.asja.org/wc/2010

   Held each spring since 1971, this conference offers concurrent morning and afternoon panels, which are ranked to help beginning to advanced writers choose appropriately. More than 100 editors, authors, agents, and publicists take part in this weekend event, which allows time for keynote speeches and networking. The 2010 theme is "Inspiration: Finding the Spark, Unlocking the Doors." *Date:* April. *Location:* New York, New York. *Cost:* $255–$385.

Anhinga Writers' Studio Summer Workshops
P.O. Box 357154, Gainesville, FL 32635
www.anhingawriters.org

   Participants in these three-day workshops choose an in-depth course in one of five genres: mainstream fiction, mystery, romance, poetry, or narrative nonfiction. Literary agents and editors are available for private meetings during the program; attendees may submit a work-in-progress for a one-on-one consultation. *Date:* July/August. *Location:* Gainesville, Florida. *Cost:* $395; one-day and half-day rates available.

Ann Arbor Book Festival Writer's Conference

500 South Main St., Ann Arbor, MI 48104

www.aabookfestival.org

Held all day Friday and a half-day on Saturday, this conference is an annual event that coincides with the Ann Arbor Book Festival. Sessions consist of lectures and individual meetings with visiting festival authors who also serve as faculty. Workshops are available in playwriting, poetry, mystery writing, creative nonfiction, and writing for children and young adults. *Date:* May. *Location:* Ann Arbor, Michigan. *Cost:* Friday sessions, $105; Saturday sessions, $30.

Annual Writers Conference at Penn

University of Pennsylvania, College of General Studies

3440 Market St., #100, Philadelphia, PA 19104

www.pennwritersconference.org

Established in 1995, this annual two-day event features more than 60 workshops and master classes, instructor book signings, a keynote address, and a reception. Among the workshops offered are autobiography/memoir, business and technical writing, journalism, children's fiction, science fiction, fantasy, and writing for teens. *Date:* October. *Location:* Philadelphia, Pennsylvania. *Cost:* $75 per workshop ($65 for past registrants); $205 per master class ($195 for past registrants). Registration fee, $25.

Antioch Writers' Workshop

P.O. Box 494, Yellow Springs, OH 45387

www.antiochwritersworkshop.com

This weeklong conference features morning lectures and afternoon intensives, with evenings reserved for readings, panel discussions, and workshops. Programs focus on fiction, nonfiction, screenwriting, playwriting, and poetry, as well as the business of publishing. *Date:* July. *Location:* Yellow Springs, Ohio. *Cost:* $610 ($550 for past registrants and local residents), plus $125 non-refundable registration fee. Manuscript critique, $70.

Appalachian Heritage Writers Symposium

Southwest Virginia Community College

P.O. Box SVCC, Richlands, VA 24641

http://appheritagewritersym.wordpress.com

Fiction, memoir, poetry, and children's writing workshops, as well as panel discussions, are offered during this two-day symposium. *Date:* June. *Location:* Richlands, Virginia. *Cost:* $50; includes continental breakfast and awards luncheon. College credits, optional.

Arizona State University Writers Conference

P.O. Box 875002, Tempe, AZ 85287

www.asu.edu/piper/conference

Classes, panels on publishing and the writing life, small group instruction, evening readings, and conversations with faculty are the main components of this four-day conference. It features workshops on fiction, nonfiction, playwriting, poetry, and children's fiction. *Date:* February. *Location:* Tempe, Arizona. *Cost:* $400. Early bird registration, $375. Small group instruction, $350.

Bay to Ocean Writer's Conference
2401 Beech St., Cambridge, MD 21613
www.baytoocean.com

The Eastern Shore Writers' Association sponsors this one-day conference of workshops, speeches, and panel discussions on topics pertaining to the craft of writing and the business of publishing. Presenters include authors, editors, publishers, journalists, freelance writers, and literary agents. *Date:* February. *Location:* Wye Mills, Maryland. *Cost:* $80; $55 for students.

Erma Bombeck Writers' Workshop
University of Dayton, 300 College Park, Dayton, OH 45469
www.humorwriters.org

"The workshop for humor writing, human interest writing, networking, and getting published," this event is held every other year. The next conference is scheduled for 2010. Past sessions covered such topics as developing and using humorous anecdotes, and humorous greeting cards. The faculty is made up of experienced, and entertaining, writers and publishing professionals. *Date:* April. *Location:* Dayton, Ohio. *Cost:* $350.

BYU Workshop on Writing for Young Readers
348 Harman Continuing Education Building, Brigham Young
   University, Provo, UT 84602
www.ce.byu.edu/cw/writing

Morning workshops are devoted to individual work, with afternoons reserved for conferences on marketing, publication, and the craft of writing fiction and nonfiction for children and teens. Readings, informal critique groups, and chat sessions with editors take place in the evenings during this five-day annual event. *Date:* June. *Location:* Provo, Utah. *Cost:* $450.

Canadian Authors Association CanWrite! Conference

www.canauthors.org/conference.html

"Applying Technology to Your Writing" is the theme of the 2010 CanWrite! Conference. Attendees will learn computer tips for making their writing life easier, and how to create PowerPoint presentations to enhance book launches. Other workshops will explore the world of e-books and explain electronic rights for writers. Fiction, nonfiction, poetry, public speaking, and writing for young adults are some of the other sessions planned. *Date:* June. *Location:* Victoria, British Columbia. *Cost:* $325 ($255–$285 early bird) for members; $365 ($295–$325 early bird) for nonmembers. One-day rates are also available.

Cape Cod Writers' Conference

Cape Cod Writers' Center

P.O. Box 408, Osterville, MA 02655

www.capecodwriterscenter.org

Over the course of five days, attendees take part in morning and afternoon courses and master classes on the craft of writing romance, mystery, poetry, screenwriting, journalism, memoir, and children's fiction, among others. Panels, faculty readings, and speeches are also scheduled during this annual conference. *Date:* August. *Location:* Craigville, Massachusetts. *Cost:* $165 per course; $150 for mentoring; $125 for manuscript evaluation; $125 for master class. Registration fee, $35 (waived for members).

Carolinas Writers Conference

South Piedmont Community College

P.O. Box 126, Polkton, NC 28135

http://ansoncountywritersclub.org/

About 250 to 400 people attend this annual event, which

focuses on the craft of writing and the promotion of reading. The program covers children's and young adult writing; fiction, including the genres of romance, science fiction, fantasy, horror, and mystery; screenwriting; poetry; marketing; and publishing. *Date:* April. *Location:* Polkton, North Carolina. *Cost:* $30.

Cat Writers Association Writers Conference
22841 Orchid Creek Lane, Lake Forest, CA 92630
www.catwriters.org

The business and technical aspects of a writing career are explored at this three-day annual conference, which also offers panels and lecture sessions on various fiction genres, nonfiction, and writing for children and young adults. Private appointments with editors from such magazines as *Cat Fancy* and *ASPCA Animal Watch* are available. *Date:* November. *Location:* Houston, Texas. *Cost:* $75 for members; $100 for nonmembers.

Celebration of Children's Literature
Chevy Chase Library, 8005 Connecticut Ave., Chevy Chase, MD 20815
www.childrensbookguild.org

Seven morning workshop sessions are held at this yearly convention, which begins with keynote speeches from editors and writers. Eight additional workshops are offered on children's and YA writing and marketing. *Date:* April. *Location:* Montgomery County, Maryland. *Cost:* $60 for Maryland residents; $84 for nonresidents. Cost includes continental breakfast and lunch.

Chautauqua Institution Conferences
P.O. Box 28, Chautauqua, NY 14722
www.ciweb.org/summerchautauqua

The Chautauqua Institution sponsors weekly workshops during the summer months. Topics include business and technical writing, playwriting, autobiography/memoir, journalism, poetry, romance, mystery, and humor writing, among others. A four-day Writer's Festival is held as well, which also features workshops along with panel discussions, readings, and lectures. *Date:* June, July, August. *Location:* Chautauqua, New York. *Cost:* $350 for Writer's Festival. Summer workshops, $95/week.

Colgate Writers' Conference

13 Oak Drive, Hamilton, NY 13346

www.cvwc.net

Veteran and novice writers alike are welcome at this annual weeklong conference. Mornings are devoted to craft talks and workshops, while afternoons are set aside for individual consultations with instructors. Panel discussions, readings, and informal conversations round out the program. *Date:* June. *Location:* Hamilton, New York. *Cost:* $995 for residential attendees; $750 for day students; $1,245 for novel tutorial students. Discounts available.

Duke University Adult Writers' Workshops

Box 90700, 201 Bishop's House, Durham, NC 27708

www.learnmore.duke.edu

Established in 1982, these five-day workshops are held every year. Workshops from the 2009 event included "Finishing Your Novel," "Creative Nonfiction and Personal Essay," and "Structure and Scene," among several others. *Date:* September/October. *Location:* Durham, North Carolina. *Cost:* $695 single; $595 double.

East Texas Christian Writers Conference

East Texas Baptist University

 Contests 351

1209 North Grove St., Marshall, TX 75670

www.etbu.edu/news/cwc/workshops.htm

In addition to one-hour writing workshops scheduled for Saturday, this conference also holds pre-conference workshops on Friday. Workshops offer intense, personal, and practical application for those willing to get directly involved in the writing process. They include "Writing Boot Camp: The Basics for a Beginner," "Putting Personality into Your Writing," and "Building a Writing Investment: Keeping a Journal." *Date:* April. *Location:* Marshall, Texas. *Cost:* Individual, $80; student, $60. Early registration (before March 19), $75. Fee covers attendance at five writing workshops, Friday evening banquet, and Saturday luncheon. Pre-conference workshops, $30 additional.

Green Mountain Writers Conference

47 Hazel St., Rutland, VT 05701

www.vermontwriters.com

At this annual weeklong conference, developing writers attend workshops run by professional authors who teach the craft of writing fiction, creative nonfiction, poetry, journalistic pieces, nature articles, essays, memoir, and biography. Working sessions and writing assignments are scheduled around readings and panel discussions. *Date:* July. *Location:* Tinmouth, Vermont. *Cost:* $525; includes lunches and farewell banquet.

Highlights Foundation Writers Workshop at Chautauqua

814 Court St., Honesdale, PA 18431

www.highlightsfoundation.org

Seminars, small-group workshops, and intensive one-on-one sessions with prominent children's authors, illustrators, editors, critics, and publishers fill the days of this annual weeklong conference, while evenings are reserved for a variety of informal and cultural activities. This conference is designed for writers at all levels, from beginning to published, who are interested in writing or illustrating for young readers. *Date:* July. *Location:* Chautauqua, New York. *Cost:* $1,785 (early bird) includes meals; additional cost for lodging.

Idaho Writers' League Annual Writers Conference

P.O. Box 303, Jerome, ID 83338

www.idahowritersleague.com/conference.html

This two-day conference offers morning and afternoon work-shops, luncheons, and a banquet. Last year's workshops included "Writing for Children and Teens," "Writing History," "How TV News Can Streamline Your Writing," and "The Western." *Date:* September. *Location:* Visit the website for location. *Cost:* $125 for members; $135 for nonmembers. One-day rates, $85–$105.

Iowa Summer Writing Festival

215C Seashore Hall, University of Iowa, Iowa City, IA 52242

www.uiowa.edu/~iswfest

Weeklong and weekend workshops are held over the course of six weeks and four weekends at this well-known annual event for serious writers. Some workshops are devoted to critiquing manuscripts that participants bring with them, others to generating new work through exercises and assignments. Writing for children and young adults, screenwriting, playwriting, poetry, travel writing, and nature writing are some of the 140 workshops offered. *Date:* June and July. *Location:* Iowa City, Iowa. *Cost:* $500–$525 per week; includes special events, Friday banquet, and Sunday dinner. Weekend only, $250; includes Saturday breakfast.

Jackson Hole Writers Conference

P.O. Box 1974, Jackson, WY 83001

http://jacksonholewritersconference.com

In addition to workshops led by novelists, creative nonfiction writers, poets, agents, editors, and publishers, this conference offers three manuscript critiques at no extra charge. The 2009 conference offered five tracks: fiction, creative nonfiction, poetry, young adult fiction, and travel and outdoor writing. This four-day event is held annually. *Date:* June. *Location:* Jackson Hole, Wyoming. *Cost:* $390; $360 early bird.

James River Writers Conference

Zero East Fourth St., Studio 24, Richmond, VA 23224

www.jamesriverwriters.com

In addition to workshops, panel discussions, and speeches, this conference offers attendees the opportunity for one-on-one meetings with literary agents or editors and first-page critique sessions. Last year's two-day conference featured workshops on the author's role in publicity, writing dialogue, music in language, "Writing Around Your Regular Life," and "Spirituality Hits the Shelves." *Date:* October. *Location:* Richmond, Virginia. *Cost:* $155; $140 early bird.

Jewish Children's Book Writers' Conference

92nd St. Y, 1395 Lexington Ave., New York, NY 10128

www.jewishbookcouncil.org

Sponsored by the Jewish Book Council, which promotes public awareness of books that "reflect the rich variety of the Jewish experience," this day-long conference is held annually. It offers presentations from authors, literary agents, publishers, and editors designed to help new as well as published authors advance their careers. *Date:* November. *Location:* New York City, New York. *Cost:* $135; $115 early bird.

Kentucky Women Writers Conference

232 East Maxwell St., Lexington, KY 40506

www.thewomenwritersconference.org

This two-day conference, held annually since its inception in 1979, attracts women at all stages of their writing careers. Workshops are limited to 12 members each. Pre-registration is required, and enrollment is done on a first-come, first-served basis. Fiction, nonfiction, poetry, and writing for young adults are among the workshops offered. *Date:* September. *Location:* Lexington, Kentucky. *Cost:* $75 for one day; $160 for two days.

Key West Travel Writing Workshop

Heritage House Museum, 410 Caroline St., Key West, FL 33040

Two full days of classes are held at this workshop, which is led by the former Editor in Chief of Fodor Travel Guides and current Contributing Editor of Frommers.com. Topics in 2010 include "Who Are Travel Writers?," "How to Get Published," and "What Is Good Travel Writing?" A roundtable critique of assignments and individual appointments round out the schedule. *Date:* February. *Location:* Key West, Florida. *Cost:* $275.

Manhattanville Summer Writers' Week

2900 Purchase St., Purchase, NY 10577

www.mville.edu/writersweek

Three-hour workshops are held each morning of this five-day conference. Participants choose from workshops offered in the categories of fiction, creative nonfiction, poetry, and writing for young readers. Afternoons are devoted to special workshops,

readings, sessions with editors and agents, and individual manu-script consultations. *Date:* June. *Location:* Purchase, New York. *Cost:* $725; two graduate credits available for an additional fee.

Mendocino Coast Writers Conference

College of the Redwoods

1211 Del Mar Drive, P.O. Box 2739, Fort Bragg, CA 95437

www.mcwc.org

This three-day conference features all-day genre intensives. Those who wish to attend one of these novel, short fiction, memoir, or poetry intensives are required to pre-submit a sample of their work, which will be critiqued in the small group sessions. Those attending only the afternoon lectures and discussions are not required to send work in advance; however, those who wish to take advantage of a 30-minute consultation with an author, editor, or agent must pre-submit 10 pages of a manuscript. *Date:* July/August. *Location:* Fort Bragg, California. *Cost:* Visit the website for fees.

Midland Writers Conference

Grace A. Dow Memorial Library

1710 West St. Andrews, Midland, MI 48640

www.midland-mi.org/gracedowlibrary/writers.html

This one-day event, held annually, features one speaker/presenter. Melissa Seitz, a creative writing lecturer at Saginaw Valley State University, presented the 2009 program, which ex-amined the pre-writing, drafting, and editing processes. Topics covered included working with prompts, shaping a rough draft, and revision. *Date:* May. *Location:* Midland, Michigan. *Cost:* Visit the website for cost information.

Northern Colorado Writers Conference

2107 Thunderstone Court, Fort Collins, CO 80525

www.ncwc.biz

More than 30 morning and afternoon workshops are offered at this conference, which is held once each year. Among the topics covered in 2009 were "Writing a Book Proposal," "How to Write and Market a Personal Story," and "Architecture of Fiction." An editor's panel, editor pitch sessions, and read and critique sessions with authors and editors were other features of the two-day program sponsored by Northern Colorado Writers. *Date:* April. *Location:* Fort Collins, Colorado. *Cost:* $225 for members; $275 for nonmembers.

North Wildwood Beach Writers Conference

www.nwbwc.com

Presentations, workshops, manuscript evaluations, contests, and a book bazaar are the components of this day-and-a-half event. Workshops cover writing for children and young adults; fiction writing, including romance; nonfiction writing, including journalism and memoir; screenwriting; and poetry. Other workshops delve into marketing and the business of publishing. *Date:* June. *Location:* North Wildwood, New Jersey. *Cost:* $75 includes breakfast and banquet dinner. Manuscript evaluations, $25.

Oklahoma Writers' Federation Writers Conference

Deborah Bouziden, Conference Chair, 8416 Huckleberry Road,
    Edmond, OK 73034

www.owfi.org

This annual three-day conference has been held for more than 40 years. Workshops generally cover writing and marketing fiction (including science fiction and thrillers) and nonfiction for

children, young adults, and adults. The theme for the 2010 conference is "Write Every Day." *Date:* April/May. *Location:* Oklahoma City, Oklahoma. *Cost:* $150; $125 early bird.

Outdoor Writers Association of America Annual Conference

158 Lower Georges Valley Road, Spring Mills, PA 16875
www.owaa.org

First held in 1927, this gathering attracts writers who specialize in informing the public about outdoor recreational activities and the responsible use of natural resources. Workshops and seminars focus on craft improvement as well as on issues of specific interest to those who write about the outdoors. Topics include the business and technical sides of writing, marketing, and publishing, and nature journalism. The five-day conference also devotes sessions to national and local news related to outdoor activities and conservation. *Date:* June. *Location:* Rochester, Minnesota. *Cost:* Visit the website for cost information.

Pacific Northwest Children's Book Conference

Portland State University
CEED, P.O. Box 1491, Portland, OR 97207
www.ceed.pdx.edu/children

At this five-day conference, participants attend morning lectures on topics such as plotting, dialogue, and revision; afternoon intensive workshops; critique sessions; first-page analyses; and faculty readings. Speakers featured in previous years included Arthur Levine of Arthur A. Levine Books and author Margaret Bechard. *Date:* July. *Location:* Cannon Beach, Oregon. *Cost:* $695–$895. University credits available.

Pet Writing Conference

The Pet Socialite, Inc., 362 Broome St., #20, New York, NY 10013
www.petwritingconference.com

Animal-interest authors and journalists gather at this one-day event each year to attend seminars and workshops about the business side of pet writing, as well as for networking opportunities with representatives of animal organizations. One-on-one sessions with agents and book and magazine editors are also available. *Date:* February. *Location:* New York, New York. *Cost:* $175; $150 early bird; $200 after January 1.

Pikes Peak Writers Conference

427 East Colorado Ave., #116, Colorado Springs, CO 80903
www.pikespeakwriters.com

This annual conference offers more than 40 workshops that focus on fiction writing for children and teens as well as for adults. In addition, agents and editors are available to attendees seeking to pitch their work. Manuscript evaluations and critique sessions round out the three-day program. *Date:* April. *Location:* Colorado Springs, Colorado. *Cost:* $295–$380; includes 6 meals.

San Francisco Writers Conference

1029 Jones St., San Francisco, CA 94109
www.sfwriters.org

San Francisco Writers sponsors this weekend conference, which features more than 40 workshops, panels, social events, and one-on-one networking with presenters. In addition, editors from major publishing houses participate in Ask-A-Pro sessions. Writing workshops include expanded tracks for poetry and children's writing. *Date:* February. *Location:* San Francisco, California. *Cost:* $695; $595 early bird.

Contests 359

Sayulita Writers Workshops

Calle Chiripas #15, Sayulita, Nayarit, Mexico
www.sayulitawritersworkshops.com

Fourteen weeklong workshop sessions are held each year in the Mexican beach town of Sayulita. Workshops for 2010 include "Contemporary Magazine Journalism," "Introduction to Travel Writing," "The Art and Soul of Food Writing," "Dramatic Writing," "Drafting the Personal Essay," and "From Memory to Story: Writing Your Life." *Date:* January, February, March, April. *Location:* Sayulita, Mexico. *Cost:* $500 per class; lodging and food additional.

Barbara Seuling's Manuscript Workshop

P.O. Box 529, Londonderry, VT 05148
www.barbaraseuling.com

First offered in 1981, this workshop focuses on writing book-length works of fiction and nonfiction for children and young adults. Over the course of five days, attendees work on daily assignments and participate in hands-on exercises, discussions, and critiques. *Date:* July and September. *Location:* Landgrove, Vermont. *Cost:* $895 includes shared lodging and meals; $25 discount for seniors and members of SCBWI.

Sewanee Writers' Conference

Cheri B. Peters, Creative Writing Program Manager, University of the South, 310G St. Luke's Hall, 735 University Ave., Sewanee, TN 37383
www.sewaneewriters.org

With a focus on fiction, playwriting, and poetry, the Sewanee Writers' Conference offers workshops that meet for five 2-hour sessions on alternating days. Over the course of the 12-day program, participants also attend daily readings, lectures on craft, panel discussions, and Q&A sessions with distinguished faculty members. Alice McDermott, William Styron, and Arthur Miller are among the faculty and visitors who took part in previous years' conferences. *Date:* July. *Location:* Sewanee, Tennessee. *Cost:* $1,700; includes single room and board.

Society of Children's Book Writers & Illustrators (SCBWI) Annual Conference

8271 Beverly Boulevard, Los Angeles, CA 90048

www.scbwi.org

This conference, first held in 1968, offers workshops, master classes, manuscript and portfolio consultations, and panel discussions over the course of its four-day program. The faculty consists of more than 20 authors, illustrators, editors, and agents. *Date:* July. *Location:* Los Angeles, California. *Cost:* Visit the website for cost information.

SCBWI Carolinas Fall Conference

P.O. Box 1216, Conover, NC 28613

www.scbwicarolinas.org

The theme of the 2009 conference was "Revision 9-1-1: Intensive Care for Your Work-in-Progress." The main event was a four-hour intensive workshop that shared techniques for fixing problems with voice, setting, plot, and character. Manuscript critiques are available for an additional fee. Visit the website for information about the 2010 conference. *Date:* November. *Location:* North Carolina. *Cost:* Visit the website for cost information.

SCBWI Florida Regional Conference

www.scbwiflorida.com

Workshops, first-page critiques, and writing and illustrating intensives are scheduled into this three-day conference, which reserves time for informal critique groups and keynote speeches on topics such as "Write What Your Heart Tells You" and "Writing Real Books in the Facebook Age." *Date:* January. *Location:* Miami, Florida. *Cost:* Visit the website for cost information.

SCBWI Kansas Fall Conference

P.O. Box 3987, Olathe, KS 66063
www.kansas-scbwi.org

Writers at all stages of their careers gather at this two-day conference to attend workshops led by editors, agents, authors, illustrators, and other prominent professionals from the world of children's and young adult publishing. Panel discussions, keynote speeches, and manuscript critiques round out the event. *Date:* September. *Location:* Overland Park, Kansas. *Cost:* Visit the website for cost information.

SCBWI MD/DE/WV Summer Conference

www2.mcdaniel.edu/scbwi

Writers and illustrators who attend this weekend conference have the opportunity to strengthen their marketing skills, glimpse the workday world of literary agents, and gain insights into running critique groups. Breakout sessions and panel discussions geared toward sharpening writing and illustrating skills are also on the schedule. *Date:* July. *Location:* Westminster, Maryland. *Cost:* Visit the website for cost information.

SCBWI Michigan Spring & Fall Conferences

www.kidsbooklink.org

The workshops at this weekend conference are led by award-winning authors and illustrators; literary agents; and art directors and editors from major publishing houses. Although the conference is open to members and nonmembers, only SCBWI members are eligible to enter the lottery for a paid manuscript or portfolio critique. *Date:* May, October. *Location:* The spring conference will be held in Lansing, Michigan. Visit the website for fall conference location. *Cost:* Visit the website for cost information.

SCBWI Nevada Fall Workshop

P.O. Box 19084, Reno, NV 89511
www.nevadascbwi.org

Novelists, picture book authors and illustrators, and poets find sessions geared toward their interests at this one-day event. Speakers in 2009 included award-winning humorists, poets, picture book authors, and novelists. Adrienne Tropp, a writing teacher, led a workshop titled "Tap into Your Inner Child," and local bookstore owners discussed "What We Sell and How It Works." *Date:* November. *Location:* Reno, Nevada. *Cost:* $55 for members; $60 for nonmembers.

SCBWI New England Annual Conference

www.nescbwi.org

Paid editor critiques, peer critiques, a query session with agents, keynote speeches, book signings, and book sales are scheduled around the workshops and writing intensives presented at this weekend conference. Among the workshops offered in 2009 were "Voice and Choice in Nonfiction," How Far Is Too Far? Sex in YA Literature," "Thoughts on Constructing a Solid Mystery," and "Picture Book Plotting, Pacing, and Paging." *Date:* April. *Location:* Nashua, New Hampshire. *Cost:* Visit the website for cost information.

SCBWI New Mexico Spring Conference

P.O. Box 1084, Socorro, NM 87801

www.scbwi-nm.org

Those who attended last year's conference were greeted with a party on Friday night, followed by first page/synopsis critiques, illustrator portfolio displays, and mini book launches. Saturday workshops and keynote speeches were presented by a literary agent, an editor from HarperCollins, and an award-winning author. *Date:* April. *Location:* University of New Mexico, Albuquerque, New Mexico. *Cost:* Visit the website for cost information.

SCBWI North and East Bay Fall Conference

www.scbwinorthca.org

This one-day conference draws children's writers at all stages of their careers. The theme of the 2009 fall conference was "From Creativity to Mastery." Attendees chose from three sessions— main, picture book, and marketing. Manuscript critiques were available for SCBWI members only. *Date:* October. *Location:* Oakland, California. *Cost:* Visit the website for cost information.

SCBWI Northern Ohio Annual Conference

P.O. Box 195, Medina, OH 44256

www.nohscbwi.org

Editors and art directors from prominent publishing houses and bestselling Ohio authors are among the presenters at this weekend conference. In addition to workshops focused on craft, attendees also have opportunities to speak with editors, network with other writers and illustrators, and catch up on the latest news from the world of children's publishing. *Date:* September. *Location:* Cleveland, Ohio. *Cost:* Visit the website for cost information.

SCBWI Oklahoma Fall Conference

P.O. Box 525, Chandler, OK 74834

www.scbwiok.org

Oklahoma writers and illustrators gather for one day of panel discussions, morning breakout sessions, and an afternoon devoted to an in-depth presentation on a single topic of interest. *Date:* September. *Location:* Chandler, Oklahoma. *Cost:* Visit the website for cost information.

SCBWI Rocky Mountain Fall Conference

www.rmcscbwi.org

In addition to workshops presented by editors from some of the best-known New York City-based publishing houses, this conference offers manuscript critiques with editors, agents, and published authors; one-on-one portfolio reviews; and first-page critiques. A weekend conference, it draws writers and illustrators from Colorado and Wyoming. *Date:* September. *Location:* Lakewood, Colorado. *Cost:* Visit the website for cost information.

SCBWI Southern Breeze Fall Conference

P.O. Box 26282, Birmingham, AL 35260

www.southern-breeze.org

Almost 30 workshops are offered at this one-day event, each led by an agent, art director, editor, or other publishing professional. The editors who take part in this conference will review submissions. *Date:* October. *Location:* Birmingham, Alabama. *Cost:* Visit the website for cost information.

SCBWI Texas: Austin Annual Conference

www.austinscbwi.com

Individual critiques and breakout sessions are held throughout the course of this one-day conference, which is brought to a close in the evening with a Texas barbecue. Manuscripts presented for critique may be at any stage of the writing process, with feedback offered on issues ranging from shaping an early draft to polishing a revision. Advanced critiques are available for more experienced writers. *Date:* January. *Location:* Cedar Park, Texas. *Cost:* $125 for members ($115 early bird); $135 for nonmembers ($125 early bird).

SCBWI Ventura–Santa Barbara Writers' Day

www.scbwisocal.org

Spotlight presentations by authors and illustrators, an editors' panel, and speeches by representatives from major publishing houses are the featured activities at this annual event. Limited space is available for manuscript or portfolio critiques. *Date:* October. *Location:* Thousand Oaks, California. *Cost:* $85 for members; $95 for nonmembers. Manuscript/portfolio critique, $45.

Solstice Summer Writers' Conference

400 Heath St., Chestnut Hill, MA 02467

www.pmc.edu/solstice

Set on the Chestnut Hill campus of Pine Manor College, this five-day conference features a faculty of award-winning authors who lead workshops on the craft of writing poetry, short stories, novels, creative nonfiction, and literature for young readers. The conference also holds seminars on the business side of writing, as well as panel discussions and faculty readings. *Date:* June. *Location:* Chestnut Hill, Massachusetts. *Cost:* $725, plus meals and lodging (available on campus).

South Carolina Writers Workshop Conference

P.O. Box 7104, Columbia, SC 29202

www.myscww.org

This weekend conference begins on Friday morning with optional intensive workshops. Saturday and Sunday are filled with interactive workshops, basic to advanced; critique sessions; and opportunities for participants to interact with the editors, agents, authors, and technology and publicity professionals who serve as faculty. The 2009 conference featured a "slush fest" with agents and editors. Workshops covered queries, historical novels, character development, and middle-grade and YA novels. *Date:* October. *Location:* Myrtle Beach, South Carolina. *Cost:* Visit the website for cost information.

Southern California Writers' Conference

1010 University Ave., #54, San Diego, CA 92103

www.writersconference.com

Dozens of interactive workshops are scheduled during this three-day conference, which also offers Read & Critique sessions that provide comprehensive, one-on-one manuscript evaluations. More than 60 authors, screenwriters, editors, and agents are among the faculty members. Workshops are held on a variety of fiction genres such as mystery and romance; journalism; children's and young adult writing; screenwriting; humorous writing; memoir; playwriting; and poetry. *Date:* February, September. *Location:* San Diego, California. *Cost:* $325–$415. Additional fees for critique sessions and one-on-one consultations.

St. David's Christian Writers' Conference

87 Pines Road East, Hadley, PA 16130

www.stdavidswriters.com

Four days of workshops led by nationally-known authors and editors are the centerpiece of this conference, which also offers one-on-one tutorials and professional critiques for additional fees. Keynote addresses and literary readings, evening meditations, and after-hours social events are other components of the conference. Workshops offered last year were "Turning Personal Experience into a Devotional Message," "Journaling to the Heart of Your Life," and "Hollywood Storytelling Tools," among others. *Date:* June. *Location:* Grove City, Pennsylvania. *Cost:* Visit the website for cost information.

Tin House Summer Writers Workshop

P.O. Box 10500, Portland, OR 97296

www.tinhouse.com/workshop

Held on the campus of Reed College, this weeklong program consists of morning workshops limited to 12 participants. Craft seminars and career panels are scheduled in the afternoons, with author readings held in the evenings. Workshops are led by the editors of *Tin House* and Tin House Books. For an additional fee, mentorships are available to participants who have completed a collection of stories or poems, a memoir, or a novel. *Date:* July. *Location:* Portland, Oregon. *Cost:* $1,000–$1,100, plus meals and lodging. Mentorship, $750–$1,000.

Wesleyan Writers Conference

Wesleyan University, Middletown, CT 06459

www.wesleyan.edu/writers

This conference welcomes all writers, from beginners to veterans. The five-day program consists of seminars, readings, panels, lectures, and optional manuscript consultations. Each seminar typically includes a lecture, a discussion, and optional writing exercises. Seminar topics include novel, short story, fiction techniques, narrative in fiction and nonfiction, poetry, literary journalism, short and long-form nonfiction, memoir, and multimedia and online work. Private manuscript consultations are available with faculty members or teaching fellows. Attendees also have the opportunity to meet with editors and agents who are looking for new writers. *Date:* June. *Location:* Middletown, Connecticut. *Cost:* $150, includes lunch and dinner.

Western Writers of America Convention
www.westernwriters.org

Workshops, panels, discussions with editors and authors, and book signings are all part of this five-day convention. Workshops focus on writing fiction and nonfiction—including writing for children and young adults—and all are geared toward preserving the rich history of the American West. The business side of publishing is also examined, as is marketing. *Date:* June. *Location:* Knoxville, Tennessee. *Cost:* $220–$235.

Willamette Writers Conference
9045 SW Barbur Boulevard, #5A, Portland, OR 97219
www.willamettewriters.com

Participants have almost 100 workshops to choose from at this weekend conference. Topics include historical fiction, self-help books, children's books, screenplays, mysteries, romance, and science fiction, among many others. Literary agents, Hollywood agents and producers, and editors are among the workshop leaders. Only those attending the conference for the full three days may submit up to two manuscripts for advanced critiques for an additional fee of $65 per manuscript. *Date:* August. *Location:* Portland, Oregon. *Cost:* Visit the website for cost information.

Winnipeg International Writers Festival

624-100 Arthur St., Winnipeg MB R3B 1H3 Canada

www.winnipegwords.com

Workshops, lectures, interviews, keynote speeches, and readings fill the days of this weeklong festival, which has been held annually since 1997. More than 50 representatives from the publishing world offer presentations on playwriting, poetry, children's and young adult writing, journalism, mystery, horror, and other topics. Programs target children as well as adults, and are presented in both English and French. *Date:* September. *Location:* Winnipeg, Manitoba. *Cost:* Visit the website for cost information.

Write on the Sound Writers' Conference

700 Main St., Edmonds, WA 98020

www.ci.edmonds.wa.us/artscommission/wots.stm

Sponsored by the City of Edmonds Art Commission, this conference is a highly anticipated regional event that fills up early. With more than 30 workshops to choose from, it draws noted authors and other publishing professionals as faculty. The program begins on Friday afternoon with pre-conference workshops, and continues with two full days of workshops and other events on Saturday and Sunday. Manuscript critique appointments are available for an additional fee. *Date:* October. *Location:* Edmonds, Washington. *Cost:* Visit the website for cost information.

Writers in Paradise

4200 54th Ave. South, St. Petersburg, FL 33711

www.writersinparadise.com

This eight-day program offers workshops on fiction, nonfiction, and poetry writing. Lectures, panels, roundtable discussions, readings, and book signings fill out the rest of the schedule at this annual convention. *Date:* January. *Location:* St. Petersburg, Florida. *Cost:* $675.

The Write Stuff
Greater Lehigh Valley Writers Group
3650 Nazareth Pike, PMB #136, Bethlehem, PA 18020
www.glvwg.org/conference

This weekend conference has been held annually since 1993. In addition to writers' workshops, it offers sessions on the business of writing, panel discussions, manuscript critiques, opportunities to meet with agents and editors, and a book fair. Workshops offered at the 2009 conference included "Writing Young Adult and Middle-Grade Fiction in the 21st Century," "A Nose for News," and "The Ten Most Common Mistakes Beginning Writers Make." *Date:* March. *Location:* Allentown, Pennsylvania. *Cost:* $100 for members and students; $120 for nonmembers. $135 for late registration.

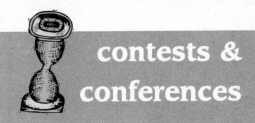

Contests for Adult & Children's Writers

Abilene Writers Guild Annual Contest
P.O. Box 2562, Abilene, TX 79604
www.abilenewritersguild.org

This annual competition open to all writers awards prizes in ten categories, including children's stories, novels, poetry, short fiction, and nonfiction. Guidelines vary for each category. Visit the website for specific information. Entry fee, $5 for short pieces; $10 for novel entries. *Deadline:* Submissions are accepted from October 1 to November 30. *Award:* First prize in each category, $100.

Jane Addams Children's Book Award
Central Michigan University English Dept., 215 Anspach, Mount
   Pleasant, MI 48859
www.janeaddamspeace.org

Honoring authors and illustrators of children's literature who reach standards of excellence while promoting the themes of peace, social justice, equality of the sexes, and a unified world, this competition is held annually. Books of fiction, nonfiction, or poetry targeting children ages 2 through 12 that were published in the year preceding the contest are eligible. *Deadline:* December 31. *Award:* Honorary certificate and a cash award.

Alligator Juniper's National Writing Contest

Prescott College, 220 Grove Ave., Prescott, AZ 86301

www.prescott.edu/alligator_juniper/submit.html

This contest accepts unpublished, original entries in the categories of fiction, creative nonfiction, and poetry. Fiction and nonfiction entries should not exceed 30 pages. Poetry, limit 5 poems per entry. Entry fee, $15. *Deadline:* October 1. *Award:* First prize in each category is $100 and publication in *Alligator Juniper*.

Sherwood Anderson Fiction Award

Mid-American Review, Dept. of English, Box W, Bowling Green
State University, Bowling Green, OH 43403

www.bgsu.edu/studentlife/organizations/midamericanreview

Sponsored by *Mid-American Review,* the literary journal of Bowling Green State University, this competition is open to all writers and accepts short story entries of high literary merit. Entries may be in any genre of fiction, but must be original, unpublished material. *Deadline:* October 1. *Award:* First place, $1,000 and publication in *Mid-American Review.* Four finalists are also considered for publication.

Arizona Authors Association Literary Contest

Contest Coordinator, 6145 W. Echo Lane, Glendale, AZ 85302

www.azauthors.com/contest_index.html

This annual contest is sponsored by the Arizona Authors Association and Five Star Publications. It accepts both unpublished and published works in several categories including short stories, poetry, essays, articles, true stories, and novels. Entry fees range from $15 to $30. *Deadline:* July 1. *Award:* Category winners, $100 and publication in *Arizona Literary Magazine.*

ASPCA Henry Bergh Children's Book Award

424 East 92nd St., New York, NY 10128

www.aspca.org/bookaward

This annual award is sponsored by the ASPCA and recognizes authors whose work promotes the humane treatment of animals while helping children understand the interdependence of humans, animals, and the environment. Entries for children to age 12 or for teens ages 13 to 17 may be fiction, nonfiction, or collections of stories, essays, or poems by one author. Illustrations are also recognized. *Deadline:* October 31. *Award:* Winners are honored at an ASPCA conference in June.

Atlantic Writing Competition

Writers' Federation of Nova Scotia, 1113 Marginal Road, Halifax
   NS B3H 4P Canada

www.writers.ns.ca

Open to writers living in Atlantic Canada, this annual competition accepts entries of YA novels, short stories, poetry, writing for children, and magazine articles/essays. Previously unpublished material only. Entry fees: novel category, $25; all other categories, $15. WFNS members receive a $5 discount on entry fees. Published authors may not enter the competition in the genre that they have been published. Limit one entry per category. *Deadline:* December 5. *Award:* First- through third-place winners in each category receive awards ranging from $50 to $200.

Autumn House Poetry and Fiction Contests

P.O. Box 60100, Pittsburgh, PA 15211

www.autumnhouse.com

Autumn House Press sponsors this annual contest that accepts collections of fiction and poetry. All fiction genres are welcome. Poetry collections, 50 to 80 pages. Fiction, 200–300 pages. Entry fee, $25. *Deadline:* June 30. *Award:* Winning entry is published by Autumn House Press, with a $1,000 advance against royalties. All entries are considered for publication.

AWP Award Series

George Mason University, MS 1E3, Fairfax, VA 22030-4444

www.awpwriter.org

This annual award series is open to fiction, creative nonfiction, and poetry. This competition is open to all writers, and specific guidelines are available at the website. *Deadline:* Ongoing. *Award:* $2,000, and publication by the University of Pittsburgh Press, University of Massachusetts Press, or University of Georgia Press.

Doris Bakin Award

Carolina Wren Press, 120 Morris St., Durham, NC 27701

www.carolinawrenpress.org

This annual award seeks fiction and nonfiction submissions on any subject, written by women. It encourages submissions from both new and established writers and accepts unpublished material only. Entries should be 150–500 pages. Entry fee, $20. *Deadline:* December 1. *Award:* From $150 to $600.

Baltimore Review Creative Nonfiction Competition

P.O. Box 36418, Towson, MD 21286

www.baltimorereview.org

This annual competition accepts original, unpublished essays in all styles. Entries should not exceed 6,000 words. Entry fee, $10; $15 includes a year's subscription to *Baltimore Review. Deadline:* From January 1 to April 1. *Award:* First place, $250 and publication in *Baltimore Review.* Second place, $100; third place, $50.

Baltimore Review Short Fiction Competition

P.O. Box 36418, Towson, MD 21286

www.baltimorereview.org

Submissions of short fiction in all genres are accepted for this annual competition. All entries will also be considered for publication in *Baltimore Review.* Entries should not exceed 6,000 words. Entry fee, $20; $25 includes a one-year subscription to *Baltimore Review. Deadline:* Entries are accepted between August 1 and December 1. *Award:* First place, $500 and publication in *Baltimore Review.* Second place, $250; third place, $100.

Josiah Bancroft Sr. Novel Contest

Dr. Dana Thomas, Writers' Festival Contests, 4501 Capper Road, Jacksonville, FL 32218

www.fccj.org

This novel contest is part of the Florida First Coast Writers' Festival. It is open to all writers and accepts original submissions of fiction in all genres. Submit first 100 pages of manuscript. Entry fee, $45. *Deadline:* Ongoing. *Award:* First place, $700 and consideration for publication. Second place, $200; third place, $100.

Berkeley Fiction Review's Sudden Fiction Contest

ASUC Publications, 10 Eshleman Hall, University of California, Berkeley, CA 94720

www.ocf.berkeley.edu/~bfr

This annual contest promotes the writing of high-quality short fiction. It is open to all writers, and accepts previously unpublished entries only. Entries should not exceed 1,000 words. Entry fee, $6 for first entry; $4 for each additional entry. *Deadline:* February 20. *Award:* First place, $200. First-, second-, and third-place winners are published in the *Berkeley Fiction Review*.

Geoffrey Bilson Award for Historical Fiction for Young People

Canadian Children's Book Centre (CCBC), 40 Orchard View Blvd.,
   Suite 101, Toronto ON M4R 1B9 Canada
www.bookcentre.ca

Books of historical fiction for young people that are written by Canadian authors are celebrated through this annual contest. Books published in the year preceding the contest are eligible for entry. Winners are chosen by a jury appointed by the CCBC. Picture books, short story collections, plots involving time travel, self-published books, and books produced by a vanity press are not eligible. Submit six copies of the published entry. *Deadline:* January 15. *Award:* Winner receives $5,000 and a certificate.

Waldo M. and Grace C. Bonderman Youth Theatre Playwriting Competition

140 West Washington St., Indianapolis, IN 46204
www.indianarep.com/Bonderman

This competition is open to all writers who participate in the Bonderman Workshop, held every other year in Indianapolis. The competition accepts unpublished plays for children. Plays for children in grades one through three should not exceed 30 minutes in length; plays for students in grade three and up must be at least 45 minutes. Submit three copies, a synopsis, and a cast list. *Deadline:* August 31. *Award:* Winners are notified in December. The top four winners receive $1,000 and a staged reading of their plays.

The *Boston Globe-Horn Book* Awards

Horn Book, 56 Roland St., Suite 200, Boston, MA 02129
www.hbook.com

These prestigious awards celebrate excellence in literature for children and young adults. A committee of three judges evaluates books submitted by U.S. publishers and selects winners on the basis of overall creative excellence. No entry fee. *Deadline:* May 15. *Award:* $500 and an engraved silver bowl.

Boulevard Short Fiction Contest for Emerging Writers

6614 Clayton Road, Box 325, Richmond Heights, MO 63117
www.richardburgin.net

Writers who have not yet published a book of fiction, nonfiction, or poetry with a nationally distributed press are eligible to compete in this annual contest. Entries have no length restrictions, but must be original, unpublished work. Entry fee, $15. *Deadline:* December 31. *Award:* $1,500 and publication in *Boulevard.*

Briar Cliff Review Writing Competition

3303 Rebecca St., Sioux City, IA 51104
www.briarcliff.edu/bcreview

This annual contest accepts unpublished entries of fiction, creative nonfiction, and poetry. Fiction and creative nonfiction should not exceed 6,000 words. Poetry entries may include up to three poems. Entry fee, $15. *Deadline:* November 1. *Award:* First prize in each category is $1,000 and publication in *Briar Cliff Review.*

Marilyn Brown Novel Award

Jen Wahlquist, English Literature Dept., Utah Valley University,
  800 West University Pkwy., Orem, UT 84058
www.uvu.edu/english/brownaward.pdf

This award is presented by the Association for Mormon Letters
and Utah Valley University. It accepts novel length entries on a
variety of subjects. No entry fee. Limit one entry per competition.
Deadline: October 1. *Award:* $1,000.

Randolph Caldecott Medal

American Library Association (ALA), 50 East Huron, Chicago, IL
  60611
www.ala.org/alsc/caldecott.html

Named in honor of the nineteenth-century English illustrator,
Randolph Caldecott, this award is presented to the artist of the
most distinguished American picture book for children published
in the preceding year. It is open to all U.S. citizens. Honor books
are also recognized. *Deadline:* December 31. *Award:* The winner
is announced at the ALA Midwinter Meeting and presented with
the Caldecott Medal at an awards banquet.

California Book Awards

595 Market St., San Francisco, CA 94105
www.commonwealthclub.org

This contest was established with the goal of finding the best
California writers and spotlighting the high-quality literature produced in the state. The competition awards 10 California authors
with medals in recognition of outstanding literary works. Awards
are presented in the categories of fiction or nonfiction for children
of various ages; adult fiction and nonfiction; poetry; and book
production. Submit five copies of entry. *Deadline:* December 19.

Award: Gold medal winners receive $2,000. Silver medal winners receive $300.

Canadian Library Association's Book of the Year for Children

66 Ash St., RR#5, Rockwood ON N0B 2K0 Canada

www.cla.org

Recognizing Canadian works of children's literature for ages 12 and under, this award is presented annually to books of fiction, nonfiction, poetry, or retellings of traditional literature written by Canadian citizens. All titles submitted for this award must be published in the year preceding the contest. *Deadline:* December 31. *Award:* Winner receives a leather-bound copy of their book and $750.

Canadian Writer's Journal Short Fiction Contest

Box 1178, New Liskeard ON P0J 1P0 Canada

www.cwj.ca

This contest, sponsored by *Canadian Writer's Journal*, accepts previously unpublished work in any genre that does not exceed 1,500 words. Awards are presented in March and September. Each entry must be accompanied by a brief author biography. Entry fee, $5. *Deadline:* April 30. *Award:* First place, $150; second and third place, $100 and $50, respectively. Winning entries are published in *CWJ*.

CAPA Competition

Connecticut Authors and Publishers Association, Dan Uitti,

P.O. Box 715, Avon, CT 06001

www.aboutcapa.com

Held annually, this contest accepts entries of short stories for children (to 2,000 words); short stories for adults (to 2,000 words); personal essays (to 1,500 words); and poetry (to 30 lines). The competition is open to all writers and accepts multiple entries, provided each entry is accompanied by an official entry form. Submit four copies of entry. Entry fee, $10 per short story/personal essay or up to three poems. *Deadline:* May 31. *Award:* First place, $100. Second place, $50. Winning entries are published in CAPA's newsletter.

Children's Writer Contests

95 Long Ridge Road, West Redding, CT 06896
www.childrenswriter.com

Children's Writer newsletter sponsors two contests each year, each with a specific theme and requirements. The themes for 2010 call for an article on a science topic for 11-year-old readers; and historical fiction for young teens. It accepts original, unpublished work only. No entry fee for subscribers; $13 entry fee includes an eight-month subscription. Multiple entries are accepted. *Deadline:* February 27 and October 31. *Award:* Cash prizes vary, with first place as much as $500. Winning entries are published in *Children's Writer*.

Christopher Awards

5 Hanover Square, 11th Floor, New York, NY 10004
www.christophers.org

These annual awards are sponsored by the Christophers, a non-profit organization with a ministry of communications. The awards recognize artistic work in publishing, film, and television that creates a positive change in society and promotes self-worth. Profiles of courage, stories of determination, and chronicles of constructive action and empowerment are accepted. All entries must be published in the year preceding the contest. *Deadline:* November. *Award:* Winners are presented with bronze medallions at a ceremony in New York City.

CNW/FFWA Florida State Writing Competition
P.O. Box A, North Stratford, NH 03590
www.writers-editors.com

Open to all writers, this contest honors authors of fiction, nonfiction, children's literature, and poetry. Entries of children's literature must be previously unpublished or self-published only. Poetry may be traditional or verse. Specific category guidelines are available at the website. Entry fees vary for each category. *Deadline:* March 15. *Award:* First- through third-place awards range from $100 to $150, and certificates.

Crossquarter Short Science Fiction Contest
P.O. Box 23749, Santa Fe, NM 87502
www.crossquarter.com

Short story entries of science fiction, fantasy, and urban fantasy are accepted in this annual competition. The contest is sponsored by Crossquarter Publishing and looks for entries that portray the best of the human spirit. Entries should not exceed 7,500 words. Entry fee, $15 for first entry; $10 for each additional entry. *Deadline:* January 15. *Award:* First place, $250 plus publication by Crossquarter. Second- to fourth-place prizes range from $125 to $50 plus possible publication.

Sheldon Currie Fiction Prize
The Antigonish Review, P.O. Box 5000, St. Francis Xavier
    University, Antigonish NS B2G 2W5 Canada
www.antigonishreview.com

The Sheldon Currie Fiction Prize is held each year. It is open to well-written, unpublished short stories of any subject matter. Entries should not exceed 20 pages. Entry fee, $25 from the U.S. and Canada; $35 from outside North America. *Deadline:* May 31. *Award:* First place, $600; second place, $400; third place, $200. The three winning entries are published in the *Antigonish Review.*

Delacorte Dell Yearling Contest
1745 Broadway, New York, NY 10019
www.randomhouse.com

Random House sponsors this annual contest that is open to writers living in the U.S. and Canada. It welcomes submissions of middle-grade contemporary or historical fiction set in North America. Submissions should be unpublished and target readers ages 9 to 12. Entries should be between 96 and 160 pages and include a cover letter with a brief plot summary. *Deadline:* Postmarked between April 1 and June 30. *Award:* Book contract with Random House; advance on royalties of $7,500; and $1,500 cash.

Delacorte Press Contest for a First Young Adult Novel
1745 Broadway, 9th Floor, New York, NY 10019
www.randomhouse.com

This annual contest looks to encourage writing in the young adult contemporary fiction genre. It is open to writers living in the U.S. and Canada who have not yet published a YA novel. Manuscripts should be between 100 and 224 typed pages. Limit two entries per competition. All entries must feature a contemporary setting and plot suitable for readers ages 12 to 18. *Deadline:* Postmarked between October 1 and December 31. *Award:* Book contract with Random House; advance on royalties of $7,500; and $1,500 cash.

Jack Dyer Fiction Prize

Dept. of English, Faner Hall 2380, Mail Code 4503, Southern
   Illinois University–Carbondale, Carbondale, IL 62901
www.siuc.edu/~crborchd/dyer.html

Open to U.S. residents, this annual competition is sponsored
by *Crab Orchard Review,* the literary journal of Southern Illinois
University–Carbondale. It is open to submissions of previously
unpublished fiction. Entries should not exceed 6,000 words. Entry
fee, $10. Limit 3 entries per competition. *Deadline:* Entries are
accepted between March 1 and April 30. *Award:* $1,500 and
publication in the Winter/Spring *Crab Orchard Review.*

Margaret A. Edwards Award

50 East Huron St., Chicago, IL 60611
www.ala.org/yalsa

This award was established by the American Library Association's Young Adult Services Association and honors a living
author for a body of work and his or her special contribution to
YA literature. The winner's writing will have been popular over a
period of time and is generally recognized as helping teens to
become better aware of who they are and their role in society.
Nominations are accepted from librarians and teenagers. All
books must have been published in the U.S., no less than five
years prior to the nomination. *Deadline:* December 31. *Award:*
$1,000.

Arthur Ellis Awards

3007 Kingston Road, Box 113, Toronto ON M1M 1P1 Canada
www.crimewriterscanada.com

The Arthur Ellis Awards were established 26 years ago to

honor excellence in Canadian mystery and crime writing. The contest is open to writers living in Canada or Canadian writers living elsewhere in the world. It accepts entries in several categories including best short story, best nonfiction, best first novel, best juvenile novel, best novel, best crime writing in French, and best unpublished crime novel. *Deadline:* January 31. *Award:* Winners receive a wooden statue at the annual awards dinner.

William Faulkner–William Wisdom Creative Writing Competition

624 Pirate's Alley, New Orleans, LA 70116-3254
www.wordsandmusic.org

This annual competition was set up to preserve the storytelling heritage of New Orleans and the Deep South. Unpublished entries are accepted in seven categories: novel; novella; novel-in-progress; short story; essay; poetry; and short story by a high school student. Entry fees range from $10 to $35 depending on category. Visit the website for complete guidelines. *Deadline:* May 1. Do not send entries before January 15. *Award:* Ranges from $250 to $7,500.

Shubert Fendrich Memorial Playwriting Contest

P.O. Box 4267, Englewood, CO 80155
www.pioneerdrama.com

This competition encourages the development of quality theatrical material for educational and community theaters. This contest is open to playwrights who have not been published by Pioneer Drama Service. *Deadline:* March 1. *Award:* Publishing contract; advance against royalties of $1,000.

Foster City International Writers' Contest

Foster City Parks and Recreation Department, 650 Shell Blvd.,

Foster City, CA 94404
www.geocities.com/fostercity_writers

Entries of original fiction, humor, personal essays, children's stories, and poetry are accepted in this annual competition. Word lengths vary for each category. Multiple entries are accepted. Entry fee, $12. *Deadline:* December 30. *Award:* First prize in each category, $150; second prize, $75.

H. E. Francis Award

Dept. of English, University of Alabama, Huntsville, AL 35899
www.uah.edu/hefranciscontest

This annual award is sponsored by the Ruth Hindman Foundation and the UAH English Department. It accepts original, unpublished short stories that are judged by a nationally known panel of editors. Manuscripts must not exceed 5,000 words. Entry fee, $15. *Deadline:* December 31. *Award:* $1,000.

Don Freeman Memorial Grant-in-Aid

3646 Wood Lake Road, Bellingham, WA 98226
www.scbwi.org

Members of the Society of Children's Book Writers and Illustrators who intend to make picture books their primary contribution to children's literature are eligible for this grant. It is presented annually to help artists further their training and understanding of the picture book genre. *Deadline:* Postmarked between January 2 and February 2. *Award:* Winner, $1,500. Runner-up, $500.

Friends of the Library Writing Contest

130 North Franklin St., Decatur, IL 62523
www.decatur.lib.il.us

This annual writing contest awards prizes in the categories of essay (to 2,000 words); fiction (to 3,000 words); juvenile fiction (to 3,000 words, no drawings); and rhymed and unrhymed poetry (to 40 lines). It is open to both published and unpublished writers, and accepts original material only. Entry fee, $3. Limit 5 entries per competition. *Deadline:* September 25. *Award:* First place in each category, $50. Second place, $30; third place, $20.

John Gardner Memorial Prize for Fiction
Harpur Palate, English Dept., Binghamton University, Box 6000,
    Binghamton, NY 13902
http://harpurpalate.binghamton.edu

This contest was established to honor John Gardner's dedication to the creative writing program at Binghamton University. It is open to all writers and accepts previously unpublished short story entries. Entries should not exceed 8,000 words. Entry fee, $15 (includes a one-year subscription to *Harpur Palate*). *Deadline:* Between January 1 and March 31. *Award:* $500 and publication in the summer issue of *Harpur Palate.*

Paul Gillette Writing Contest
Pikes Peak Writers, P.O. Box 63114, Colorado Springs, CO 80962
www.ppwc.net

Open to writers who have not yet published book-length fiction or short stories, this contest accepts entries in categories such as children's books, YA novels, romance, and historical fiction. Entry fee, $30 for members; $40 for nonmembers. Critiques are available. For book submissions, include first 15 pages and a synopsis; short stories to 5,000 words. Describe the target market. *Deadline:* November 1. *Award:* $100 or a refund of the Pikes Peak Conference fee. Second place, $50; third place, $30.

Glimmer Train Contests

1211 NW Glisan St., #207, Portland, OR 97209

www.glimmertrain.org

Glimmer Train sponsors a variety of contests, each held two or four times a year. They are Family Matters, Fiction Open, Short Story Award for New Writers, and Very Short Fiction. Lengths vary. Entry fees, generally $15-$20. *Deadlines:* Vary. *Award:* First place award ranges from $1,200 to $2,000 and includes publication in *Glimmer Train*, and 20 copies of the issue with the winning story.

The Golden Kite Awards

8271 Beverly Blvd., Los Angeles, CA 90048

www.scbwi.org

The Golden Kites recognize excellence in children's fiction, nonfiction, picture book text, and picture book illustration. SCBWI members whose work has been published in the year preceding the contest are eligible. Editors and art directors of the winning titles are also recognized. *Deadline:* December 15. *Award:* $2,500 and a Golden Kite statuette. Honorable mentions receive plaques. The editor and art director of the winning title receive $1,000.

Lorian Hemingway Short Story Competition

P.O. Box 993, Key West, FL 33041

www.shortstorycompetition.com

Writers of short fiction whose work has not been published in a nationally distributed publication with a circulation of 5,000 or more are eligible to enter this competition. It accepts original, unpublished short stories of up to 3,000 words. There are no restrictions on theme. Entry fee, $12 for entries postmarked by April 1; $17 for those postmarked between April 2 and May 15.

Deadline: May 15. *Award:* First place, $1,000. Second and third place, $500.

Highlights for Children Fiction Contest
803 Church St., Honesdale, PA 18431
www.highlights.com

This annual contest sponsored by *Highlights for Children* accepts original short fiction up to 500 words. The competition is open to writers over the age of 16. Clearly mark FICTION CONTEST on manuscript. *Deadline:* January 1 and January 31. *Award:* $1,000 and publication in *Highlights for Children.*

Insight Magazine Writing Contest
55 West Oak Ridge Dr., Hagerstown, MD 21740-7390
www.insightmagazine.org

This annual contest looks for inspiring, thoughtful writing with a strong spiritual message. Submissions with references to the Bible are encouraged. It accepts unpublished material in categories including student short story, general short story, and student (under age 22) poetry. True stories are also eligible. No entry fee. Short stories should range from 1,500 to 2,000 words. Poetry, to one page. *Deadline:* June 2. *Award:* From $250 to $150, and publication in *Insight.*

Barbara Karlin Grant
8271 Beverly Blvd., Los Angeles, CA 90048
www.scbwi.org

The Barbara Karlin grant was set up by SCBWI to recognize and encourage aspiring picture book writers. It is presented to an SCBWI member who has not yet published a picture book. Works of fiction, nonfiction, retellings of fairy tales, folktales, or legends are eligible for consideration. Manuscripts should not exceed eight pages. No entry fee. New applications and procedures are posted on the website each year. *Deadline:* March 15. *Award:* $1,500. Runners-up, $500.

Coretta Scott King Awards

50 East Huron St., Chicago, IL 60611-2795

www.ala.org

Honoring Martin Luther King, Jr. and his wife, Coretta Scott King, for their courage and determination, this award promotes the artistic expression of the African American experience through literature and graphic arts. The awards are given to African American authors and illustrators for inspirational and educational contributions to children's and YA literature. *Deadline:* December 1. *Award:* A framed citation, $1,000, and a set of *Encyclopaedia Britannica* or *World Book Encyclopedia*.

E. M. Koeppel Short Fiction Award

P.O. Box 140310, Gainesville, FL 32614

www.writecorner.com

Unpublished fiction in any genre is the focus of this annual competition open to all writers. Submissions should not exceed 3,000 words. Entry fee, $15; $10 for each additional entry. *Deadline:* October 1 to April 30. *Award:* $1,100.

Long Story Contest International

White Eagle Coffee Store Press, P.O. Box 383, Fox River Grove, IL 60021

http://members.aol.com/wecspress

This worldwide competition was established to select a long

literary story for publication. Unpublished single stories, multi-part stories, and self-contained novel segments are eligible. The judges place no restrictions on style, method, or subject matter. Entries should be 8,000–14,000 words. Entry fee, $15. *Deadline:* December 15. *Award:* $1,000.

Magazine Merit Awards
8271 Beverly Blvd., Los Angeles, CA 90048
www.scbwi.org

SCBWI sponsors this annual award in recognition of outstanding original magazine work written for young people. It accepts published entries in the categories of fiction, nonfiction, illustration, and poetry. No entry fee. Submit four copies of each entry, showing proof of publication date. *Deadline:* December 15. *Award:* Winners in each category receive a plaque.

Mayhaven Awards for Children's Fiction
P.O. Box 557, Mahomet, IL 61853
www.mayhavenpublishing.com

This annual competition encourages the writing of high-quality material for children. The competition is open to all writers and accepts entries written in English only. Entry fee, $50. *Deadline:* December 31. *Award:* Winner is published by Mayhaven, and receives royalties. Second place, $200; third place, $100.

Memoirs Ink Writing Contest
10866 Washington Blvd., Suite 518, Culver City, CA 90232
www.memoirsink.com

Held twice each year, this contest accepts original personal essays, memoirs, or stories based on autobiographical experiences. Entries must be written in first person. The contest is open to all writers, but accepts submissions in English only. Entries may be up to 1,500 words for the February contest; and to 3,000 words for the August contest. Entry fee, $17. Multiple submissions are accepted. *Deadline:* February 15 and August 15. *Award:* $1,000. Second place, $500; third place, $250.

Michigan Literary Fiction Awards

839 Greene St., Ann Arbor, MI 48104-3209

www.press.umich.edu

The University of Michigan Press sponsors this annual contest for writers who have published at least one literary novel or story collection in English. It welcomes original submissions of short fiction collections and novels. No entry fee. Entrants should include a copy of their published book and the manuscript; 100 pages, minimum. *Deadline:* Postmarked between February 1 and July 1. *Award:* Publication and a $1,000 advance.

Mid-American Review Creative Nonfiction Award

Dept. of English, Box W, Bowling Green State University, Bowling Green, OH 43403

www.bgsu.edu/studentlife/organizations/midamericanreview

Honoring excellence in the field of creative nonfiction, this competition is open to all writers. It accepts original, unpublished creative nonfiction submissions of up to 6,000 words. Entry fee, $10. *Deadline:* October 1. *Award:* $1,000 and publication in *Mid-American Review.*

Milkweed Prize for Children's Literature

Milkweed Editions, 1011 Washington Ave. South, Suite 300, Minneapolis, MN 55415

www.milkweed.org

Fiction for readers ages 8 to 13 is the focus of this annual competition that is sponsored by Milkweed Editions. The prize was established to encourage authors to write for this important age group. It looks for submissions with high literary merit that embody humane values and contribute to cultural understanding. No entry fee. *Deadline:* Ongoing. *Award:* Publication by Milkweed Editions; $10,000 advance.

Minotaur Books/MWA Competition
175 Fifth Ave., New York, NY 10010
www.mysterywriters.org

Open to all writers who have not yet published a novel, this competition is sponsored by Minotaur Books in conjunction with the Mystery Writers of America. It accepts original, book-length manuscripts in which murder or another serious crime is central to the plot. *Deadline:* November 30. *Award:* Publishing contract from St. Martin's Press/Minotaur Books; $10,000 cash advance against royalties.

Mythopoeic Society Fantasy Award for Children's Literature
306 Edmon Low Library, Oklahoma State University, Stillwater, OK 74078
www.mythsoc.org

Honoring outstanding fantasy books for young readers that are written in the tradition of J. R. R. Tolkien and C. S. Lewis, this award is presented to picture books through YA novels, adult fantasy, and scholarly books. Books and collections by a single author are eligible for two years after publication. *Deadline:* February 28. *Award:* A statuette.

National Book Award for Young People's Literature

National Book Foundation, 95 Madison Ave., Suite 709, New
    York, NY 10016
www.nationalbook.org

The National Book Award recognizes outstanding literature for
young people as well as adults. Fiction, nonfiction, and collections
of single-author short stories and essays are eligible. All entries
must be published in the U.S. during the year preceding the contest. This competition is open to U.S. citizens only. Entry fee,
$125. Entries must be submitted by publishers. *Deadline:* Entry
forms due June 16; books or bound galleys due in August. *Award:*
Category winners, $10,000; 16 finalists receive $100.

National Children's Theatre Medal

280 Miracle Mile, Coral Gables, FL 33134
www.actorsplayhouse.org

Held yearly, this competition is sponsored by the Actors'
Playhouse at Miracle Theatre. It welcomes the submission of
unpublished scripts that are appropriate for children ages 5 to 12.
Submissions should feature a cast with no more than 8 adults,
who may play multiple roles. Works that received limited production exposure, workshops, or staged readings are encouraged, as
are musicals with simple settings that appeal to both children
and adults. Running time, 45 to 60 minutes. Entry fee, $10.
Include sheet music for musicals. *Deadline:* April 1. *Award:* $500
and a full production of the play.

The John Newbery Medal

American Library Association, 50 East Huron St., Chicago, IL 60611
www.ala.org/alsc

This prestigious medal is presented to honor the year's most distinguished contribution to American literature for children up to the age of 14. Titles eligible for consideration must have been written by a U.S. author and published in the year preceding the contest. Books are judged on literary quality and overall presentation for children. Nominations are accepted from ALSC members only. *Deadline:* December 31. *Award:* The Newbery Medal is presented to the winning author at the ALA midwinter banquet.

New Millennium Writings Award

P.O. Box 2463, Room M2, Knoxville, TN 37901

www.newmillenniumwritings.com

This annual contest is sponsored by *New Millennium Writings,* a literary journal. It accepts entries in the categories of short-short fiction, fiction, nonfiction, and poetry. It accepts previously unpublished material, and material that has been published online or in a print publication with a circulation of under 5,000. Short-short fiction, to 1,000 words. Fiction and nonfiction, to 6,000 words. Poetry, to three poems, five pages total. No entry fee. *Deadline:* November 15. *Award:* $1,000.

New Voices Award

Lee & Low Books, 95 Madison Ave., New York, NY 10016

www.leeandlow.com

Encouraging writers of color who have not published a children's picture book, this annual award is sponsored by Lee & Low Books. It welcomes original material that addresses the needs of children of color, ages five to twelve. Fiction and nonfiction entries are accepted, but folklore and animal stories are not. Entries should not exceed 1,500 words and must be accompanied by a cover letter with the author's contact information and relevant cultural/ethnic information. Limit two submissions per entrant. No entry fee. *Deadline:* December 31. *Award:* Publishing contract with Lee & Low Books, and $1,000.

NWA Nonfiction Contest

10940 S. Parker Road, #508, Parker, CO 80134

www.nationalwriters.com

The National Writers' Association established this award to recognize and encourage the writing of high-quality nonfiction. Submissions are judged on marketability, originality, research, and reader interest. Entries should not exceed 5,000 words. Entry fee, $18. Multiple entries are accepted under separate cover. *Deadline:* December 31. *Award:* First place, $200. Second place, $100; third place, $50.

NWA Short Story Contest

10940 S. Parker Road, #508, Parker, CO 80134

www.nationalwriters.com

Original, high-quality short stories in any genre are accepted for this annual contest. It accepts previously unpublished work only. Entries should not exceed 5,000 words. Entry fee, $15. Multiple entries are accepted under separate cover. *Deadline:* July 1. *Award:* First place, $250. Second place, $100; third place, $50.

Once Upon a World Children's Book Award

1399 South Roxbury Drive, Los Angeles, CA 90035

www.wiesenthal.com

This competition was established by the Museum of Tolerance to recognize and reward books that inspire positive change. It accepts nominations for books that are published during the year

preceding the contest that are suitable for ages six to ten and convey messages of tolerance, social justice, social and personal responsibility, and/or diversity. The competition is open to fiction and nonfiction. No entry fee. *Deadline:* April. *Award:* $1,000.

Orbis Pictus Award for Outstanding Nonfiction for Children
Kim Ford, 6617 Westminster Road, Memphis, TN 38120
www.ncte.org

This award for excellence in children's nonfiction recognizes books used in kindergarten through eighth-grade classrooms that are characterized by outstanding accuracy, organization, design, and style. Eligible titles must be published in the year preceding the contest. Nominations may come from National Council of Teachers of English (NCTE) members, or the general education community. Textbooks, historical fiction, folklore, and poetry are not eligible. To nominate a book, write to the committee chair with the author's name, title of book, publisher, copyright date, and a brief explanation of why you liked the book. *Deadline:* December 31. *Award:* A plaque at the NCTE Convention.

Pacific Northwest Writers Association Literary Contest
PMB 2717, 1420 NW Goldman Blvd, Ste. 2, Issaquah, WA 98027
www.pnwa.org

Sponsored by the Pacific Northwest Writers Association, this annual contest accepts unpublished entries in several categories including young writers; screenwriting; mainstream novel; adult short story; juvenile short story; story/picture book; inspirational; and romance. Each entrant receives two critiques of their work. Entry fee, $35 for members; $50 for nonmembers. Limit one entry per category. *Deadline:* February. *Award:* $150 to $1,000.

PEN Center USA Literary Awards

269 South Beverly Dr., #1163, Beverly Hills, CA 90212

www.penusa.org

Writers living west of the Mississippi River are honored for their literary achievements through this annual awards program. Entries that have been published in the year preceding the contest are accepted for nomination in the categories of children's literature, fiction, creative nonfiction, journalism, drama, teleplay, research nonfiction, poetry, translation, and screenplay. Entry fee, $35. *Deadline:* December 31. *Award:* Category winners, $1,000.

PEN/Phyllis Naylor Working Writer Fellowship

588 Broadway, Suite 303, New York, NY 10012

www.pen.org

This fellowship provides support for promising authors in the field of children's or YA fiction. Eligible authors will have published at least two, but no more than five titles in the last ten years. Likely candidates are those whose books have been well-reviewed but have not achieved high sales volume. Nominations are accepted from editors and fellow writers and should include a detailed letter of support; a list of the nominated author's published work and reviews; and a description of the nominee's financial resources. Three copies of no more than 100 pages of a current work must also be submitted. *Deadline:* Postmarked between September 1 and January 14. *Award:* $5,000 fellowship.

Phoebe Fiction Contest

MSN 2D6, George Mason University, 4400 University Dr., Fairfax, VA 22030

www.gmu.edu/pubs/phoebe/fiction_contest.htm

This annual contest is sponsored by *Phoebe,* the literary journal of George Mason University. It accepts unpublished short fiction. Entries should not exceed 7,500 words. Entry fee, $15. *Deadline:* December 1. *Award:* $1,000 and publication in *Phoebe.*

Pockets Annual Fiction Contest

P.O. Box 340004, 1908 Grand Ave., Nashville, TN 37203-0004
www.pockets.org

This contest is sponsored by *Pockets* magazine. The competition is open to all writers and looks for previously unpublished entries ranging from 1,000 to 1,600 words. It accepts entries in most fiction genres, with the exception of biblical and historical fiction. No entry fee. *Deadline:* Postmarked between March 1 and August 15. *Award:* $1,000 and publication in *Pockets.*

Edgar Allan Poe Awards

Mystery Writers of America, 1140 Broadway, Suite 1507, New
   York, NY 10001
www.mysterywriters.org

The Mystery Writers of America sponsors these annual awards, which are considered among the most prestigious awards for mystery writers. They are presented for work published in the year preceding the contest in several categories including: best fact crime, best YA mystery, best juvenile mystery, best first novel by an American author, and best motion picture screenplay. No entry fee. *Deadline:* November 30. *Award:* An Edgar Award is presented to each winner at a banquet; cash award.

Prairie Fire Press Contests

423-100 Arthur St., Winnipeg MB R3B 1H3 Canada
www.prairiefire.ca

Two annual competitions honor works of creative nonfiction and short fiction. Creative fiction entries should not exceed 5,000 words and must be unpublished. Short fiction, to 15,000 words. Entry fee, $31. *Deadline:* November 30. *Award:* First prize, $1,250. Second prize, $500; third prize, $250. Winning entries are published in *Prairie Fire* magazine.

Michael L. Printz Award for Excellence in Young Adult Literature

50 East Huron St., Chicago, IL 60611

www.ala.org/yalsa/printz

This award recognizes excellence in YA literature. Fiction, nonfiction, and poetry titles that target ages 12 to 18 and were published in the preceding year are eligible for submission. ALA committee members may nominate titles. Entries are judged on overall literary merit, taking into consideration theme, voice, setting, style, and design. Controversial topics are not discouraged. *Deadline:* December 1. *Award:* An award seal, presented at the annual ALA midwinter conference.

Prism international Literary Nonfiction Contest

Creative Writing Program, University of British Columbia,
    Buchanan E462, Main Mall, Vancouver BC V6T 1Z1 Canada

www.prism.arts.ubc.ca

This annual contest honors excellence in literary nonfiction. Entries of creative nonfiction may be on any subject, and should not exceed 25 double-spaced pages. *Deadline:* November 30. *Award:* Grand prize, $1,500 and publication in *Prism international*.

Prism international Short Fiction Contest

Creative Writing Program, University of British Columbia,

Buchanan E462, Main Mall, Vancouver BC V6T 1Z1 Canada
www.prism.arts.ubc.ca

This competition is open to all writers, with the exception of those currently enrolled in the creative arts program at the University of British Columbia. It looks for original, unpublished short stories to 25 double-spaced pages. Entry fee $25 (includes a one-year subscription to *Prism international*). *Deadline:* January 29. *Award:* Grand prize, $2,000 and publication in *Prism international*. Three runner-up prizes of $200 are also awarded.

Roanoke Review Fiction Contest

221 College Lane, Salem, VA 24153
www.roanoke.edu/roanokereview

This annual contest is sponsored by the literary journal of Roanoke College and looks to encourage the writing of short fiction. It is open to all writers. Entries should not exceed 8,000 words. Entry fee, $15. *Deadline:* November. *Award:* First place, $1,000. Second place, $500. Winning entries are published in the spring issue of *Roanoke Review*.

San Antonio Writers Guild Writing Contests

P.O. Box 34775, San Antonio, TX 78265
www.sawritersguild.org

This competition accepts entries in the categories of novel, short story, essay, memoir, and poetry. It accepts previously unpublished submissions only. Word limits vary. Visit the website for complete information. Entry fee, $10 for members; $20 for nonmembers. *Deadline:* October 1. *Award:* First place, $100; Second place, $50; third place $25.

David B. Saunders Creative Nonfiction Prize

Cream City Review, Dept. of English, University of Wisconsin-
   Milwaukee, P.O. Box 413, Milwaukee, WI 53201
www.creamcityreview.org/submit

Original, unpublished entries of creative nonfiction are accepted for this annual competition. Entries should not exceed 30 pages. Entry fee, $15. *Deadline:* December 1. *Award:* $1,000 and publication in *Cream City Review.*

The A. David Schwartz Fiction Prize

Cream City Review, Dept. of English, University of Wisconsin-
   Milwaukee, P.O. Box 413, Milwaukee, WI 53201
www.creamcityreview.org/submit

Sponsored by the literary journal of the University of Wisconsin, *Cream City Review,* and Karry W. Schwartz Bookshops, this prize is offered annually. The competition accepts previously unpublished works of fiction. Entries should not exceed 30 pages. Entry fee, $15. *Deadline:* December 1. *Award:* $1,000 and publication in *Cream City Review.*

Seven Hills Writing Contest

P.O. Box 3428, Tallahassee, FL 32315
www.twaonline.org

Sponsored by the Tallahassee Writers' Association, this annual contest offers prizes in the categories of best short story, memoir, essay, and children's literature. The competition is open to all writers and accepts unpublished, original entries only. Entry fee, $10 for members; $15 for nonmembers. *Deadline:* Between January 1 and September 30. *Award:* Publication in *Seven Hills* literary journal. First place, $100; second place, $75; third place, $50.

Mary Shelley Award for Imaginative Fiction

Rosebud Magazine, N3310 Asje Road, Cambridge, WI 53523
www.rsbd.net

Established to promote all forms of speculative and imaginative fiction in a literary context, this contest accepts entries of science fiction, horror, fantasy, and mystery, as well as entries that stretch beyond the boundaries of these genres. Entries should be between 1,000 and 3,500 words. Entry fee, $10. *Deadline:* October 15. *Award:* First place winner receives $1,000 and publication in *Rosebud.* Four runners-up receive $100 and publication.

Kay Snow Writing Contest

9045 SW Barbur Blvd., Suite 5A, Portland, OR 97219
www.willamettewriters.com

This annual competition encourages writers to reach their personal goals. It accepts original, unpublished entries in the categories of adult fiction and nonfiction, juvenile short story or article, poetry, screenwriting, and student writing. Entry fee, $10 for members; $15 for nonmembers. Word lengths vary for each category. Visit the website for complete category guidelines. *Deadline:* April. *Award:* $50 to $300. The Liam Callen award, in the amount of $500, is given for the best overall entry.

Society of Midland Authors Awards

P.O. Box 10419, Chicago, IL 60610
www.midlandauthors.com

Authors and poets who reside in, were born in, or have strong ties to any of the 12 Midwestern states are eligible to enter this annual contest. Awards are presented for adult fiction and nonfiction, biography, poetry, and children's fiction and nonfiction. Entries must have been published in the year preceding the contest. No entry fee. *Deadline:* January 30. *Award:* Cash award and a recognition plaque.

So to Speak Contests

George Mason University, MSN 2C5, 4400 University Dr., Fairfax, VA 22030

www.gmu.edu/org/sts/contest/php

So to Speak, a feminist literary journal, sponsors this contest for fiction, nonfiction, and poetry. Entries may also be memoirs or vignettes. Fiction, to 5,000 words. Nonfiction, to 4,000 words. Poetry, no line limits; two to five poems per submission. Entry fee, $15. *Deadline:* Nonfiction and poetry deadline, October 15. Fiction deadline, March 15. *Award:* $500 and publication in *So to Speak*.

SouthWest Writers Annual Contest

3721 Morris NE, Albuquerque, NM 87110

www.southwestwriters.org

This annual contest is sponsored by SouthWest Writers and honors distinguished unpublished work in a variety of categories including: novel, short story, short nonfiction, book-length nonfiction, children's book, screenplay, and poetry. Entry fees range from $25 to $45. Manuscript critiques are available for an additional fee. *Deadline:* May 1. *Award:* $50 to $150.

Stanley Drama Award

Wagner College, One Campus Road, Staten Island, NY 10301

www.wagner.edu/stanleydrama_drama/

The Stanley Drama Award was set up to encourage and reward aspiring playwrights. The competition is open to original, full-length plays or musicals, or a series of two or three related

one-act plays that have not been professionally produced or published as trade books. Musical entries must be accompanied by an audio cassette or CD. Entry fee, $30. *Deadline:* October 31. *Award:* $2,000.

Sydney Taylor Manuscript Competition

Aileen Grossberg, 67 Park St., Montclair, NJ 07042
www.jewishlibraries.org

This annual competition is open to original fiction containing Jewish content targeting children ages 8 to 11. Entries should deepen a child's understanding of Judaism. Manuscripts should be between 64 and 200 pages. Short stories, plays, and poetry are not eligible. No entry fee. Limit one entry per competition. *Deadline:* December 15. *Award:* $1,000.

Utah Original Writing Competition

617 East South Temple, Salt Lake City, UT 84102
www.arts.utah.gov/literature/comprules.html

Since 1958, this annual competition has been honoring Utah's finest writers. It presents awards in several categories including YA book, novel, personal essay, short story, poetry, and general nonfiction. The competition accepts unpublished entries from residents of Utah only. Word lengths vary for each category. Check the website for complete information. No entry fee. *Deadline:* Postmarked by June 27. *Award:* $300 to $1,000.

Jackie White Memorial National Children's Playwriting Contest

309 Parkade Blvd., Columbia, MO 65202
www.cectheatre.org

This contest is sponsored by the Columbia Entertainment

Company and was established to encourage the writing of plays for children and families. Roles that challenge and expand acting talents are strongly encouraged. Submit only previously unpublished and unproduced material. Entries must be full-length plays (60- to 90-minute running time) with well-developed speaking roles for at least seven characters. Entry fee, $10. *Deadline:* June 1. *Award:* $500 and possible production of the play.

Laura Ingalls Wilder Medal

American Library Association, 50 East Huron St., Chicago, IL 60611
www.ala.org/alsc

Every other year this award is presented to honor an author or illustrator whose body of work has contributed substantially to children's literature. It is open to books that were published in the U.S. during the year preceding the contest. Nominations are made by ALSC members. The winner is chosen by a team of children's librarians. *Deadline:* December 31. *Award:* A medal is presented to the winner.

Tennessee Williams Fiction Contest

938 Lafayette St., Suite 514, New Orleans, LA 70113
www.tennesseewilliams.net

This competition is open to writers who have not yet published a book of fiction. It accepts entries up to 7,500 words by hard copy or through the website. Entries are subject to blind judging. Author's name should not appear on manuscript itself. Include a cover letter with story title, name, and full contact information. Entry fee, $25. *Deadline:* November 15. *Award:* $1,500 and publication in *New Orleans Review.*

Tennessee Williams One-Act Play Competition

938 Lafayette St., Suite 514, New Orleans, LA 70113

www.tennesseewilliams.net

This annual contest recognizes and rewards excellence in one-act plays from writers around the world. The winning script should require minimal technical support and a small cast of characters. Entry fee, $20. Multiple entries are accepted. Plays should run no longer than one hour and must have been previously produced or published. *Deadline:* November 15. *Award:* $1,000 and a full production of the play. Second place, $200; third place $100.

Paul A. Witty Short Story Award

International Reading Association, P.O. Box 8139, Newark, DE
   19714

www.reading.org

The International Reading Association presents this annual award to a short story that was published in a magazine for children during the previous calendar year. Submissions should be of the highest literary merit. No entry fee. *Deadline:* December 1. *Award:* $1,000.

Work-in-Progress Grants

SCBWI, 8271 Beverly Blvd., Los Angeles, CA 90048

www.scbwi.org

Each year SCBWI offers several grants to children's writers to complete projects that are not currently under contract. Grants are available to both full and associate members of SCBWI in the categories of general work-in-progress; contemporary novel for young people; nonfiction research; and previously unpublished author. All applications should include a 750-word synopsis and a writing sample of no more than 2,500 words from the entry. *Deadline:* Submit beginning October 1. *Award:* $1,500; runners-up, $500.

WOW! Women on Writing **Flash Fiction Contests**
www.wow-womenonwriting.com

This e-zine presents quarterly flash fiction contests to inspire creativity and communication and provide recognition to its winners. All styles of writing are welcome. Entries should be from 250 to 300 words. Accepts entries through the website only. Entry fee, $10. *Deadline:* February 28; May 31; August 31; and November 30. *Award:* Winner, $200. Second place, $150; third place $100.

Writers at Work Fellowship
P.O. Box 540370, North Salt Lake, UT 84054-0370
www.writersatwork.org

Writers at Work, a non-profit literary arts organization, sponsors this annual fellowship that recognizes emerging writers of fiction, nonfiction, and poetry. Writers not yet published in the category of their entry are eligible to submit original work. Entries are judged by faculty members. Entry fee, $20. *Deadline:* March 1. *Award:* $1,500 and publication in *Quarterly West.*

Writer's Digest **Annual Writing Competition**
4700 East Galbraith Road, Cincinnati, OH 45236
www.writersdigest.com

This annual competition calls for entries in many different categories including children's fiction, short stories, screenplays, and plays. It accepts previously unpublished work only. Entry fee, $10. Multiple entries are accepted. *Deadline:* May 15. *Award:* Grand prize, $3,000. Other prizes are also awarded.

Writers' League of Texas Annual Manuscript Contest

1501 W. 5th St., Suite E2, Austin, TX 78703

www.writersleague.org

This annual novel contest accepts original, unpublished entries in the categories of mainstream fiction; middle-grade; YA; mystery/thriller; science fiction; historical or Western; and romance. Entry fee, $50. Include a one-page synopsis along with the first 10 pages of entry. *Deadline:* Varies. Check website for details. *Award:* Winners are invited to a meeting with an editor or agent at the Writers' League of Texas Agents and Editors Conference.

Writing for Children Competition

Writers' Union of Canada, 90 Richmond St. East, Suite 299,
    Toronto ON M5C 1P1 Canada

www.writersunion.ca

Canadian writers who have not yet published a book are eligible to enter this competition from the Writers' Union of Canada. It was established to encourage new Canadian talent in the field of children's literature. Entries should not exceed 1,500 words. Entry fee, $15. Multiple entries are accepted. *Deadline:* April. *Award:* $1,500 and submission to three children's publishers.

Paul Zindel First Novel Award

Hyperion Books for Children, P.O. Box 6000, Manhasset, NY 11030

www.hyperionchildrensbooks.com

Named for the bestselling author, this annual award honors contemporary and historical fiction set in the U.S., for readers ages 8 to 12. Manuscripts should reflect the cultural and ethnic diversity of the country. Submissions should be between 100 and 240 pages. *Deadline:* April 30. *Award:* Book contract with Hyperion Books for Children; $7,500 advance on royalties; $1,500 cash.

index